THE GIRL FROM LEAM LANE

Piers Dudgeon is a writer, editor and photographer. Born in 1949, he worked for ten years as a publisher in London and then started his own company, publishing a number of bestsellers with authors as diverse as Daphne du Maurier, John Fowles, Edward de Bono, Shirley Conran and Susan Hill. Since 1989 he has worked as a journalist and written nine works of non-fiction. In 1993 he moved with his wife and three children to a village on the North Yorkshire moors, where he is setting up a residential school for writers and artists.

The Girl from Leam Lane

The Life and Writing of CATHERINE COOKSON

Piers Dudgeon

HEADLINE

First published in 1997
by HEADLINE BOOK PUBLISHING

First published in paperback in 1998
by HEADLINE BOOK PUBLISHING

10 9 8 7 6

ISBN 0 7472 5660 8

Typeset by Avon Dataset Ltd, Bidford-on-Avon, Warks

Printed and bound in Great Britain

HEADLINE BOOK PUBLISHING
A division of Hodder Headline PLC
338 Euston Road
London NW1 3BH

Contents

Acknowledgements

The author would like to thank all the picture sources, which include Catherine Cookson, The Beamish North of England Open Air Museum, the Borough of South Tyneside, Brian Duff/*The Daily Express*, Newcastle Libraries & Information Services, The Northumberland Record Office, The Gibson Collection, Getty Images, The Bede Gallery, Gateshead Libraries and Arts Department, *The Newcastle Journal*, The North Tyneside Libraries and Arts Department, Scottish and Newcastle Breweries and *The South Shields Gazette*. While every effort has been made to trace copyright sources, the author would be grateful to hear from any unacknowledged sources.

CHAPTER ONE

Wednesday's Child

The night of Tuesday 19 June 1906 gave way to a warm, early-summer day on Tyneside, a light wind from the south preventing the diffuse clouds from settling into a pall over the river and keeping the temperature to a happy sixty-five degrees. Inside number 5 Leam Lane, one of a cluster of houses by the south-west corner of Tyne Dock itself, the atmosphere was anything but clement, however. For Kate's time had come.

Kate Fawcett was in her prime. She was an attractive woman in her mid-twenties, not pretty, but beautifully built: strong, with an innate feminine softness, her azure eyes, abundant brown hair and dark curving brows crowning a laughing, earthy personality, which had smitten the father of the child about to be born and warmed her to nearly everyone who came within her orbit.

At this stage in her life, one characteristic only seemed to tell another story. Kate's left foot flapped inwards slightly when she walked. It was a manner of walking which in no way detracted from her briskness of step, a barely noticeable blemish; but a kind of sad emblem, to those who knew, of the stressed and impoverished root-stock on which this singular beauty had been produced. As a child, Kate had walked the streets of Jarrow barefoot and one time had aroused such pity in a woman that she had given the girl a pair of boots.

Forty-one years later, Kate Fawcett's daughter, born that balmy day of 20 June, would recreate the goings-on in number 5 Leam Lane. In the opening pages of the manuscript of *Kate Hannigan*, her first novel, Catherine Cookson described her own birth. It was a dramatic debut performance, and a good deal more was spawned in those pages than Kate Hannigan's daughter, Ann, which is Catherine's middle name.

As the fictional Kate spreads her legs for a torturous labour the cry goes up for hot water, towels and sheets, accoutrements of the laundry with which, by the time she came to write this novel, Catherine was particularly at home. There is a doctor in attendance, Rodney Prince, but within the first few lines of dialogue we are introduced to a woman who embodies this fledgling author's talent for bouncing her female characters off the page to live for real in our imagination.

Midwife Dorrie Clarke is a fat, pugnacious, caustic, gin-soaked gossip, a busybody with a sharp tongue, and full of resentment. But she has an agile brain and a turn of phrase so tellingly true that she cannot but be real. In a matter of a few pages of Dorrie's thoughts and repartee with Dr Prince we have not only their own characters laid out before us, but those too of Kate's acquiescing mother, Sarah, her bully of a father, dark, dour Tim Hannigan in the room downstairs, and a sense of the whole hellish, impoverished world in which they move, riddled with religious superstition and cruelty.

It is the birth of a rare talent indeed.

Kate Fawcett's real father, William, was not in any way the model for Tim Hannigan's character. William, a Jarrow steelworker and faithful Catholic, had married Kate's mother, Rose, in the 1870s. They had produced five daughters, only three of whom – Sarah, Kate and Mary – had survived their teens. In the room downstairs at the time of Catherine's birth would have been Rose's second husband, John McMullen, whom she had married in 1890. The couple lived together first in Jarrow, then in Nelson Street, Tyne Dock, before arriving at number 5 Leam Lane.

John McMullen was the stereotypical Irish Geordie, a figure on which it is all too easy to hang the sins of every drunken Irishman since famine first drove his compatriots unwillingly to these shores. John was one of triplets in a family of thirteen from southern Ireland, and had served in the Indian Army before marrying Rose. Two of his brothers still lived in Jarrow, just west along the river from Tyne Dock. 'At that time, Jarrow seemed to be peopled with Irish,' Catherine would recall. 'Palmer's Shipyard provided many of them with work, as did the smaller yards along the Tyne.' John, who worked the ships in Tyne Dock, loading and unloading iron ore, was imbued with a set of mind-bendingly confused values. A Roman Catholic with a deeply ingrained hatred of Protestants, he never went to church and exercised an irrational suspicion of sanctimonious piety in anyone who did.

An ability to mesmerise people with a point of view riddled with obvious discrepancies is a not uncharacteristically Irish trait. It relies for success on an emotional conjuring trick – charm mingled with conviction giving blarney the semblance of truth. There was no sorting John out, either in conversation or in a fight. Both he and later his only son, also named John but known as Jack, born in the year of his marriage to Rose, were well known around the docks for their fighting. John did not, however, hit women. For them he reserved an inspired vocabulary of obscenities, never more imaginatively explored than when he was drunk, which was often.

One of his favourite songs when he came home three

sheets in the wind was the Irish 'Comaylia', which he would conduct with Dennis, a two-foot-long iron poker. This same poker would also be used to knock pictures off the wall until only one remained: a portrait of Lord Roberts sitting on his horse with an Indian servant standing beside him. Whatever this archetypal British Imperial soldier, born in India, educated at Eton and Sandhurst and much decorated for his services to the Empire in India, Afghanistan and South Africa, excited in John McMullen – presumably his hatred of all that was British – he would use this image to give vent to his spleen, before standing in front of the window and letting rip with: 'Sing us an Irish Comaylia, sing us an Irish tune. For Patsie Burke has buggered his work, all by the light of the moon . . .'

His wife, Rose, suffered this, and a good deal worse besides, with remarkable fortitude. Family photographs make Rose look hard, and there is no doubt that she could be hard, particularly on her daughter Kate. But her stiff face is a sign of the stoicism which her life had bred in her. Rose kept her own counsel, but her feelings ran deep, particularly for her new granddaughter, who would open up Rose's great store of natural wisdom, comfort and love in a way that quite possibly she had never experienced before, or at least not for some time.

Whatever had been Rose's feelings for John when she married him in 1890, he had effectively rescued her children from the shame and squalor of begging on the streets and Rose from virtual slave labour at the Jarrow Puddling Mills. The real poor in the nineteenth and early twentieth centuries were the widows and unmarried mothers, women and girls with no men to bring in the money, when pay sufficient to keep a family was only available to men. Work at the mills, where pig iron was converted into wrought iron by heating it to very high temperatures to oxidise the carbon, was gruelling, ill paid and reckoned to be one step away from the workhouse or an early death.

Marriage to John raised Rose's standard of living, but she was poorer with him than she had been with her first husband. Even so, John managed to sustain a reputation for hard work and lay the blame for any lack of it at someone else's door. In this John could justifiably call on truth as his witness. Jobs were indeed hard to come by, the problem being underemployment as much as unemployment. Today dockers are retained on a minimum wage, but until the decasualisation of the docks they got paid only when there was work for them to do. Wages were intermittent and dependent on ships coming in. There was always a pool of labour – men unpaid, and uncertain of when they would be paid – hanging around the dock offices a few minutes' walk from Leam Lane, opposite a line of public houses which stood wall to wall down the whole street.

This precariousness was at the root of John's drink problem, which in turn threatened the family's solvency further. Drink was a serious problem all over Tyneside, but was a scourge in those families, like the McMullens, that were already near the breadline. For them drink was a catastrophe if it meant that money for necessities could not be found. Nevertheless, when he was taken on, John worked hard and for a pittance of a wage. He would come home at the end of six ten-hour shifts, his moleskin trousers red and wet up to the thighs from shovelling ore, with only three shillings and fourpence in his pocket. As a result, like his mates, he felt entitled to stoke his ego at home with the northern working-class myth of male primacy, and did so for all he was worth.

The myth kept the Fathar, as he was known, firmly in charge. He was waited on hand and foot. 'In those days,' recalls Catherine, 'a man went out to work and that, in his mind, was enough; the house and all that was in it was the woman's task, and it lowered a man's prestige if he as much as lifted a cup.' Rose and her daughters would dutifully walk the three miles from Jarrow, where they lived, to the dock gates with the Fathar's bait, and back again, at times barefoot but always uncomplaining. In Catherine's memory, the Fathar's tea at home was a similar occasion for acquiescence. A scout would be posted to calculate his coming to the minute, the idea being to present him with his meal (haddock and mash or steak, eggs and chips) piping hot on the plate, and, more especially, to time – to the second – the boiling of an egg which always preceded the meal, not hard-boiled, but done to a turn so that the yoke was runny but right.

There was little or no sense of servility among the women, perhaps because they realised deep down that, as Hal says in *A Dinner of Herbs* (1985), 'Man was so made he needed a mother in some form or other until the day he died.' After all, the primary role of woman as procreator, feeder and sustainer harks back to a myth far older than that of male primacy, even to the dawn of time when man worshipped a Goddess creator of the world and the idea of a male creator was patently absurd. On Tyneside men's work was non-inspirational. It was the women who provided that dimension to life – and in the kitchen, which was their sole domain, they knew as much about hard work as their menfolk, using it or the wash-house to bring in extra money from cooking or laundering, or taking in lodgers.

Kate Fawcett and her elder sister, Sarah, had both left school and started work at the age of twelve, Kate first with a butcher in Stanhope Road, east of Tyne Dock. Her job was in the wash-house, where she beat clean her employer's bloodied work clothes in a tub with a poss-stick. Her hours were from six-thirty in the morning to late at night, six days a week; her wages, half a crown.

The sisters were very different from one another. Like Sarah, Kate was a hard worker, and both were dominant women. But there the likeness ended. In those days Kate was gay, warm, large-hearted, while Sarah enjoyed none of these traits, her downright manner doing little to warm Catherine to her when she came along. By then, though, Sarah was married and had every reason to appear hard, having fared badly in the marriage stakes through following her heart rather than her head. Her story is a sad one, but it does suggest that in her youth she may have had more about her.

'Just before I was born,' Catherine recalls, 'Kate got a letter from Sarah saying that she had fallen for this pit lad who was about half her size – for Sarah was a big woman – and she was distressed,' a comment which indicates that marriage was usually regarded as a potentially profitable institution. Kate wrote back to her: 'Marry him whatever you do, it doesn't matter whether you live with orange boxes for the remainder of your life, marry him . . .' Unfortunately for Sarah, Kate's words were prophetic. 'Her young husband went stone deaf early in the marriage and couldn't work, and from then on she had to bring up her growing family without aid.'

Sarah's life was one of unending toil. 'When the Catholic school came out at four o'clock she had to take her youngest child with her, also called Sarah – my youngest cousin, who is still alive today – and scrub and clean the classrooms, and cleaning meant cleaning in those days.' The couple had seven children, including four boys who worked down the pit at Birtley in the Durham coalfield. There were few moments of respite, and life was grim – but not as grim as Sarah seemed to make it when Catherine visited. 'When I was staying there in my young days, she sent me to the slaughterhouse for a pint of blood to make blood puddings. The very name recalls the picture which makes me feel sick. We never got on. I didn't like her, but I admired her because of the way she worked for that family.'

Mary, the youngest Fawcett daughter, made a better catch, though it appears that he wriggled on her line for a while. Her husband, Alec, was a crane driver. He was a good man, but it had been a shotgun wedding, and once again Kate was involved. 'Mary knew that had she not been carrying Jack, her first son, and Alec had to marry her, he would have taken Kate because he had always liked Kate right up to the end. It should happen that years later they were both staying with Teresa, their only daughter, when Alec took ill and died, and he died in Kate's arms because Mary wasn't a woman to put up with sickness, and especially a dying man.'

Mary never liked Kate. She was jealous of her because of Alec and did her damnedest to get even, as Catherine remembers. 'In her bedroom was the latest in dressing tables; it had two swing mirrors. On a Saturday morning, as a child, I would move them from side to side, seeing my reflection in different ways. And I also went through all the little drawers in that piece of furniture and through being a nosey parker I caused a rift between the sisters that lasted for a few years. Because in one of the drawers I found a letter addressed to Kate. It was from the man she was going to marry after the 1914–18 war. He was now a prisoner in Germany... There was hell to pay. How Mary had come across the letter could only be surmised; perhaps she had taken it from the postman. She was a bitch of a woman, was my Aunt Mary. She was envious of anyone getting on, above her family.'

Mary had had dreams of bettering herself, and when she was married and living in East Jarrow, she vented her frustration at having failed to realise them on anyone she could find lower than herself in the social pecking order – a family called Robson, for example, who lived upstairs. 'The man must have been dead for years. The youngest was a boy called

Tommy. Mrs Robson had an older son who I imagine went
to work and kept them meagrely.' Mary delighted in being
better than the Robsons and took every opportunity to drive
her advantage home. 'The day Tommy was fourteen he went
down the pit, and Mary bragged to Kate that every time the
poor lad was on night shift, she banged and clattered the fire
irons and everything else to keep him awake. Moreover, such
was Mary's temperament that days were allotted for the use
of the wash-house and poor Mrs Robson had dared to light
the fire under the boiler in the wash-house on a day that
wasn't hers. And my dear aunt went in and raked all the
burning ashes from the grate and threw them in the yard.
You can't imagine such things happening, but they did.'

Always desperate to keep up appearances, Mary maintained her house better than any other in the neighbourhood.
'She had a lovely front room,' Catherine remembers. 'There
was a carpet, on which there was a three-piece suite, and
above all a lovely old spinet.' But the preposterous lengths
Mary went to in order to protect the veneer betrayed her
obsession with social status. Catherine recalls bringing her
husband Tom to visit Mary, years later. 'I was carrying my
first baby, it was during the second war. We came on the
Friday night to see my mother and on the Sunday went to tea
at Aunt Mary's. Tom couldn't believe it – she had knitted
leggings for the legs of this enormous mahogany table.'

In Catherine's fiction Mrs Flannagan is the archetypal
upstart. She and her daughter Sarah, something of a chip off
the old block, appear in *Fanny McBride* (1959) and the Mary
Ann series. Once, knowing that Catherine had had a neighbour of the same name, I asked her whether she had based
the character on a particular person. 'Did I know any Mrs
Flannagans? Oh, yes. In any community you'd find a Mrs
Flannagan, and the Mrs Flannagan who lived opposite Fanny
McBride in that book wasn't a patch on my Aunt Mary!'

Marriage was just about the only way for a girl to get on in life in those days. It was well-nigh impossible to make it on one's own; marriage was the fast track up or out. A girl might marry a striver and work with him at a small business, a shop perhaps, which could lead to bigger things – like Alice Fairbrother in Catherine's novel *The Upstart* (1996). Samuel Fairbrother was originally a cobbler, and rose to become the owner of a chain of shoemaking shops and a very rich man. Alice had made what would have been regarded by her contemporaries as an inspired choice of husband, and it is fair to assume that all three of the Fawcett sisters had at some time dreamed of such a conquest, coming as they did from so impoverished a background.

In 1901 or 1902, long before Mary was married and four or five years before Catherine was born, Mary and Kate went to work in a pub, The Ravensworth Arms in Lamesley, a village near Gateshead. Both lived in. Kate must have liked this job; she enjoyed the company of people and they enjoyed hers. Mary was a housemaid, while Kate worked in the bar. It was this division of responsibilities which handed Kate the chance of a lifetime to meet her ticket to success. For The Ravensworth Arms at Lamesley – visited, incidentally, by Robert Bradley at the start of *The Moth* (1986) – while not by any stretch of the imagination the gateway to high society (indeed, many of its patrons were pitmen), nevertheless offered a better opportunity for meeting people than grinding a tub full of clothes in a butcher's wash-house.

Kate's opportunity arose in 1903. She was serving in the saloon bar when an unusually well-dressed man appeared through the door. He wore a black coat with a collar made of astrakhan lambswool, a very choice trim. The coat alone would have been enough to cause the likes of Mary and Kate to double-take, but the effect was embroidered by a high hat, black kid gloves and a silver-mounted walking stick.

It is not difficult to imagine that after the man's first appearance the Fawcett sisters would have shared a giggle in their attic room above the pub. But his visit was repeated, and then became a regular event. Always he would take a table in the saloon bar, always Kate would serve him, and they began to strike up a rapport. The girlish giggles ceased, and Kate and her gentleman friend began a serious affair.

For Kate it was a dream come true. In Catherine's novel *Fenwick Houses* (1960) we get a glimpse of how such a man might have affected a girl from Kate's background. For Christine Winter it is his physical presence which impinges first, his bearing and the nonchalant fall of a scarf over his shoulder – and, of course, his accent. He is an alien presence, supremely self-assured but gentle with it. He is not a boy, like Christine's other male friends, and yet he is not much older than them. He has a fluency about him, an easy charm, and he is a stranger, apparently, to cynicism and self-interest. Above all, Christine's gentleman encourages Christine to be herself. It is her *self* that he loves. The barrier of class is not swept away, it is denied existence, dismissed as a figment of her imagination. Disarmed, Christine allows him to make love to her. She becomes pregnant. But when next she seeks him out, for the first time going to what she believes to be his home, no one has ever heard of him. The fairytale is over and the stark truth is delivered by Don Dowling: 'some bugger has given her a bellyful and skedaddled.'

Kate Fawcett's affair with Alexander Davies, which is the name he gave to her, lasted for two years. It was consummated once. Like Christine, Kate became pregnant. Marriage was proposed. Plans were made in Newcastle for their new life together. Then one day Alec, as he was known, called at the McMullens' house when Kate was out. He left an address for her to contact him, but when Kate went in search of him no one there had ever heard of him. She never saw him again.

11

In *Fenwick Houses*, Christine's response to this desertion is fury: 'I could feel malevolence so powerful that I seemed to smell it, it was like a stench.' It was in this frame of mind that Kate had given her matrimonial advice to her sister Sarah. She ended the letter: 'Don't go through the hell that I'm going through.'

Kate's pregnancy changed her life, and her demeanour, for ever. But of course Kate wasn't alone in her 'hell'. She was pregnant with Catherine. Kate's resentment was Catherine's emotional initiation into the McMullen family. As she said to me recently, 'I must have been greatly desired, mustn't I?' And things got no better even after she was born.

CHAPTER TWO

⬡⬡⬡

A Bellyful of Trouble

Catherine's baptism certificate and the formal registration document of her birth, dated a week late, bear testimony to the frantic state that Kate was in at this time. She had delayed because registration meant officially admitting that Catherine had been born out of wedlock. Today, when partners and single parents are as respectable as married parents, it is difficult to appreciate the shame Kate felt. When it came to the baptism certificate, the usual practice in South Shields was to describe the new lamb in the fold as 'bastard child of . . .', followed by the mother's name only. In fact, on Catherine's birth registration and baptism forms, the father's name was entered. When the error was discovered it seems the authorities were a bit kinder than usual. 'When someone spotted that my father was "not known", they just scratched his name out.'

The reason why Kate registered the wrong birth date of 27 June, having finally plucked up courage to go and register at all, was that 'she was afraid there'd be trouble that she was a week late in going.' The poor were so downtrodden in those days that they nurtured an inordinate fear of the police; 'they would go to extraordinary lengths to cover up the slightest misdemeanour.' Kate's fear was also a sad expression of the disgrace that was visited upon any girl in those days for mothering an illegitimate child.

Illegitimacy was of course a sin, and the Church policed society in a way it no longer does today. 'Divn't dee what I wouldn't dee unless ya want the priest after ya,' Catherine writes in *The Blind Miller* (1963), beautifully capturing a fundamental rule for all girls in Tyneside with the finger-wagging rhythms of her native idiom.

In 1851, according to one religious census, Tyneside had a particularly low church attendance, and Roman Catholicism was poorly represented. The Irish constituted the main body of Catholicism, but they were far fewer than the Nonconformists and tended to live a rather separate existence – islands in a sea of Protestantism. Nevertheless, the local Catholic priest, like the local doctor, was a very real judgemental presence within the Irish community.

Father O'Malley, who appears in *Kate Hannigan* (1950) and *The Fifteen Streets* (1951), is based on Father Bradley, the strict Roman Catholic priest at Tyne Dock church in Catherine's childhood days. O'Malley keeps his people firmly under the yoke, whether or not they actually go to Mass. He condemns Kate Hannigan's new clothes as a sign of her immorality – how else could she have afforded them? – and Dr Prince records three cases of hysteria in a month among children whose 'little heads' O'Malley has filled with fears of hell and purgatory. In *The Fifteen Streets* Christine Bracken accuses O'Malley of policing people's thinking and confirming them in their poverty and ignorance by insisting upon blind acceptance of their position in society, rather than encouraging them to think for themselves. Again, in *Kate Hannigan*, O'Malley is only there to stop people thinking; 'for, if she once started thinking, she and her like wouldn't put up with things as they were.' In *The Black Velvet Gown* (1984), set in the nineteenth century, Grandmama Diana Gullmington shows that the role of the church as social policeman is rooted in history. She scorns as absurd the idea that members of the lower classes possess reason (minds of their own), and sees the placing of human beings in a social pecking order (the great English class system) as God's work.

In Father O'Malley's world, fornication is the greatest sin of all, and in *Fenwick Houses* Father Ellis reduces Christine Winter to abasing herself on the ground before him, begging him not to inform her mother that he has come upon her fornicating with her gentleman lover. In so vengeful a religious atmosphere as this, Father Bradley of Tyne Dock church will not have turned a blind eye to Kate's sin with Alexander Davies.

A family with no father spelled poverty, too. Without Kate's wage the McMullens would find it difficult to survive. John was already in his fifties and his son Jack was only sixteen when Catherine was born. The family was faced with a pretty clear set of options, the first of which was to put Kate and Catherine in the workhouse.

The workhouse, the austere brick building of Harton Institution, with its tall chimneys, imposing central tower, stone breaking yard at the back and flat-faced asylum nearby, was a fearful presence in the lives of the poor. In a case of illegitimate birth, the bastard child would be separated from its mother, and the mother would be kept in the workhouse for fourteen years, unless her people took her out.

Fear of the workhouse, like fear of the Church, had strong historical roots. In *The Dwelling Place* (1971), fifteen-year-old Cissie Brodie makes a home for her three brothers and five sisters in a cave on the fells after the death of their parents from cholera, rather than capitulate to the poor law custodian, a man called Riper. In *Our John Willie* (1974), another novel set in the nineteenth century, we have a clear sense not only of the ignominy of the workhouse, but of the cruelty meted out there by working-class officials upon their own kind. In the McMullen household dread of the workhouse had a more immediate source: John McMullen had first-hand experience of its harsh regime, breaking stones there for a shilling a day. There was no doubt about it, Kate would have to continue in work – a decision which would cut her off from her child, for if she was to make a difference to the family finances, it would mean living out, in service.

These were some of the immediate practical consequences of Catherine's illegitimate birth. Another, no less real, was what people thought. Illegitimacy was a mark of disrepute as prominent as the dash of white hair on the heads of the illegitimate children of Thomas Mallen in *The Mallen Streak* (1973). One might think that, being near the bottom of the pile, the McMullens would have had less reason than most for embarrassment at the arrival of an illegitimate child. But that is to misread the situation. Respectability was important whatever social level you were on. In Catherine's novel *Hannah Massey* (1964), set in the 1930s, Hannah, whose main concern is to rise up the social scale, is so appalled at the thought of disgrace when it appears that her daughter, Rosie, has been living in London as a whore (which she hasn't) that she sets fire to her savings (her passport to posh Brampton Hill) and commits suicide.

Among the lower levels, indeed, respectability was often hardest fought for, as a little diversion on this theme in *Fanny McBride* suggests. Fanny is bemoaning the fact that her family has grown up and her favourite son, Jack, has moved out to get married to a 'Hallelujah' (Protestant) called Joyce Scallen, which will leave Fanny alone in the house with her other son, Phil, whom she regards suspiciously as an upstart, always making himself different with his reading and copying of fine ways, like standing up when a woman enters the room. The narrative moves forward with the arrival of Fanny's friend Mary Prout, who is suffering from 'a bad leg'. It is clear from Mary's tearful expression that she is in something of a stew, and it emerges that the doctor has laid her off work. What Mary does for a living is not immediately made clear. All that we are told is that it is largely a sit-down job, which she doesn't want to lose. Sit-down jobs are hard to find and Mary will surely lose hers if she has to take time off, for whoever replaces her won't want to hand such a peach of a job back when she's better.

Gradually it becomes clear that Mary is cautiously suggesting that Fanny take on her job for the duration. Mary can depend on her friend to play fair and relinquish the job when she is fully recovered. Moreover, it is an obvious solution to Fanny's need for a change and something to do now that Jack has left. But why Mary makes the suggestion in so roundabout a way is baffling – until Fanny twigs and explodes with a bellow of a laugh. Mary, it transpires, is responsible for taking the tickets in the ladies' public lavatory, wiping the seats and seeing that no one holds the door for a friend to save her having to put a penny in the slot.

We naturally assume that Mary has been pussy-footing around before offering Fanny the job because of the ignominy of such an occupation. That, certainly, is the kind of reaction Fanny expects from Phil when she tells him about it later. But nothing could be further from Mary Prout's mind. The problem as Mary sees it, and the reason for her stealthy approach, is how the higher-class defecators will react when they have to lower themselves before the lowest. She is concerned that Fanny doesn't dress respectably enough to take the job on! 'Not that you can't when you like, Fan. But you know what I mean, Fan. You'd have to put your corsets on.'

The whole business of class and respectability was immensely complex on Tyneside. The catch-all term 'working-class', beloved of the Labour movement as it rose to power in the twentieth century, obscured an intricate hierarchy within the workforce which was reflected in workers' families at home and turned life for some (such as Catherine's Aunt Mary) into an all-absorbing game of social snakes and ladders. Classifying all the dock workers and all the coal miners, who worked the seams of the Durham coalfield just a few miles from the docks, as working class imposed a uniformity which they certainly did not feel.

Among shipyard workers, for example, fitters, platers and boilermakers did not think of themselves as labourers. In *Kate Hannigan*, the trimmers at the dock gate stand in groups a little apart from the main workforce as they wait in the hope of being taken on. Skilled workers might earn twice or three times as much as unskilled workers, their families would have different social lives and they probably worshipped at different places. Similarly, among miners, the hewers (the coal cutters who did the hard manual work) were a very different breed from the surface workers. There were pitmen who became deputies or overmen in the collieries, and dockers who became foremen and charge hands in the shipyards. Promotion of this sort spelt job security and probably a bigger income and a corresponding rise in status in the community for their families.

Nor was there one homogeneous popular culture. On the one hand, a minority – but a very important one, with more than its fair share of influence – were devotees of church or chapel: against drinking, gambling and smoking. On the other hand, there were pub- and club-goers, who didn't go to church. So you had two sorts of divisions: the economic division, for example between the hewers and other types of mine workers, and the cultural divisions within each of these groups between drinkers and non-drinkers, chapel attenders and non-chapel-going men.

With this sort of keener focus we can begin to appreciate

that there were lines of defence, positions worth protecting or improving on, at a multitude of levels within the so-called working class. There were different outlooks and expectations, too. Within each stratum there were the social climbers, who maybe went to church or chapel for no genuine religious reason but because it was 'the thing to do', or (like Aunt Mary) found other ways to appear to be on a higher level than their neighbours. Then there were those unconcerned with self-promotion, who thought perhaps that the most important thing in life was how far their racing pigeons could be made to fly. At the very lowest level, strivers – people whose one purpose in life was to keep their heads above water – existed alongside the hard cases, the no-hopers, whose daily lives were dominated by poverty and, as John McMullen's life was already and Kate Fawcett's was soon to become, by drink.

It was impossible to appreciate all these fine distinctions unless you lived among them, as Catherine did. Those who lived just outside the Fifteen Streets in her novel of that name considered people living there 'to be of one stratum, the lowest'. But the people inside this stratum knew that there were all kinds of different levels.

Most people lived in rented 'houses', either 'upstairs houses' or 'downstairs houses'. They were called houses by virtue of the fact that each housed an entire family, even though upstairs and downstairs belonged to the same building. In an 'upstairs house' there would be four rooms for habitation, in a 'downstairs house' only three. In the Fifteen Streets, the lower stratum lived 'one step from the Workhouse' at the bottom end, where each 'house' had only two rooms and all were alive with bugs. These families usually arrived after they had been turfed out of a better 'house' for non-payment of rent.

Where you lived and the size of your house was a mark of

your social position, and even the smallest advances were hard won. As Catherine showed in *A Grand Man* (1954), if you moved out of a house with a communal backyard, such as Mulhattans Hall, to a house which had a backyard divided into two distinct areas (one for the upstairs family and one for downstairs) you had 'a right to feel that [you] were socially on the up-grade'.

The McMullens scored badly on practically every scale: house, drink, religion, John's underemployment, his violence, his uncouth tongue, and lack of money. They were not, however, quite at the bottom of the pile. The Kanes, for example, were so poor that little Mary Ellen used to come in to borrow Kate's boots. There were still ways in which the McMullens could fall, and Kate had found one of them.

Also, when Kate came home and informed John and Rose that she was pregnant, the social disgrace was exacerbated by the unfulfilled expectation of her intended marriage up several classes, which had probably set tongues wagging in the neighbourhood. For private lives were public property. The environment in which the McMullens lived was incredibly insular – in *Pure as the Lily* (1972) Alec Walton is deemed a foreigner by workers in Wallsend a few minutes away across the Tyne. In so isolated a community, gossip thrived: neighbours 'just had to get a hold of a thread and by the time they had finished it was a hawser, iron-bound at the ends'. There were, no doubt, some within the McMullens' insular circle who capitalised on Kate's misfortune at her family's expense. There was nothing so enjoyed in a community replete with upstarts as an upstart fallen; and that was how Kate in her plight was viewed. Years later, when Catherine declared herself too good for service, a neighbour, Mrs Waller, would say, 'She's got ideas about herself, that one. She'll end up the same as big Kate!'

Whether or not Kate was subjected to violence at the

hands of her stepfather when she came home and announced that she was pregnant remains unrecorded. But one night when Kate's sister Sarah had failed to return home as arranged from Newcastle, he pursued her into the backyard with a horsewhip. John, of all people, would have found the ignominy to which Kate had subjected the family hard to stomach.

Whatever happened to Kate on the fateful day when she made her announcement, once the dust had settled an arrangement was agreed with John and Rose. Not only was Kate to return to work, in service, but henceforth Rose was to be Catherine's mother and John her father. Rose was forty-eight years old at the time; John was in his fifties. Kate, at twenty-four, would see her child only on her day off. There was no bonding between Catherine and her natural mother. Indeed, one of Catherine's earliest memories is of Rose tearing her away from Kate when the young mother arrived home and gathered her daughter into her arms. Psychologists today believe mother–child bonding to be a crucial development stage for both parties. Until 1913, when Catherine turned seven, she believed Kate to be her elder sister.

CHAPTER THREE

⟨⟨⟨⟩⟩⟩

The Apprenticeship Years

Since the coming of the railway and the dredging of the Tyne in the 1850s, both banks of the river had changed beyond recognition. Hamlets and villages had grown into towns; fields had given way to shipyards, to iron, steel, glass and chemical works and other factories. A multiplicity of railway lines now snaked their way over four of the five slime-dripping arches at Leam Lane End on to the great dock staithes, and as little Katie lay in bed at night she could hear the horns of ships and the creaking and groaning of shunting trains. She was indeed a child of the Tyne.

But industrial Tyneside was little more than half a century old, and there were still reminders of the displaced agriculture of earlier days. On the north side of the Leam Lane hamlet was a blacksmith; on the south, two shops and a pub known as The Twenty-Seven, because this was where the local men docked when they had finished loading and unloading on the twenty-six staithes. The McMullens' house was next to the pub. Beyond lay the gasworks and then, a quarter of a mile or so higher up the bank, a few bigger houses, then the little country school at Simonside, which Catherine first attended at the age of four and a half. 'The country began at Simonside,' Catherine recalls. 'A lot of people would laugh in disbelief today, but it was open land then, mostly given over to turnips or taties. There was a pub

23

called The Robin Hood, and nearby a stream, and it was here that courting couples would walk on a Sunday. I remember that I was sometimes used as camouflage when my Aunt Mary was courting – she was not supposed to be courting this man who became my Uncle Alec. I also have a memory of cowslips then. You don't see many cowslips in the south in the fields somehow, but there you'd see cowslips.'

Opposite the school at Simonside was a farm, from where the farmer would drive his cows past Katie's home to the slaughterhouse in South Shields. On one occasion a cow, terrified by the sound of a tram emerging from the arches at Tyne Dock, escaped from the herd and found its way up the steps to the rooms above the McMullens' home in Leam Lane occupied by a family rather appropriately called Angus. Leaning out of an upstairs window, Mrs Angus shrieked her defiance at the cow's intrusion. But the cow had the last word, quietly evacuating its bowels on the landing floor.

However unforgiving Rose was towards Kate for bearing an illegitimate child, she loved Catherine, and in the first six years of her life the little girl knew security. Rose's love may not have been a natural mother's, but it had a sound, formative influence. Gran Carter in *Hamilton* (1983), while not Rose, suggests something of what Catherine derived from her grandmother's care. She is a warm, caring figure-head, full of old-world lore, and the safety zone to which her granddaughter, Maisie, runs.

Rose would sing to Catherine the only song she knew, about the pleasure of love growing older and fading away 'like the morning dew'. She would tell her what she remembered of Tyneside back into the mid-nineteenth century and repeat other tales she had heard as a child, which took her even further back, to the roots of her culture. Even John managed fairly well to keep his oaths in check when

Catherine was around, and though she would later have to contend with his drunkenness, she was never afraid of him. A clue to their relationship lies in a ritual he enacted every time he came home for his tea. The ritual turned on that egg which always preceded his meal. He would have Catherine sit beside him at the table, top the egg and give her the best of it to eat. While at the time she never understood why she wasn't given an egg of her own, years later she would thank John for his 'voiceless love'. From her grandparents Catherine received possibly a richer influence in the first years of her life than she would have had from her real parents had Alexander Davies had the character to take Kate on. Richer not, of course, in a pecuniary way, but in a way that few who lived in middle-class luxury in Westoe Village, east of Tyne Dock, would know. But it did not last.

Nearly two years after she had started at Simonside School, in June 1912, the McMullens moved from Leam Lane to East Jarrow. It was a move of less than a mile that took them to an odd collection of some fifty houses – two terraces and three streets, William Black Street, Phillipson Street and Lancaster Street – which went under the name of the New Buildings and had been built in the 1880s by the nearby Hedworth (known as the barium) chemical works. I say 'odd' because, while downriver lay noisy, dirty Tyne Dock and the congested industrial town of South Shields, and upriver crusading Jarrow, whose population had increased tenfold in the previous fifty years, the New Buildings – a spit from the Jarrow Road – formed an island community contained within high black wooden palings and surrounded by open space. On the east side of William Black Street was a field of corn, and I have a turn-of-the-century photograph of boys chasing a hay cart trundling past Simonside Terrace at the north end – an image which owes more for its effect to nostalgic ideas about the rural idyll than to industrial

Tyneside in the raw. To the south of William Black Street was another open space, which took in the end of adjacent Phillipson Street and gave on to a field and market garden. Next to Lancaster Street on the west side was waste land belonging to the barium chemical works, where gypsies camped, real old-time travellers. Once, when Catherine was a girl, their head man invited her to take to the road with them; the smell of water on the hot ash of their fires still lives with her to this day. Then, to the north, the eye was released into the mighty river itself, free to range some three-quarters of a mile over to Howdon on the opposite bank.

First stop for the McMullens was an upstairs house in William Black Street. Catherine remembers making the trip with their few bits of furniture, sitting on Jackie Halliday's coal cart next to the mangle, with her feet dangling over the back. (Nearly sixty years later Jackie Halliday, a man with no legs, would inspire the character of Amos in her 1971 novel *Feathers in the Fire*.) The following month they moved again, to a downstairs house in the same street, number 10; this was to be Catherine's home from the age of six until she was twenty-three. Aunt Mary lived at number 30 after she married Alec, and Great Aunt Maggie, Rose's sister, lived at number 26.

Years hence Catherine would stand on the site of number 10, which had fallen before the bulldozers, and gather up the memories of what her grandma had meant to her. It was a sad, nostalgic moment. I have a picture of Catherine on that day, standing where the kitchen had been. Confusion is written on her face, perhaps a little helplessness too. Of all the images of the old days which flooded through her mind it was that of Rose which was the most vivid. 'The tears rolled down my face and I went back to the car and wrote down the vivid impression I had got of her:

Me granny sat in a wooden chair
She had a stiff face, wrinkles and straight black hair,
But if ever I needed comfort I found it there.
Between her knees each day she'd have me stand,
And look me head for nits, and I'd play the band
Until she said, "Here's a bullet
Mind you don't choke yourself
It'll stick in your gullet." '

That summer of 1912, Rose fell ill and Kate was recalled to
run the house. It was the start of a new period in Catherine's
life and it couldn't have been more different from what had
gone before.

Catherine's complex feelings about her 'sister', Kate, are
well suggested by two incidents, both of which are also
indicative of the extraordinary nature of Catherine's awareness at this time.

The first occurred immediately after the decampment to
East Jarrow. Kate was living in at her job with a baker in
Chester-le-Street at the time, and no one had even bothered
to tell her of the move. Perhaps the move had been very
sudden; perhaps it was a sign of how estranged Kate had
become, though she came home regularly, invariably bringing
parcels of food from the baker with her. Now she had come
to the New Buildings to find out where everybody was.

Catherine had tied a rope to a lamp-post in the street and
was whirling around it, singing a song to herself, lost in a
world of her own, when suddenly she caught sight of Kate
coming towards her. At this instant Kate seemed utterly
beautiful to her, approaching as it were out of a mist. She
was a good-looking woman, as I have described, but at that
moment Catherine seems to have had an insight into the
depth of that beauty, into its sources that lay beyond physical
attraction. I was reminded of this story when I saw that

27

Catherine's first novel is dedicated to Kate as a woman 'who found her expression through me'.

The second incident occurred when Catherine emerged one Saturday afternoon from the Crown cinema, where she liked to see the penny matinée. (Catherine walked the streets on her own from the age of five.) Again she saw Kate coming towards her; but this time it was an altogether different vision, 'a sickening revelation'. Kate was drunk, her speech slurred, her laugh raucous, her walk unsteady. Catherine was ashamed to be seen with her. That Kate had turned to drink is the saddest comment on the manifold effects of being jilted by the father of her child because it very soon became a serious problem which would colour her relationship with Catherine to the day Kate died.

As befitted a downstairs house, the McMullens' quarters in number 10 consisted of three rooms, which were now home to Rose, John, Kate, Jack and Catherine. In the front room were six chairs, a couch, a centre-legged oval table, a desk-bed and a double brass bed set in an alcove. In the middle of the kitchen, whose window looked out on to the backyard (shared with the people upstairs), was a large table, covered with some sort of artificial material which today would appear to be plastic; a smaller oblong baking table stood in front of the window, and to the side of the black range fireplace with its steel fender was the Fathar's wooden armchair. A chest of drawers stood against the wall opposite the window and baking table, and by the wall opposite the fireplace was a six-foot wooden 'saddle' or settle, which was sometimes used as a bed. There was one bedroom, where at this stage Catherine slept with her mother.

In the yard was a tap, a staircase to the upstairs house and hen crees, which stretched the length of the side wall to a coal-house at the bottom end, where there were two dry 'ash' lavatories (one for each 'house'). These would be emptied by refuse workers or 'scavengers' using a long-handled shovel inserted beneath the pan through a hole in the back lane wall. The McMullens' washing was done in a poss-tub in a wash-house opposite the lavatories, next to the staircase.

The upstairs 'house' was occupied by a family named Romanus. Jim Romanus was a trimmer in the docks; his wife, a secret toper, drank herself to an early death. Mr Romanus used to knock her about, but no one ever intervened. Neighbourhood gossips were always ready to spread the word as to what was going on, but no one saw it as their business to interfere. So much for the myth of the supportive, close-knit working-class community; in reality it was very much everyone for themselves.

To help make ends meet, Kate took in washing, which was hung out to dry on a line in the back lane and had to be removed hurriedly when the cry went up that the coal cart was coming through. Also, though it sounds incredible in such a small 'house', she took in lodgers. This necessitated different sleeping arrangements: John and Rose in the front room, Catherine and Kate top to tail on the settle in the kitchen and all the lodgers in the bedroom with Jack. There could be as many as nine or ten people living in the three-room house at any one time, for sleeping five lodgers was not unheard-of.

In fact, there doesn't seem to have been anything unusual about these crowded conditions. In 1921 42.3 per cent of Jarrow's population lived in 'overcrowded' accommodation; two adults per room was rated normal, i.e. not overcrowded, and children didn't count in the statistics. And, as with virtually every other statistic for Tyneside at this time, the historical context put the figures in perspective. However bad things were for Catherine in William Black Street in the second decade of the twentieth century, they had been worse for her people a century earlier.

Overcrowding was a major cause of disease, and health problems on Tyneside remained among the worst anywhere in the country. When, according to the Annual Report on Jarrow in 1949, the national infant mortality rate was 32 per 1,000, the Jarrow figure was almost double that.

With normally seven – sometimes nine or ten – occupants of 10 William Black Street and only one, non-flushing lavatory in the yard, visits by the scavengers must have needed to be fairly frequent. However, the main problem for the McMullens seems to have been sheer lack of room to move about. From an early age this sparked in Catherine a particular ambition: 'We had lodgers all the time and I promised myself then that I was going to give myself a very nice, big house with plenty of space.' It is incredible to me that this child, living in so difficult a situation, should make such an apparently absurd promise to herself. For a promise it was: never just a dream. As soon as she began to earn even a small wage she started to put money by. This she added to the pennies she had saved by walking instead of taking a tram when out on messages for Kate. Poverty bred care with money (though absolutely no interest in it for its own sake), and she stashed her hoard in a secret place in the outside lavatory. Later, with the help of these savings, she took out insurance policies which, at the age of twenty-seven, when she was earning the very good wage for a woman of three pounds, six shillings, would enable her to buy a fifteen-roomed house of her own.

The lavatory was more than her bank, however; it was the only place you could be alone, and became a kind of sanctuary for Catherine. Away from the crowded house, she could sit on the white wooden seat, which stretched the whole breadth of the lavatory and half its depth, and lose herself in her thoughts, occasionally peeling the flaking whitewash off the walls and absent-mindedly watching it fall on to the brick floor below. So precious were these moments alone, that the intrusion, without warning, by a refuse worker was especially hard to bear. Suddenly she would hear the rasp of the hatch in the back lane wall being lifted by a 'scavenger' and dart up from the seat, pressing herself, eyes closed, against the door, as the searching long-handled shovel appeared beneath the seat where, a moment before, she had been sitting. It was an assault upon her private world which filled her with such revulsion that she recalled it in her first novel, giving her memory of the desecration of her 'little square house' to Annie Hannigan to disperse the memory. Seven years after *Kate Hannigan* was published, however, she showed that she bore no grudge against refuse collectors. In *Rooney* (1957), her dustman hero is given his 'day of happiness': 'I thought . . . surely they are entitled to one day of love . . . Every working man is entitled to that!'

When Kate first came home to take over the running of the house from Rose, Catherine was a self-confident little six-year-old and the centre of attention at home. It won't have been by chance that she was selected from among her contemporaries at Simonside School to play the Faerie Queen in the Christmas concert. 'My part was the biggest and the best, and I was the prettiest bairn of the lot.' One can hear her saying it with a twinkle in her eye, but it was probably true that she was a cocky little thing at this point in her life. She wasn't spoilt – there wasn't the money to spoil her – but she was loved, and her situation as a child with parents very much older than her and no brothers and sisters to play with, no one of her own age in the house, marked her out as unusual among the children of the New Buildings.

Rose, by this time fifty-four years of age and wearied by the grind of life at subsistence level, seems to have given Catherine an unusually 'old' head on her young shoulders; a teacher at her school even referred to her as 'granny'.

Remembering Rose's song about love fading away 'like the morning dew' as clearly as if she had heard it sung to her only yesterday, she remarks how clearly the words 'spoke of the disillusionment of life'. That was her grandma's mood, not striving at the beginning of adulthood but world-weary, experienced, thinking back over life as she made her way to the journey's close.

It is the classic picture of the only child, with the added dimension of much older parents. This early environment made Catherine not only more adult, but more self-centred – she loved nothing better than to perform her leading role, recite her lines and sing and dance in the kitchen with the clippy mat rolled back and with her grandma and granda, Kate, Jack, Mary and Alec as her appreciative audience. It also made her more self-reliant, more self-motivated, and more innocent of the social conventions of play with other children, the give and take which comes naturally to brothers and sisters. And lastly, it made her more imaginative. The only child – of necessity – tends to create its own world inside. For as long as she could remember, Catherine had been able to see pictures, real live pictures, in her imagination. She was already reading too: not only comics but her 'first real book'. This had been lent to her by the daughter of the caretaker at school and she treasured it so much that she managed somehow never to give it back. For years, whenever they passed on the street, Catherine didn't dare look the girl in the eyes lest she remember that she still had it.

Catherine wasn't a lonely child at this stage. Like other children of the New Buildings, she often went out to play in the streets after tea. She was one of the crowd; and yet she was somehow different. It is not difficult to see her having her say over what should be played or who should occupy centre stage. They would play round the street lamps or in the open space in front of the terrace or on the bank of Jarrow Slake ('the Slacks'), a huge tidal pond across the Jarrow Road from the New Buildings, running from the barium chemical works maybe a quarter of a mile to the sawmill not far from Tyne Dock. It was used for storing timber; great lengths of wood floated on the water's surface when the tide was in. Here the children played a favourite (and dangerous) game of 'piano', deftly jumping from one bobbing beam to the next, trying not to get their feet wet.

At Christmas, like the children in *The Wingless Bird* (1990) who gaze at the sugared mice in the Conways' confectionery shop window, the kids would gather outside Cissie Affleck's shop at the corner of Phillipson Street, wondering at the festive delights they saw there. And at any time, a little group might be found huddled in the chimneypiece on the outside wall of the Richardsons' house, 'used as headquarters for deady-one by the boys', or by the girls as shelter for a game of shops, as Catherine would recall in *Maggie Rowan* (1954). In the novel it is little pieces of coloured paper which pass for currency in the imaginary shop. In reality bits of broken bottle, preferably coloured, or of china, passed as the 'boody', which represented the wonderful sweetmeats on sale in Cissie Affleck's.

One night, a little more than a year after Catherine arrived in the New Buildings, a grasping hand snitched a prize piece of green glass from her boody pile. Outraged, Catherine squared up to the culprit and accused her of the robbery. 'If you don't give me back me boody I'll go and tell me ma about you, so I will!' Whether the other girl saw an opportunity to redress the balance of power which had been upset by the advent of this cocky little girl from Leam Lane or whether she felt she had it coming to her, in one short sentence she tore Catherine's childhood world apart. The girl put her face close to hers and sneered, Catherine didn't even know who her ma was; Rose wasn't her ma, she was her grandma; Kate was her ma, and the 'old sod' she thought was her da, he was her granda. Then she drew her trump card and let fly with – '*You ain't got no da!*'

With no gratuitous exaggeration this spiteful girl, on whose shoulders falls the weight of Catherine's grief, occupies a place in her story akin to that of Judas in the garden of Cedron. For the episode at the chimneypiece on the outside wall of the Richardsons' house, which climaxed in the crowd of children taking up her persecutor's chant, not only sent Catherine immediately into a spiral of uncertainty, fear and loss, but began her long nightmare voyage to nervous break-down and afterwards to a destiny which would put her name on the lips of millions, the story of suffering and triumph which it is my purpose to tell.

Catherine's immediate reaction was not only that of a secure child suddenly informed that she is adopted; it was a complete loss of faith in those whom she had loved and who had loved her. It was the negation of all that had been true. Then came questions about her identity which, at seven years old, she couldn't fully form, let alone understand. Worse, she bottled up her new-found knowledge. She didn't even put it to Rose or Kate, for she felt shame in her heart that the drunken woman whom she had thought of and, yes, loved, as a sister, but not revered, should be the mother of all that she, Catherine McMullen, was. Men could get drunk, even a sister could get drunk, but a ma . . . How could she even think of Kate as her ma? Kate was a person, a grown-up sister; she was not a ma. Suddenly the smell of whiskey on Kate's breath when she leant over her was a repulsive thing. Mothers didn't drool and laugh like a docker; mothers were warm, comforting.

Kate and Catherine had never bonded as mother and daughter. How could they suddenly bond now? Catherine continued to call Rose her ma until Rose died, and Kate never managed to pick up the pieces of their fractured relationship. It was a two-way passage to nowhere. In her ninety-first year, Catherine put it to me this way, with characteristic honesty and even humour: 'I think Kate rejected me from when I was born. She went through hell, having to come home to that little two-roomed house in Leam Lane where her drunken stepfather and half-brother and mother existed. I think I rejected her when I was seven and learnt that she wasn't just our Kate, a relation, she was my mother. But she was never a mother to me. She didn't know how to be a mother. For instance, she wouldn't even tell me the facts of life. When this great, terrifying incident [the onset of menstruation] happened she ran up the street to her sister Mary, who had to come down straight away and pacify me and tell me the facts of life. I was thirteen at the time. Kate was never made to be a mother, and the fact is nor did I want her to be my mother when I realised she drank. Poor little orphan of the storm, one could feel sorry for her . . .'

The episode round the chimneypiece marked the beginning of a quest by Catherine for her own identity that would take many years to complete. It began with a trip to her refuge, the lavatory. In her first novel she gives this to Annie, Kate Hannigan's illegitimate daughter, whose persecutor is named, perhaps with an ironic sidelong glance to the long-term positive elements of the affair, as Cissy Luck. Annie, like Catherine, had supposed that her grandparents, Sarah and Tim Hannigan, were her parents, and that her mother, Kate, was her sister. She flies to her sanctuary in the backyard, but there is no place that her 'queer sense of shame, inexplicable' does not penetrate.

By the time she came to write *Maggie Rowan* (published four years after *Kate Hannigan*) her illegitimate heroine, Maggie, who has been told that she is not Nellie Rowan's daughter but the offspring of Polly Harkness, a whore in Pinwinkle Street, asks, ' "Who am I?" but with a difference.' Maggie does not ask who her parents are – she knows that – but from which of them she has inherited the dominant characteristics 'of her complex self'.

When Catherine was sixteen, her Aunt Mary gave her a full description of her father as she remembered him when he used to visit Kate at The Ravensworth Arms. The picture Mary painted was so unlike anything that Catherine had imagined – Kate had never spoken of him; only once had she ever referred to him, and that only obliquely – that it quite lifted Catherine out of herself. This man, her father, she now realised, had been someone out of the ordinary, out of her class; not some docker or pitman, but a man of mystery and style, a gentleman, who was part of her. She did make some attempts to find out who he was, where he was, even promising a boyfriend, a pit lad 'who ran a betting book on the side', that she would marry him if he managed to find her father. She confesses now that she had no intention of honouring the deal, 'knowing full well that if he did find my father that boy would not see me for dust. Because my father, being the gentleman I had been given to understand he was, would take me away to his big house and have me educated . . .'

The main effect Mary's news had on Catherine, however, was to cause her, like Maggie, to look at herself differently, to consider what there was of her father in her and where it might lead. She embarked on a serious strategy of self-improvement to give whatever traits or genes she had from him the best chance of development over those of her mother, who represented her other side, the side she wanted desperately to eclipse. It was a recipe for disaster psychologically and caused her an enormous amount of grief.

Mary's story, Catherine believes, was related to her in

order to hurt Kate, 'to make me more ashamed of her', in comparison with who *he* was. But, as we shall see, so greatly did the whole idea inspire Catherine that it did lift her out of her impoverished situation. Her absent father, she has written, 'pushed and pulled me out of the drabness of my early existence'. And who is to say whether, as she believed, her father *was* responsible for what marked her out as different, her 'power to convey awareness, this painful sensitivity . . . without which what I sensed in others would have remained an indescribable mass of feelings'? Who is to say what part his genetic legacy had in her talent as a writer? All that is certain is that she does have this remarkable talent, unique among her known kin.

By the time she came to write *The Glass Virgin* (1970) and *The Girl* (1977), Catherine's quest for identity had become altogether more sophisticated. The mothers of Hannah Boyle and Annabella Lagrange, both lowly creatures, trick their gentleman lovers – Matthew Thornton and Edmund Lagrange respectively – into believing that they have fathered their girls out of wedlock, giving their daughters into Matthew's and Edmund's care and an upbringing beyond their wildest dreams. In these novels Catherine's theme is the perversion of nature by so-called civilised attitudes which mark out a bastard as base and so warp human instinct that natural mothers must give their daughters away. Significantly, however, when the girls realise what has been going on they are not consumed by a desire to find their real parents, nor to establish their own identities through heredity. They are, rather, driven by a need to take responsibility for their own lives, to become free agents, free from all the perverse interferences which have so far dictated their lives, free to be *themselves*. That Catherine reached such a stage in her own quest enabled her, following her breakdown, to draw utterly honestly, and therefore convincingly, upon the rich, autobiographical vein which feeds her novels and transforms her work from fairy story into an exploration of human needs and endeavour, valid for all times and all people.

In the same year, 1913, that Catherine learnt who her real mother was, Kate began sending her on errands to feed the very habit that stood between them, and soon this became a daily task. There would have been plenty of other drinkers in the New Buildings, but no one other than Kate sent their child to a pub to get their beer. To begin with Catherine would be given a couple of empty bottles to fill; then, when she was eight and reckoned to be old enough to carry it, Kate gave her a gallon stone jar which would have been used originally to hold vinegar. It was so big, and so heavy when full, that Catherine would have to rest it on her hip on the return journey and pause regularly to rest it on the ground. She would have to take this Grey Hen, as it was called, as far afield as Hudson Street, a mile away, past the dock arches into South Shields, where there was an 'outdoor' beer shop.

Catherine did what she could to make Kate see what she was doing. One occasion sticks in her memory because it was the only time Kate ever mentioned her father until a few days before she died. 'I can see myself standing with my back against the wall,' she told me, 'in the corner of the kitchen and openly defying her by staring at her silently and refusing to budge. It was then she cried at me, "Don't you look at me with his eyes." It must have been at that point that the longing for a father grew in me.'

The pressure on Kate was clearly enormous. She had no life of her own to speak of. Her toil with lodgers, with laundry, with cooking and keeping the house together saw to that. She was a rat in a trap. But to inflict this humiliation, even victimisation upon Catherine as a young girl (it went far beyond sending her for the beer, as we shall see) cannot be so excused.

There were times of laughter, but they too leave a sour taste in the mouth. 'Oh yes, we laughed,' Catherine told me, 'we laughed at the most simple things. Word of mouth was the only form of communication then and Kate had sayings. But they were naughty sayings – very naughty sayings when I think of them now. And I used to say them because I thought they were funny sayings, until I was about fourteen when I realised they meant something else.'

Inevitably the drinking put an additional strain on the family's finances, leading to instances of petty crime. Along with everyone in her class, Catherine was asked by her teacher one day to bring in a length of flannelette to make a nightie. Kate did not have the money to buy it. Weeks passed and Catherine kept reminding her that the date was fast approaching when she would have to produce this flannelette at school. Finally, at the eleventh hour, Kate took her to a shop in Jarrow and, before her daughter's eyes, picked up a part bale of material, stuffed it under her coat and left smartly, with the astonished girl tripping behind. On the way home, Catherine had to ask Kate to stop while she vomited by the side of the road.

The incident shows just how close to the wind the McMullens with Kate in control were sailing. 'Necessity, through time and circumstances, made life,' Catherine wrote in *The Obsession* (1995). But necessity did not drive all the Tyneside poor to crime, as an incident which followed an injury to her hip in the playground at school shows.

'I have never before told what I am about to say now. It had been snowing during the week and on this particular day, Kate put into my hand a ten-shilling note and a bass bag and told me to go to Tyne Dock and get three bottles of beer . . . She put the note into my hand – I cannot remember having a purse or a bag during my childhood or my early teens. I carried the money in my hand and I brought the change back in my hand. Now that day she did not give me a halfpenny for a tram to Tyne Dock, because likely she hadn't another penny in the house. So I had to walk. The terminus of the Jarrow car was about twenty feet from the actual police box that guarded the big dock gates. Here the driver would take a pole and turn the long overhead leads round to what had been the back of the car and link it to the wires above. The passengers for the return journey would be standing against the iron railings that bordered the dock shipping offices. The dock gates, the Jarrow tram and the shipping offices seemed to be a full stop between East Jarrow and Tyne Dock, and from this point Shields seemed to begin. Straight in front of the dock gates was a steep bank bordered on one side by public houses and on the other by part of the shipping offices, where the men used to line up in order to be picked for jobs on the boats. This steep bank led to the station, my school and my church. But off it led Hudson Street, where there was the outdoor beer shop and the butchers.

'On this particular day I knew that I could not walk up that bank. My leg was aching terribly and I was trailing my foot. Now, at the bottom of the bank there always stood a paper boy. And what did I do? I went up to this boy and I asked him would he go a message for me as I had a bad leg and couldn't walk up the bank. He said he would, so I placed in his hand the ten-shilling note and the bass bag. What I went through as I waited for that boy to return were ages of eternity filled with terror, knowing what Kate would do to me when I managed to get back home and tell her what I had done. That boy returned with the three bottles of beer and the change, and I gave him a penny. I recall he was poorly clad and freezing with the cold because it was a bitter, bitter day. All that I remember about him otherwise was that he kept hopping from one foot to the other, and although my

The girl from Leam Lane. Despite the shame, anger and recrimination that heralded her birth, in the first six years of her life Catherine knew security.

The map shows Tyne Dock and East Jarrow, where Catherine lived from her birth in 1906 until she left the North in 1929. She was born in the southwest corner of the dock on the south side of Leam Lane (marked Leamlane End on the map), where it funnels out on to the Jarrow Road.

Southwest from her place of birth, Leam Lane became Simonside Bank and led up to Simonside School, which Catherine attended from four-and-a-half. 'In those days the country began at Simonside,' Catherine recalls.

To the west of Leam Lane End can be seen the New Buildings, the island community to which she moved in 1912 – William Black Street (where she lived), Phillipson Street, Lancaster Terrace, and the posh end, Simonside Terrace, closest to the Jarrow Road. On the far side of the Jarrow Road (to the north), lay the Jarrow Slake or Slacks (the timber pond) and the River Tyne.

Travelling west along the Jarrow Road brought you to the barium chemical works and then Jarrow; travelling east led you under the five 'slime-dripping' arches to the dock gates. The first arch was a bridge leading to a timber yard, the other four carried trains on to the loading bays of the dock itself.

Directly opposite the dock gates the map shows Hudson Street, where Catherine went for Kate's liquor; second left can be seen Bede Street, where Bob Gombertz had his pawn shop. Hudson Street led to the railway station and Tyne Dock church and school, which Catherine attended from 1916, and then to Brinkburn Street, where she would also go for Kate's beer and where, much later, Kate lived. Further southeast, just off the map, the workhouse still stands where Catherine was employed from 1924 until 1929.

From right to left: Catherine's step-grandfather, John McMullen, whom she knew as her father, the prototype Irish Geordie on whom it is all too easy to hang the sins of every drunken Irishman since famine first drove them unwillingly to these shores. Then comes John's son Jack: sixteen years of age when Catherine was born, he grew into a handsome hulking docker and wanted more from his half-sister Kate than virtue allowed. On the left is John's wife, Rose, Catherine's grandma, whom she first knew as her mother.

'Clothes-poor on Tyneside', the photograph was taken in 1890, the year that John McMullen married the widow Rose, rescuing her children from the shame and squalor of begging on the streets and Rose herself from slow death at the Jarrow Puddling Mills.

The bustle of Shields harbour in the late nineteenth century. After the coming of the railway in the 1840s and the dredging of the Tyne a decade later, both banks of the Tyne changed beyond recognition. Hamlets and villages grew into towns, fields became shipyards, iron, steel, glass and chemical works and other factories. It was into this industrial world that Catherine was born in 1906.

The little girl who is standing across the road from the house, number 5 Leam Lane, where Catherine was born, seems to beg identification with her.

Looking westwards, away from Tyne Dock, at the point where Leam Lane funnelled out on to the Jarrow Road. Catherine was allowed to wander Tyne Dock from the age of five and would follow this coal truck and pick up any fallen coals to take home for the fire.

Tyne Dock itself, as it appeared when Catherine was born in 1906, a few miles from where North and South Shields face each other across the mouth of the Tyne and the river flows into the North Sea.

Children discerning treasures on the shoreline at Broad Landing in 1910 as a tug makes its way upstream. Even as Catherine lay in bed at night she could hear the horns of ships and the creaking and groaning of shunting trains as they snaked their way over the arches on to the great dock staiths. She was indeed a child of the Tyne.

On the move. Catherine remembers sitting with their few bits of furniture on the back of a flat cart for the trip (less than a mile from Leam Lane) to the island community of the New Buildings in East Jarrow, where Rose, John, Jack and Catherine moved in June 1912.

Boys chasing a hay cart, trundling past Simonside Terrace at the north end of the New Buildings in 1910. Catherine lived on adjacent William Black Street from 1912 until 1929 when she was twenty-three. Although in the heart of industrial Tyneside, the countryside was less than a mile away

Catherine with Rose in the doorway of number 10 William Black Street. Rose had a sound, formative influence on her charge and Catherine returned her warmth and wisdom with a child's love for its real mother, which made it all the more devastating when, in 1913, Catherine discovered who her real mother was.

situation was poor, that boy's was much worse. I never told Kate of this episode because she would have gone mad to think that I had been such a fool as to trust a paper boy.

'Over the years I have thought of that incident. A ten-shilling note would have been a fortune to that child because he was only about ten or eleven years old. He was cold and likely hungry and likely one of a large family, all in the same boat.

'That incident has grown in my mind with the years. If miracles could be handed out to honesty then there was one.

'Whether it was that Christmas or the following one, I don't know. But there occurred another incident, as opposite to that of the paper boy's as could be possible. There must have been little money in the house and Kate sent me to the pork butcher's in Jarrow. It was a half-penny tram drive and it was near Dee Street. She put a shilling into my hand this time and told me I was to get sixpennyworth of bones and threepennyworth of trotters and scranchums, bits of odds and ends of crackling, odd pieces of fat. I knew that the shop sold penny dips. This was a bun with a piece of pork cracklet in it. But she didn't go in for such luxuries. Again I remember it was snowing.

'The shop was full, and on this day there seemed to be a lot of commotion. I was standing near the end of the counter, waiting my turn to push up to give in my order. My feet were cold and I was stamping them against the sawdust on the floor. I happened to glance down between the legs around me and saw a piece of paper sticking out. I picked it up and saw that it was a ten-shilling note. Then I realised what the commotion was about further along the counter. People were looking among the sawdust, scraping their feet, and a woman was crying that she'd had it, she'd had it. 'Twas then I realised that they were looking for this ten-shilling note that she had dropped.

'I recall that it was very dirty and crumpled because it had been trodden on and nobody had noticed that I'd picked anything up. They were all looking towards the commotion. I pushed my way through the throng and held out the now straightened but still crumpled ten-shilling note and said, "Are you looking for this, Missis?" The commotion stopped; the woman turned on me, grabbed the money out of my hand and glared at me – then handed it over the counter and picked up her purchases and was gone. I can't recall any comment being made on what I had done, but when I got back home I put my bag on the table and said to Kate, "I found a ten-shilling note on the butcher's floor." I can see her now. She stopped dead in what she was doing, put her hand to her head, then made a sign of the cross and she said, "Thanks be to God!" She held out her hand and I said, "Well, I gave it back to the woman." At this she just stared at me, stared and stared. Then she suddenly sat down and all I recall is that she bent her head.'

Kate's 'Thanks be to God!' and the hanging of her head at the waste of that ten-shilling note speak volumes about the financial difficulties the McMullens were in. Catherine never had the things which many of her contemporaries enjoyed. It became routine at Christmas to pack her stocking with vegetables, just one or two presents lying in the top. One year, to Catherine's painful disappointment, it was all vegetables. She never had new clothes and was mortified by Kate making her wear a costume coat of thick serge material, far too big for her, with great ballooning sleeves which came in at the wrists and made her look like a bat when she raised her arms. When it was worn out, Kate replaced it with a thick blanket of a coat she'd picked up somewhere, off-white with splurges of red, pink and blue in blotches and stripes. Deeply ashamed of it, Catherine wore it only once.

Yet poverty alone cannot explain why Kate used Catherine

as gofer for all her more degrading tasks, in particular for regular trips to the pawn shop. Catherine's readers will recognise in this Katie O'Brien of *The Fifteen Streets*, to whom she gives the utter degradation of her own regular trips to Bob Gombertz, the Pawn. It wasn't until she was eleven years old that it finally came home to Catherine that the reason Kate sent her was to avoid the shame of it herself. The pawn shop, where clothes were hocked for cash, was a cheap and viable moneylending operation for families in need. But in a community where respectability was all, it was deeply humiliating for the child to be seen by women cleaning their front doorsteps (an obsession in the New Buildings as elsewhere), carrying the tell-tale parcel in her arms.

It should be emphasised that the New Buildings was a mixed community and that its isolation made it a breeding ground for affectation and snobbery. The three streets and the two blocks in Simonside Terrace housed a mixture of families ranging from the lower working class right through to lower middle class and even some middle-class people, who would probably have preferred to have lived in Harton village on the upmarket east side of Tyne Dock. There were the destitute clothes-poor, like the O'Briens in *The Fifteen Streets* or in real life the Kanes, whose daughter would borrow Kate's boots. At the other end of the scale were the Larkins, who lived in two houses at the end of Simonside Terrace (the terrace was the place to be). The Larkins were middle-class people, who at one time had a stake in the barium chemical works and sent their daughter to a boarding school. Catherine glimpsed this girl only once, as she was alighting from a taxi – 'equivalent to a guttersnipe watching the Queen pass' is how Catherine remembers it. Many years later, when this girl had grown up and moved to France, she visited England, bringing her own daughter with her, and let it be known at a banquet at Langley Castle that she had been a friend of Catherine and played with her in her youth. Word of this got back to Catherine, who was living with her husband Tom Cookson nearby, and when Catherine received her in their home the visitor again insisted on their relationship. 'Funny what fame will do.'

For the young Catherine, as messenger, the eyes of anyone on her as she carried that parcel to the pawn, whether higher or lower in social terms, spelt ignominy. As with the beer, she was the only child who was made to do it, and she came to dread Kate asking her to stay off school in the morning, sometimes pleading (when the rent was due and there was no money in the house), at other times shouting at her if she tried to refuse. Going to Bob Gombertz's pawn shop in Bede Street meant passing underneath the arches at Tyne Dock and running the gauntlet of dockers waiting to be taken on. They stood in their huddles right up Hudson Street to where the road divided. Everyone knew her as 'old John's bairn'; everyone knew what she was carrying in her arms – or Catherine had convinced herself they did. To avoid their greetings or stares, she embarked upon an elaborate strategy to throw them off the scent.

If she could, if she had a halfpenny for the fare, she would take a tram up Hudson Street, right through to the railway station, where she would disembark and emerge down the steps by the station as if she were arriving by train, then walk back down Hudson Street towards Bede Street. Fortuitously there was a back lane separating Bede Street from adjacent Nelson Street and she would duck down there, entering the pawn shop through the rear door. She would then pass right through the shop and emerge into Bede Street by means of Gombertz's front door and study his shop window as if she were there to buy. After a period of time, judged to be sufficient to have convinced her audience what she was (or wasn't) up to, she would enter the shop through the front door once more. She might even take the deception further, rummaging through the goods for sale inside.

Whether the deception was successful is hardly the point. Quite possibly her audience were totally unaware of what was going on, or if they did notice were very confused. But the pains she took in constructing this strategy give us all the insight we need into her personal agony – particularly as it was only a matter of time before Gombertz annihilated all pretence by asking what she'd got to exchange. Then her emotions were twisted still further by the need to negotiate, for Kate invariably compounded her anguish with a demand that she try to squeeze him for a little extra that week. She was rarely successful, and so the trip home was fraught with more anxiety about what Kate would say.

What Catherine dreaded perhaps even more than people looking down their noses at her was the other response she detected as these trips became regular: pity.

The difference between love, compassion and pity is a theme repeatedly explored in her novels, recently in *The Obsession*. When Dr Falconer proposes marriage to the obsessive Beatrice Steele and tries to analyse his feeling for her, he realises that it isn't passion but isn't sure that it is love either. 'Was it . . . compassion perhaps? Yes. Yes, compassion. But even more than that. Pity? Well, no, no. She wasn't the kind of person you could pity. She was too strong . . .'

Starved of mother love, Catherine began to loathe being on the receiving end of its poor relation, pity, because it marked her out as weak, which she prided herself she was not. She was always fighting against her fears and anxieties, right from the age of seven. Above all, it was important to her that to the other customers in the shop she appeared quite in control of the situation. So, on the outside, whatever she was feeling inside, she played the extrovert, the consummate actress. Once, when taking her place in the pawn shop queue, a woman stroked her rich auburn curls and said, 'Eeh! but you have bonny hair!' Catherine's response was as sharp as a dart. Lifting her full head of hair with her hand she brought the woman's attention to the darker hair at the nape of her neck. 'That's nearly black,' she said, 'Me da must have been a nigger!'

On cue, the woman had howled with laughter. But with the sobering distance of time the incident is rather less humorous than it is revealing. Catherine tells me that she knew little or nothing about the racism which was rife in the area, but clearly she was well versed in the racist undertow of day-to-day conversation. What the incident reveals is an extrovert actress adept at self-effacing humour. In so many of her novels humour transforms pathos, and we can see it at work here, while she suffered inside at the ignominy of her trip to the Pawn. It is a brave, even courageous, performance for such a tortured little girl, and it wouldn't be wasted. This incident, she told me, inspired her novel *Colour Blind* (1953), and readers may fancy that they can hear the raucous laughter of the woman in the pawn shop in the mouth of Kathie McQueen, whose huge breasts and hanging stomach literally reverberate with it.

Catherine had no one with whom to share her feelings until she was in her teens, and even then she felt guilty, disloyal, doing so. Those who were moved to pity her were not moved to do anything about it. This was a community of gossips who kept trouble at arm's length. No one had any idea how Catherine felt. Her shame that they might, and her extrovert behaviour, saw to that, and Kate's widespread popularity protected her from criticism. Kate was a different person in company and people responded to her humour, her generosity, her ability to be the life and soul of the party. No one looked deep inside her, any more than they did inside

Catherine – particularly not in Kate's case, because she was the life and soul of the party when in drink, and people needed people like Kate. When Catherine wrote her autobiography *Our Kate* (1969) to cleanse her own soul of the bitterness she felt, she rewrote it eight times to make it palatable. Nevertheless, it remains a forceful indictment of her mother. Yet after publication Catherine received countless letters from men who said what a wonderful woman Kate must have been, one even expressing his regret that he had not met her, for surely they would have been married.

Perhaps people take out of a book what they want to believe. True, Kate was generous and warm. When she had what she needed – a drink – you couldn't come across a more generous soul. And yet it was then that Catherine couldn't abide her, for she knew that it wasn't Kate, and it certainly wasn't her ma. But there were other times, just a few, when she became what she might have been if her life had run differently, and I will come to them. Catherine has written, 'Kate had a depth in her that attracted me' – shades of that vision when Catherine was dancing round the lamp-post . . . If her life had been different, if she hadn't turned to drink, then I have a feeling that Catherine wouldn't have had to turn to Mary's gilded image of her father to identify what gave her the inspiration to write; nor, perhaps, would she have suffered the terrors of breakdown before she found herself capable of being a vehicle for Kate's expression, as she put it in the dedication to her first novel. Catherine not only saw but came to understand this depth in Kate. What others saw – the raucous bonhomie – was not the real Kate at all.

'When I made a name for myself I made a short visit from Hastings, where I then lived, to the north to give a talk in South Shields. I stayed with Sarah [her Aunt Sarah's youngest daughter], and as I hadn't time to visit all the relatives, she kindly got them all together and gave a party for me. It was an awkward situation, since some of them I hadn't seen for twenty years. Sarah, I know, was so proud to have a famous cousin and she did me well with a beautiful tea. Then there we were, all in her sitting room, talking about the family and all saying how they had liked Aunt Kate. Oh wasn't Aunt Kate a joker. She was the best practical joker that ever lived (if I hated Kate for nothing else I hated her for her awful practical jokes). How merry she was. How kind she was. Always had a welcome when you went to see her. And the life and soul of any party. On and on it went, and then, quite quietly, I said, "Yes, Kate was all that, I know. But then you hadn't to live with her. You didn't know the other side." Like a shot of a gun one of the sons sprang up and said, "Don't you dare say a word about my Aunt Kate. You're not fit to wipe her shoes."

'Imagine the silence that followed. My poor cousin Sarah didn't know where to put herself . . . They knew nothing about Kate, especially he who had opened his mouth. Oh, he liked his Aunt Kate. When he left the pit (because it was too much like hard work) and he was broke, Kate was always forthcoming with a sixpence or a shilling to get a drink. Oh yes, he liked his Aunt Kate. And since then I've hated that fellow. He was the first person who had ever insulted me in public (and belonging to my family!). From that day I disowned him in my mind. I have never felt spiteful against anyone in my life, but I felt it against that man and I still do.'

Violence is part of the rough fabric of Tyneside culture and is a fearsome aspect of Catherine's novels. 'In those days,' she once told me, 'it was not unusual for the man of the house to use a belt, often with the buckle end, on members of the family. There was violence in our household, massive rows.' John never hit Catherine, but Kate did. She would be sent to her bedroom . . . to wait for it. The last time Kate raised her hand to her daughter was when Catherine was about sixteen: she threatened to hit her back, and did. There was friction, too, between Kate and John, especially after Rose died. 'I can see Kate standing there in the doorway with the frying pan, a huge, iron pan about fourteen inches across, a big pan for an open fire. I can see her with it raised above her head. I can't remember what the row was about, but it was after that that we went up to Aunt Mary's and stayed. I remember I laid on a shakey-down on the floor and I remember thinking, wouldn't it be nice to be always here; it'd be heaven.'

Some of the most savage incidents in Catherine's novels, which arise out of the underswell of real violence and cruelty running through Catherine's formative years and which measure her rage and repulsion at all that beset her in the first two decades of her life, occur in *The Girl*, in which Hannah Boyle is whipped senseless by her 'adoptive' mother, Anne Thornton, who in turn is whipped by her husband, Matthew; in *The Whip* (1983), in which Emma Molinero is bound in an attic and flailed mercilessly by Luke Yorkless (a novel of sexual repression and sometimes sadistic violence to which I will return); and in *A Dinner of Herbs*, in which Hal Roystan is trussed up like a chicken in a barn and left by the psychotic Mary Bannaman to die a slow death. The most masterly creation in *Fenwick Houses*, a first-person narrative – unusual for Catherine, is the character of Don Dowling, a study in repressive behaviour traceable to his extravagant, even perverse, mothering by Phyllis. We learn towards the end of the novel about the tortures to which he has subjected his brother Sam since he was a four-year-old. But the development of this psychopathic character is subtly done throughout, the first sign a rabbit nailed alive to a tree. I recall Catherine telling a story of how a woman in the neighbourhood of William Black Street chopped the tail of a puppy half off simply because it raced through her legs while she was cutting meat.

In *The Blind Miller* we have much of the coarseness which oppressed Catherine as a child, including the effect of whiskey on Kate, seen here in the beleaguered Sarah Bradley. This is a powerful novel, perhaps her best in conveying a sense not only of a life of squalor, but also of the mesmerising, primitive currents which flowed beneath the surface of life. The hopeless degradation is caught in a picture that first comes to Sarah as a hallucination when she has taken an overdose of cough medicine, and thereafter comes back to her time and time again. In this image, all the inhabitants of the Fifteen Streets are wallowing and choking in a sea of mud, which we recognise as the timber pond of the Jarrow Slacks when the tide is out. So many of Catherine's early books, through which she performed an extraordinary operation of self-purification, are full of such imagery, drawing us more deeply into her subconscious than the literal connections with the environment in which she was brought up.

Then there is the anatomical imagery, which again emphasises the uncompromising physicality of life and at the same time its truth. Sarah isn't simply embarrassed when she is first introduced to the nice young man called David Hetherington. Sweat 'bursts into her oxters'. This word 'oxters' – armpits – so unusual a piece of northern dialect that it is bound to have most of her readers sit up, occurs frequently in her novels (as do hunkers). What its use does here is to express the animalism of the scene, so successfully as to have us almost smelling the poor girl's sweat. Elsewhere Catherine uses the word as a wonderful leveller. In a society bursting with snobbery and prejudice, everyone has oxters, irrespective of race, caste or creed, and sweat bursts regularly in all of them. We get the feeling that our world too might be a better, more truthful place if we came to terms with our oxters and put the purveyors of deodorant out of business.

But then, besides the animalism, we have the animism, the primitive immaterial force which is all-inspiring, as when David's exciting, sensuous brother John takes Sarah racing the moon, he running wild against the wind 'like a great lolloping bear', she beside him caught fast in his iron grip. Poor, kind David will not stand a chance against this. The sexual hunger of his wife for John fairly crackles off the page. And yet what we feel is that sex is their response to the force, not the force itself.

For violence (and appalling prejudice, which is what in this novel sets Catherine up for the violence) it is difficult to imagine a more powerful scene than Pat Bradley's taking a belt to his daughter Phyllis, Sarah's sister, for going with an Arab called Ali.

'The Arabs first came to Shields in the crews of ships in the nineteenth century. Up until just before the war more than half the crew would have been Arab,' Catherine told me. 'Then what would happen is that one or two would start a boarding house and the men from the ships would stay there. In the docks, if there weren't Arabs, there were Swedes, a tremendous number of Swedes, and there were negroes and Russians, the big burly captains. There was everything there, and not once did anyone handle me, even though at that time there was a tremendous fuss about the white slave trade, girls being picked up and whisked away.' But race, like class and religion, 'was an opportunity not to be missed' by the bigots in the community, though 'there was just as much race prejudice between negroes and Arabs as there was between blacks and whites.'

Corstorphine Town was the Arab quarter in Shields. 'Despite what I said in Bob's pawn shop, I didn't know anything at that time about immigrants or how different one was from another.' But the Arab quarter did occupy a special place in Catherine's memory for another reason. 'Betty was a pet hen,' she told me. 'She was twelve years old, she had rheumatics and couldn't walk but could still lay eggs. When she died, me granda couldn't eat her, but he wasn't going to lose on her so he sold her to one of the Arab boarding houses in Corstorphine Town.'

Another Betty ends up in Corstorphine in *The Blind Miller* – Betty Fuller. Her mother empties a chamberpot over her head when she returns home after going out with an Arab, and the whole neighbourhood rises up against her. But this is nothing compared to Pat Bradley's wrath when he takes his buckled belt to his daughter, Phyllis, unleashing all the prejudice, cruelty, envy and morbid self-interest with which Catherine invests his character (morbid, for, as Sarah says, he wants his daughter Phyllis for himself). He whips her so hard that her jumper and skirt lie in shreds 'and the seat of her bloomers was all black as if she had been dragged around the yard.'

Catherine's description of this terrible act, effective as it is in the novel, draws additional power from the way it is contrasted to the love between the teenage sisters, Bradley's daughters. It is a relationship for which Catherine, the only child, longed in her increasingly alienating environment at home. Phyllis and Sarah sleep together in the same bed, they share all their secrets, they enjoy each other's company on a ferry-ride across the Tyne with an innocence otherwise hopelessly absent from a community eaten up by prejudice and fear.

In *Hamilton* a mother is guilty of even worse cruelty to her child. Maisie Carter was born of a cross-class liaison with a Rochester from Wellenmore Terrace, who left home when Maisie was two. Already disfigured physically (Maisie has one arm shorter than the other), she is beaten up so badly in her early teens by her mother, after a visit (expressly forbidden) to her warm-hearted Gran, that the girl's face is still swollen after a week, when the family doctor, Dr Kane, chances to call. While I was reading this novel, Catherine happened to telephone me. I had been wondering what the source could be for this kind of extreme fictional violence between a mother and daughter, and Catherine told me a story about Kate which answered my questioning pretty effectively.

The incident occurred after Catherine had left the North and moved to Hastings in Sussex and after Kate had come to live with her there. It was Christmastime, the year 1932. Kate had arrived at Hastings station drunk and had been drinking heavily ever since. Catherine had started a row with her about her heavy drinking, but when she realised that everything was coming to a head tried to back-track; she didn't want to spoil Christmas. But Kate had already gone too far to retreat. She lined up four bottles of spirits on the sideboard. One was her husband David's rum (she had married a sailor called David McDermott nine years earlier); another was her own whiskey; the other two contained gin and vodka. Kate then took a half-pint mug, poured more or less equal portions from each bottle into it and, mixing it all up, downed the whole explosive cocktail in one. Beside the fire were her husband's boots – hobnailed working boots, which David wore to work at sea, with short nails with large heads set proud of each sole to keep him steady on the metal grid floor of the hold. As the battle between the women raged, Kate took first one of these boots and then the other and hurled them at her daughter with all the anger of a lifetime. Catherine was staggered. The first missed her, but she felt the slipstream of the second on her face. A few millimetres closer and she would have been maimed like Maisie.

There are few things more unsettling for a young child than to hear its parents row, especially when they are out of sight and the row is about sex. Violence heard through the wall can set up home in the imagination, engendering a kind of voyeuristic fear which lingers longer, for example, than abrupt chastisement. In *Fenwick Houses*, the rows Christine Winter hears through the wall between her Aunt Phyllis and Uncle Jim, who has a woman in Bog's End, form the girl's earliest impressions of sex. Likewise, in *Kate Hannigan*, little Annie hears Tim Hannigan's voice, 'low and terrible with menace', met by her grandma's pleading, 'full of something that struck the greatest terror into Annie's heart'. Both scenes arise from Catherine's own experience as a child, listening to precisely this scene between grandma and her drunken stepgrandfather, as Rose struggled to fight John off.

For Kate, after Catherine's conception, sex was non-existent until she married David McDermott in 1923. Among the lodgers who came to William Black Street soon after she took up the reins of the household from Rose in 1912, one Jack Stoddart (who introduced David to Kate) was a contender for her hand, but old John would have none of it. Kate had blotted her copybook. Sex was the cause of the mess they were in. For Catherine, as she grew from a girl into a young woman, this fear and restraint sat uneasily alongside her earlier experiences of sexual menace heard through the wall, and the deviant images she picked up elsewhere. Even today she remembers vividly the occasion when she was waiting for a tram by the dock gates and, hearing raucous laughter, looked across the road to where there was a public convenience. 'To my horror I saw a woman come out of the public lavatory opposite with three men.' Then, in 1914, the year after the traumatic revelation of her illegitimacy, Catherine was sexually molested by an Irish lodger from next door, a man who had been going to marry Kate.

It was a Saturday night; Rose and John were out. Catherine was only eight, and Kate was supposed to be looking after her, but she had left her to go and fetch some beer. The man sat Catherine on his knee – she hadn't thought it strange, didn't her granda always sit her on his knee? But then he picked her up and laid her on the settle and began smothering her with kisses. It was a terrifying experience for the little girl – 'I can still hear myself screaming.'

She remembers little of what occurred until after Rose and John returned. In the ensuing fight Rose was 'knocked clean under the table . . . For me there are blocks, absolute blocks in my childhood. I have tried to get past them but I can't . . . I wasn't abused. It was what I saw and knew he intended . . . I can't remember who I told or what I said because there is a blank there. I knew that if I told anyone me granda would kill him as he would an old man in a shop who wouldn't give me the change until I kissed him. I was wise enough to know this, that there would be terrible consequences because, you know, he really loved me . . . I must have said something to me granda. The Irish lodger disappeared from the house next door the following morning.'

Childhood abuse is the subject of *The Cinder Path* (1978). The setting is Northumberland, and the novel opens around 1908–10. Charlie McFell is the fulcrum. Charlie's father, Edward, is a warped personality, damaged by his own father, William, who had bought Moor Burn Farm in 1858. Here, first Edward and then his children, Charlie and Betty, were brought up. One of Edward's earliest memories is of his father, William, sadistically throwing him down on to the rough surface of a cinder path and beating him with a birch. The pain and humiliation to which William regularly subjected Edward (and any young miscreant on the farm) are made doubly wounding by the knowledge that he had laid the path for the purpose. This strangely symbolic black strip of sharp cinders led, otherwise uselessly, from the McFells' farm to the burn which gave the farm its name. The dead-end track was never trodden; no one could possibly want to walk it. It led nowhere, other than remorselessly into the dark, obsessional reaches of William McFell's mind, and on, as the novel opens, into the mind of his son, Edward.

This time it is young 'Ginger' Slater, a workhouse boy, who gets the treatment, while Charlie and young Polly Benton look on, voyeuristically but appalled. Confirming our subliminal interpretation of William's and Edward's obsessional behaviour as sexually motivated, the event mingles with heartless suggestions by Edward that it's about time young Charlie got laid, and that, apart from this, he should think about marrying Victoria Chapman of neighbouring Brooklands Farm (so that the two properties might be joined).

Polly Benton lives in a stone cottage on Moor Burn Farm with her mother, also called Polly, who has been Edward's unhappy and unwilling means of sexual release for years. Jim Benton, utterly dependent on the McFells, has been in no position to complain. Now Edward has a mind to select young Polly as similar instrument for his son, Charlie. There is a well of sickness and depravity so deep at Moor Burn Farm that any show of parental emotion towards Charlie, even by his mother, is suspect, a cause of embarrassment. For even in his mother the show of affection has a selfish source, merely fulfilling her needs. Charlie is rendered clinically bereft of feeling by his father, the vacancy in the tunnel which leads to the bottom of this well of depravity, to the place where lies the monster which, at any moment, we know will swallow Edward up.

When it does, it is young Polly's brother, Archie, who precipitates Edward's fall. Archie rigs up a rope across the path which he knows Edward will shortly ride. He means to unseat him and so save his sister. But Edward's fall from his horse breaks his neck. Again Charlie, in the position of voyeur, watches it happen. Charlie returns Archie to his sister and mother, and makes them swear a pact never to tell what has happened. Charlie has every reason to be glad that his father is dead. But when he takes his leave of them and disappears so that Edward's death may be discovered without implicating himself or the Bentons, he weeps over the 'slaughter'.

It is a strange opening, a raw and sensitive account of childhood abuse. There is compulsion and voyeurism, repression and secrecy, love and deep, deep hurt. But the literary tool Catherine uses – the image of the cinder path, her central 'device' – is itself so odd (it seems to belong to some sort of weird, sadistic public school regime) that you are left in no doubt that whatever psychological blocks Catherine has about her abuse and rank exposure to sex as a child, they are rolled aside in the novels, where her subconscious is in control.

This was never more apparent than in *Colour Blind*. After reading it, her mother Kate was astonished. She had had no idea that Catherine had been aware of her brother Jack's incestuous advances to her, which had begun when Kate moved into William Black Street and took control of the household. Catherine herself was even more surprised, because consciously she had had no idea about Jack either.

Jack, the fourth regular member of the McMullen household, about whom little has so far been said, was a handsome, hulking docker, 'swarthy like a gypsy', and eight years Kate's junior. There appears to have been no girlfriend on the scene during his short life (he was killed in action in the First World War aged twenty-eight): Jack spoke of women, joked about them, but they never materialised. At the time of which I am writing, around 1912–13, Kate and

Catherine were sleeping in the same bed. Catherine was six. One night she remembers awakening to find Jack, his face close to Kate's, whispering her name repeatedly. This scene is actually recorded in a later novel, *Fenwick Houses*, presumably after Kate had read *Colour Blind* and told Catherine what Jack had been up to that night. But in the earlier narrative, where Matt McQueen's passion for his sister Bridget drives her 'whisky-mad' and eventually destroys Bridget's relationship with the negro Jimmy Patterson, there is so true a portrayal of Jack's desire for his sister that Kate assumed Catherine must have known about it. When Catherine denied this, Kate said, 'Well, you must have taken it in as a child.'

Catherine took it all in, all the secrets, all the repressed desires and fears, but for her own sanity's sake blocked much of it out from conscious thought until, years later, it was released in the novels.

Kate had lifted a veil from Catherine's misted memories of rows between Jack and Kate that seemed to be about nothing. The truth of what lay behind this friction, never suspected on a conscious level, had been known, deep down. Like the time Kate was on her knees clearing out the ashes of the fire and Jack, close to her, was shaking his fist, before he suddenly dashed to the bedroom and, reluctantly this time, Kate had sent Catherine out for the beer . . .

Following the episode at the chimneypiece Catherine's response to the revelation of her illegitimacy had been shame and fear, the fear of 'not belonging'. She countered both by immediately attempting to establish a new, more acceptable identity. She had considered pretending to her classmates that her Uncle Alec, Mary's husband, was her da. He was quite bright, good at crosswords and that kind of thing, and of course, as Mary never ceased to remind everyone at number 10, they were distinctly better off and more respectable than the McMullens. But Catherine decided to go for broke and instead to opt for Dr James McHaffie, the family doctor. There's quite a nice irony in this, for in a sense in those days doctors 'fathered' all illegitimate children, as childbirth was almost always carried out under the aegis of the family doctor at home. But the attraction of McHaffie for Catherine was that he was good-looking, had a car and, like all doctors, was middle class. Doctors and priests were, indeed, just about the only middle-class presence in the lives of lower working-class families. So McHaffie it would be.

She regaled her classmates with stories of the big house she lived in, the servants and horses and cars, and then one day she was all set for school and McHaffie happened to be in the house visiting her granda, who had injured his leg at work. As Catherine was ready for off, so was he, and oh, the kindness of Fate, he offered her a lift in his car. When she alighted at the school gates, her classmates couldn't believe their eyes as little Catherine glided past them with a 'There! What did I tell ya? We have got a motor.' Unfortunately her teacher called her bluff by suggesting in front of the entire class that perhaps Catherine could supply the horn for Father Christmas's sleigh from her father's motor car... It was an unnecessary put-down, but the story does give us the germ of an insight into Catherine's personality and her relationship with the school.

She once wrote a poem called 'My First Pair of Boots'. Boots were the basic piece of equipment for the poor. They stood between you and the cold wet road. A child called Steve is so proud to own a pair that he sticks one foot out in the aisle between the classroom desks so that his teacher will notice them as she walks past. But even when Mulligan blurts out, 'Are you ganna tyek 'em off when ya gan t'bed?', Miss Platt refuses to pay any attention to them. Such pride, such sparkle, such trusting optimism and good humour are all contained in Steve. But Miss Platt just won't play the game – until after the lesson, when Steve hangs back from the rest and, touching his sleeve, she looks down at the boots and says, 'They're grand boots, whoppers; keep 'em clean, Steve.'

Catherine was not a child you could ignore. The best of her teachers would bring her on, make something out of her eager, sparky side. Later, Miss Barrington would be one of these: she leapt at the challenge and gave Catherine something to chew on, gave her an appreciation of the beauty of words. But it is not difficult to see why mundane Miss Caulfield, full of her own self-importance, a kind of mother duck who liked her ducklings to form an orderly line behind her, would slap her down. For Miss Caulfield, Catherine's spark was not a challenge but a threat.

And so we come to Mary Ann, the heroine of a series of eight novels, published between 1954 and 1967, and the embodiment of Catherine's imaginative individuality at this time. Mary Ann has her own little world worked out inside, and she sparkles with it. *A Grand Man* opens in the school yard with her boasting about her 'great big house'. Like Catherine, Mary Ann tells tall stories about her family and their wealth and station to compensate for their poverty and her father's drinking, which has brought them to the lowest of the low, Mulhattans Hall. It wasn't lies she was telling, Mary Ann reassures herself, 'it was more in the nature of a story.' Mary Ann wants everyone to play her game, and why shouldn't they? Most other people's games look pretty silly. Hadn't she watched her own dear grannie, through a slit in the back lavatory door, as she snitched the cream from her neighbour's pint of milk before replenishing the deficit with milk from her own pint? If that was the level of life, then Mary Ann's game was without doubt better. Her tall stories and the promise of an invitation to her big house one day win her offers from her classmates of 'a stot of me ball', the loan of a 'thick skipping rope', a share in a classmate's 'bullets' (sweets). But alas for Mary Ann, as for Catherine, there were girls who had been brought up on the upstart game and were more experienced at it; in Mary Ann's case the chief among these was Sarah, the daughter of Mrs Flannagan, the most notorious upstart in the neighbourhood, who also happens to live opposite her and knows the truth of where she comes from.

Catherine's boasting may have celebrated her imaginative side, but if she thought it was going to win her friends she was sadly mistaken. In 1915, a year after she had been molested by the lodger and nearly two years after the traumatic episode at the chimneypiece, she took another big knock. She was as yet only nine years of age.

One of her schoolmates, a girl from Phillipson Street, which backed on to William Black Street and shared the same back lane, was throwing a birthday party and distributed invitations to all the clan . . . except Catherine. She was sure hers would come. Why wouldn't it? They were mates, after all, weren't they? But as the party approached and still no invitation appeared, Catherine began to feel uneasy. Reverberations of the feelings aroused by the episode at the chimneypiece stirred within. Kate knew something was up, and Catherine knew Kate knew; but no words passed between them until the day of the party. It was a Saturday, Catherine's day for the matinée at the Crown cinema. She announced to Kate that she wouldn't be going, got dressed up in a clean pinny and left by the back door, Kate's words – 'It's no use, hinny, it's no use!' – following her out. But Catherine was made of stronger stuff than Kate. She opened the backyard door into the lane and stood there watching her friends opening their backyard doors one by one and making their way across the lane to the back staircase of the upstairs house in Phillipson Street where the party was to be held. Not one of them said a word to her. Finally, when all had fallen quiet again, Catherine walked steadily up to the girl's yard door, opened it, crossed the backyard, walked up the staircase and, with extraordinary courage (or face), rapped on the back door.

In no time a group of squealing children seemed to fill the open doorway, all eyes on Catherine as she asked, could she come in? The ball was in her little hostess's court. Even taking into consideration what a cocky little show-off Catherine could be, it was surely inconceivable that she would not be let in. But the ball came back fast and low, and with a spin on it that destroyed Catherine. Her ma said she couldn't come.

Why?

Because Catherine 'ain't got no da'.

It must be nigh on a hundred per cent certain that the little girl's mother had said nothing of the sort. We are not looking here at adult prejudice against illegitimate children, we are looking at the cruelty of one child to another. Drawing back from the scene, we are looking at Catherine's alienation, her rejection at nine years of age from the world in which she moved, and, once more, a denial of the validity of her own inner world. Those fears engendered by the chimneypiece episode had been utterly confirmed.

In Catherine's response, however, we are looking at something else, the kind of mettle that would one day raise her up out of this place altogether. The experience would have crushed a lesser child, recommending to her perhaps a strategy of back-tracking, of seeking humiliatingly to inveigle her way back into her friends' good books, or of retreating into herself. Catherine did none of these. She came out fighting. 'From this time the fight started within me . . . I bossed, bullied and slapped out . . . I was bent on showing them, showing the lot of them.'

In the novels, Mary Ann resorts to the same aggressive tactics towards Sarah Flannagan, and we also find this side of Catherine in another of her little fictional heroines, Mary Ellen in *A Dinner of Herbs*, who had 'a tongue that would clip clouts and a head on her that would fit her granny, the things she comes up with'. In real life, when Lottie Christopher wouldn't lend Catherine her skipping rope she dragged it off her and then, when Kate appeared off the tram, threw it at poor little Lottie so that Mrs Christopher appeared at the McMullens' front door complaining that Catherine had thrashed her with it. If anyone refused to fall in line Catherine would challenge them to a fight. Once she even pushed a boy into the Slacks. Mothers, even fathers, started calling at number 10 to complain, and inevitably it all came to a head when she tried it on with someone bigger than her, one Olive Swinburne, who put her on the floor. Henceforth Catherine thought twice about giving physical vent to her feelings.

Catherine's aggression was grounded in fear and sadness – fear not of her classmates but of not belonging; sadness at their rejection of her and at what seemed to her the only possible retort, her rejection of them – all serving to intensify the fear and love 'which combined to cause the feeling of utter sadness' in her relationship with Kate at home.

Fear, bred of a combination of apprehension and anxiety, 'was the single most important emotion of my childhood,' Catherine told me, 'and it still is, right up to this very moment. I feared Kate's drinking to an exaggerated point.' It wasn't drinking itself that got to Catherine; old John's drinking didn't have the same effect. It was the fact that it was her ma who was doing it and, more especially, that she couldn't hold her drink. Her sister Sarah could, but not Kate. It took no more than a glass or two to transform Kate into the misty-eyed, slovenly, word-stumbling caricature of herself which people who dropped in accepted without a word, but which in Catherine's eyes turned her into another person. It was bad enough when there were just the two of them together, but at family gatherings the effect on Catherine was pure shame as Kate strained to hit the top notes of 'Thora', her favourite song, 'her head well back, that slack lower lip of hers wobbling. I really longed to die on such occasions.'

Fears born in the kitchen of number 10 stayed with Catherine for many years after she had left William Black Street. Talking to me in 1985, long after suffering nervous breakdown, she recalled the period from 1945 when these fears had been joined by a whole nightmarish set of others – the fear of losing her husband, of doctors, of operations, of 'blood-spattered floors and blinding arc lights', fear of going mad. 'I turned into a solid block of fear.' The dark shadows of this time stay with her even today. 'You never get rid of a breakdown. The sediment of it lies in your subconscious; an incident, a word, or even a place can stir that sediment again and there you are back full of terror... of what? You can't explain, except, in my case, it is aggression, deep aggression, against my early suffering, against my mother, against someone who did me a great evil that I have never written about because the result of it was I learned how to hate, to hate with such intensity that I knew that if I let it have the upper hand my future life would be ruined.'

It all started here, in the back streets of the New Buildings and in the kitchen of number 10, before she was even into her teens. In *Colour Blind* Catherine uses the cruelty of little Rose-Angela's playmates to show that human nature, even in ones so young, insists upon conformity. Being different is not allowed. Rose-Angela's difference is that she is a half-caste. She'll never go to heaven because she 'ain't white'. Rosie is special because she gives us an insight into the physical effect which Catherine's feeling of rejection had on her: Rosie's nervous system is 'like a highly tensed wire'. The fears of her own childhood produced the same state in Catherine, but with one difference: later, much later, she would use it creatively. The 'painful sensitivity' to which Catherine attributes her creativity was not appeased by her writing; I once asked her whether her writing helped her to recover from her breakdown and she replied, 'No, not in the least. My mind was still in torment, mentally and physically, fourteen hours a day at least.' But she put her painful sensitivity to work, which for us, at least, is the reward of the apprenticeship years.

CHAPTER FOUR

❦

Birth of Imagination

'The feeling of aloneness I felt on the day of that birthday party was felt deep inside of me and I shall always have it. I can be jolly. I can be the life and soul of the party. But I can understand these men who are always very jolly and then go and commit suicide. I talk to everybody and people think that I am such an extrovert, Kitty is this, Kitty is that, Kitty is the other, but Kitty was born with this feeling of aloneness. I can't say that I was the first person to use this word, but what I mean by it is in contrast to loneliness. There is a great difference between the two. It is being *a thing apart*.'

To this bright little girl, rejected and possessed of this alienating feeling of aloneness, the area of Jarrow, Tyne Dock and Shields which she tramped on her 'messages' to the pawn shop or pub for Kate seemed a desolate place. It is an image which occurs many times in her books. In *The Fifteen Streets* John O'Brien, shunted into work at the docks, can't understand why he doesn't welcome the sunshine, until one day it dawns on him that the sun showed the place up for what it was. On an overcast day, 'the docks, the coal dust, the houses, the rattling trams, and the people all seemed to merge into one background.' But when the sun shone, they stood out, 'dirty, stark, tired'. Lonely and lost, he asks, 'What did it all mean, anyway? What was living for?'

The Gambling Man (1975) opens with possibly the best

description of the Tyne Dock area anywhere in Catherine's fiction. It is a Sunday; everything outside is cold, silent, resting. Desolation is laid in thick layers on her canvas, her palette dispensing sounds, sensations, even moral intimations, as 'the first flat flakes of snow . . . dropped to rest in their white purity on the greasy, coal-dust, spit-smeared flags.' As Rory the rent man goes about his business he meets bootless children with snotty noses, black-shawled women with arms crossed against huge, sagging breasts, flat, downtrodden faces creasing into forced smiles of welcome and a false, chattering clannishness, aware that eviction may be only one more week away.

Almost all the messages Catherine ran for Kate would involve her walking past the sawmill and on beneath the five Tyne Dock arches, the heart of dockland which separated East Jarrow from Shields. Here, in this dark, dismal, subterranean world, where slime dribbled 'in rivulets of green' down the brickwork walls 'as black as a singed bloater', the channels of her creative imagination were opened. On one occasion, at the age of five, she was walking under the arches, alone as usual, when someone unwelcome appeared in the distance. To avoid whoever it was she crossed over the road, put her face to the blank wall and walked sideways until they had passed. What she saw with her mind's eye when her face was up against the cold, wet bricks was a picture, a real technicolour picture as clear as day of a better life in a better place, prosperous, genteel, and with herself dead centre. She would repeat this tactic whenever the occasion required. It never failed.

The same arches were also the site of a more mysterious vision. She was walking westwards this time, on her return to East Jarrow. She had passed through the first arch nearest the dock gates and emerged into the dim light, grey, polluted, in parts defeated altogether by shade from the high dock wall and the steep bank leading up to the railway, when she noticed a beautiful boy walking towards her. He occupied the same position as her but at the other end of the tunnel of arches. They each had an arch through which to pass before they would meet. As she walked on a feeling of pure joy swept through her. It was so strong and so suffused her that she became transfixed by the image of the boy. She couldn't take her eyes off him. Then a strange light, a kind of visual equivalent of the feeling inside her, seemed to spread from the boy, a white light which grew in strength and power until it overcame the tunnel of gloom and welcomed her in. When she came to, she was emerging from the last arch, alone. Retracing her steps a pace or two, she looked back down the tunnel and saw that the boy – she knew who he was; his name was Hughie Axill – was also emerging into day at the other end.

Catherine gave this experience to Mary Walton, the heroine of *Pure as the Lily*, who, after forty years of disaster, was to recognise Hughie Amsden's eyes as those of her childhood crush, who had dissolved into white light in the same way. She describes the light as pure, 'love before it was touched by hand, or marred by life; love as pure spirit'.

It was a spiritual experience, spiritual in the true sense; illuminating of love in the novel, but in real life, to Catherine, an affirmation of a capacity, even a readiness, to achieve a state of inspiration beyond conscious control. It would be forty years before she came to realise what that meant to her as a writer. Then she would be sitting in a cold drawing room in another town, her mind a void, convinced that she would never write another word – and the whole story of *The Fifteen Streets* came to her, 'right from the opening to the very last words. Every character, every incident . . . It was all there.' And, as we shall see, she just accepted it . . .

There, beneath the rawness of everyday life, in the

subterranean world of the Tyne Dock arches, the channels of creative inspiration had been opened. The conditions had been right for it to happen. Almost one hundred years earlier, the imagination of a boy, alienated, lonely and cast adrift in the city of London, had been whetted beneath the dark arches about the Adelphi. There was no white light, but his imagination had taken flight, as he recorded in his heavily auto-biographical novel *David Copperfield*. There is, indeed, much to be learned about the flowering of creative imagination from a comparison of Catherine Cookson and Charles Dickens at around the same time in their lives.

Dickens, like Catherine, had a bright, sparky personality but found it difficult to mix with his contemporaries. There was something different about Dickens, something which set him apart from his fellows. He was 'a queer small boy', a poor 'Robin Crusoe' on an island of his own. Again like Catherine, he was 'a child of singular abilities: quick, eager' and sensitive, painfully sensitive – 'soon hurt mentally', as he put it. Both were also consummate actors and dogged by illness; and, significantly in terms of the development of their imaginations, both were set loose alone in their places of inspiration – London and Tyneside – at a young age, their senses sharpened by rejection and loss.

Dickens was born on 7 February 1812, and at first enjoyed a period of security, initially at Portsea and then at the family home in Chatham in Kent. But his father had fallen badly into debt, and the family had to move to a 'mean, small tenement, with a wretched little back-garden abutting onto a squalid court', at 16 Bayham Street in Camden Town, in London. By 1824 his father's financial position was so bad that he was arrested for debt and incarcerated in the Marshalsea prison. Shortly afterwards his wife and three of their children joined him there in rooms, as was the way, but left Charles, at twelve years of age, to fend for himself. There was no question of his continuing at school, and he went to work in a boot-blacking factory, 'a crazy, tumbledown old house, abutting ... on the river, and literally overrun with rats.

'It is wonderful to me how I could have been so easily cast away at such an age,' he wrote. No one made any attempt to rescue him. He writes of 'the deep remembrance of the sense I had of being utterly neglected and hopeless, of the shame I felt in the position; of the misery it was to my young heart ... My whole nature was so penetrated with the grief and humiliation ... I know I do not exaggerate, unconsciously and unintentionally, the scantiness of my resources and the difficulties of my life.'

The causes of Dickens' dispossession may be different from those in Catherine's case, but the consequences – rejection, alienation, misery, humiliation, shame – are the same negative emotions, dark currents awaiting transformation into light by a child thrown upon its own resources.

To this lonely, hungry twelve-year-old boy, London, like Catherine's Tyneside, is desolate too – a 'Wilderness!', exclaims Cheeryble to Nicholas Nickleby: 'It was a wilderness to me once. I came here barefoot – I have never forgotten it. Thank God!' Dickens' solitary introduction to the streets of London came in the form of a twice-daily walk between his lodgings in North London and the factory in the Strand. Then, becoming more adventurous, he ventured out on his own into Soho and Covent Garden, wide-eyed, watching, observing ...

Like a child lured by the hot flame of a candle he knows he mustn't touch (but does so all the same), Dickens embraces 'wild visions of prodigies of wickedness, want and beggary'. Likewise, Catherine's imagination was stirred by characters she saw every day in Jarrow, Tyne Dock and Shields. 'It was what I soaked up during those years spent in and around

East Jarrow, Jarrow and South Shields. Like a great sponge
I'd taken it all in . . .'

London was a bigger, stranger and more terrifying place
to Dickens than the docklands of Catherine's experience was
to her, known kindly by the dockers as 'old John's bairn'. But
just as Dickens came to his vision of London a lonely child,
rejected and humiliated by loss, so Catherine came to hers of
Tyneside with her imaginative processes similarly scored so
that the spirit of the place took hold. It wasn't simply that
the place was desolate but that she was peculiarly receptive
to its desolation, and drawn to transform it. The novelist and
biographer Peter Ackroyd wrote in the introduction to my
book *Dickens' London* that the metropolis was a place of
darkness, imprisonment and suffocation to the author, transformed out of necessity. The opening scene in Catherine's
Kate Hannigan is so strong a portrayal of the spirit of
Tyneside by its authorial witness that the book's eventual
publisher, Murray Thompson at Macdonald, threw it on the
scrap heap after reading the opening pages, believing that it
would put off readers. Fortunately it was rescued by his
secretary who, caught by the power of those same pages,
took the manuscript home and stayed up half the night
reading the rest.

The faithful autobiographical content of this first novel
reveals Catherine's artistic purpose. She is exorcising her own
demons. Tyneside has taken on the shape of her own fears, as
London did for Dickens, and now out of necessity she must
transform it. The very form of the novel, which recounts the
pivotal events on successive Christmas Eves, suggests her
purpose. Even among such poverty and squalor, families
came together on Christmas Eve in a spirit of celebration.
And yet there is no sense of a fairytale happy ending. Kate
Hannigan is no Cinderella, Dr Rodney Prince no Prince
Charming.

The doctor's vocational mission to Tyneside, belittled by his wife Stella, who is locked out of our sympathies by her cruel treatment of him and her inability to look beneath the surface to see what made people like Kate tick, is crucial. It has the effect of drawing him, and us, into a whole new dimension of Tyneside life, something deep in the subconscious of its people, embodied in Kate Hannigan and illuminated by her creator, who shines the 'white light' of her imagination upon it. Early on, the newcomer Rodney Prince is envious of the rapport between Dr Davidson and Kate, realising that it hinges on what has motivated him to work with the poor of Tyneside, the deep-rooted spirit of its people, something he cannot put into words. By the end of the narrative, when Rodney and Kate come together, he understands what it is, and that is what this novel is about. Catherine once described it as 'the element of their origin that comes from far back and threads the people of this particular area', a something she could feel in the emotions of her characters when she was writing them down, 'their voice . . . their laughter, their humour, their sorrows and their joys'. It is the same primitive force which she divined in her mother, which is the reason why she dedicated this novel to Kate, 'who found her expression through me'.

At odd times of the year Kate Fawcett would join other women of the New Buildings, dress up in men's clothes and parade round the streets, beating tin cans and singing. Even Aunt Mary would join in. The sudden inexplicable loosening of the bonds of restraint and respectability amazed Catherine. 'There was a primitive weirdness about this, which I recall whenever I hear the Kerry Piper's song.'

Then there were the occasions when Kate, stone-cold sober, would suddenly snatch Catherine by the hand and dash off into the night with her, racing the moon along the Slack bank, running, jumping and laughing as the wind tore at her hat and the moon bathed her face in its pale, haunting light. When finally they came to rest in each other's arms, it was as if the moonlight had washed all the pressures of their lives away. It was primitive, moon-struck madness, one of those moments of release when Kate became what she might have been; its echoes in Sarah and John's escapade in the moonlight in *The Blind Miller* suggest that Kate's pregnancy may have come of this. The image of the moon in poetic mythology as fount of inspiration merges with Catherine's excitement and her unusual closeness to her mother to give us, above all, a sense of partnership in Catherine's artistic creativity. These were rare moments indeed.

By the time Catherine was eight or nine, the sometime little extrovert had acquired a talent for self-denigration that bore witness to a marked inferiority complex. But the extrovert remained all that was visible on the outside. All the negative emotions which Kate had aroused in her – the fear, the feeling of sickness born of anxiety, 'the awfulness . . . the fear and the love which combined to cause the feeling of utter sadness,' as Catherine put it in *A Grand Man*, she bottled up inside. Once, repulsed by the stench of whiskey on her mother's breath as Kate leant over to kiss her, Catherine told her that she hated her. But in saying it she felt utter sadness. Every emotion was a two-sided coin: never one feeling without the other. Later she would write of happiness as 'the seedbed' of pain, and in her novels the opposite is invariably true, as love is born out of bitter division. Imbibing this strange cocktail of love and hate brewed by her mother, however crippling at the time, proved to be a necessary development for the artist in her. Kate taught Catherine how to hate as well as how to love, and showed her that these emotions are inextricably intertwined. Eventually, after years of heartache and distress, Catherine would understand this fundamental principle of life – that there can be no love without hate, no good without evil, because without their antitheses, love and good are meaningless concepts. Without hate, love cannot *be*. And without such polar opposites there can be no process of transformation, no purpose in life at all.

'The law of opposites' is a phrase Catherine uses aptly as a chapter heading in *The Menagerie* (1958), and time and again in the novels she calls on it to resolve the discordant forces in her characters' lives. Later she would discover in her love for the man who was to become her husband that, 'in the channels where the intangible but real life runs', opposite poles are as one. Understanding this was critical in her life as in her art. It bred in her a sense of how the opposing principles on which the harmony of the universe depends interact and complement one another, and it is this insight which inspires the shape of all her novels.

Catherine's talent for resolving the fears and healing the fractured lives of the characters in her novels, where love and hate are at work in all kinds of social divisions within her culture, was first rehearsed in Kate's kitchen. While aggressively squaring up to her persecutors at school, she took another tack in number 10 William Black Street. Desperate to transform the bitterness inside the family, she began to use her centre-stage role to resolve the situation at home. 'I felt responsibility for the people in our kitchen,' she says. 'I could always see both sides of an argument. I could always see two sides because of what was in me. That's what I played off.'

In *A Grand Man*, little Mary Ann Shaughnessy manages to prevent the break-up of her parents' marriage and, through her manipulation of Mr Lord, a gruff, difficult old man, hopelessly unfulfilled in spite of his wealth, she rescues her family from penury. The creation of Mary Ann gave Catherine a series of eight hugely popular novels in which she expressed her growing sense of her own purpose, first enacted in the kitchen of number 10. Besides the obvious parallels between the character of Mary Ann and the innocent, sparky, extrovert side of Catherine as a little girl, the author's identification with her is spelled out in the naming of Mary Ann's grannie as Mrs McMullen. Mary Ann's love for her family, her father in particular, is her motivation, just as Catherine's deep-down love for her family and need for harmony to resolve her fears motivated her desire to transform the shambles at home.

In *The Lord and Mary Ann* (1956) we find the Shaughnessys ensconced at Mr Lord's farm. Since they arrived, her da has not resorted to drink, her ma is not just bonny but become beautiful, her brother, Michael, is happy at his swanky new school, and in the kitchen at night great larks are had with every member of the family playing a part. This is Catherine's ideal, which she herself did taste at times, in 'short rests between battles', as she refers to them, when she would sit, curled up on the corner of the fender in front of the fire, reading a book, her granda at the table, cheating himself at patience, Jack reading the paper, Kate ironing or baking. At these times she glimpsed 'a fleeting sense of security'. But for the most part it was a dream.

So important a healing influence did Catherine become at home that soon everyone came to rely on her to deal with her drunken granda. She was the only one who could settle John when he was in drink. 'When three sheets in the wind he was manageable, but only by me.' When he came in at night Kate would rouse her from a deep sleep and say, 'Get up, hinny, and get your granda to bed!' Bleary-eyed, she would shuffle into the kitchen and coax him into his bed, peeling off his longjohns, hoping against hope that he wouldn't burst into song.

To her granda Catherine was as 'pure as the lily in the

dell'. This was one of his favourite songs, usually sung when he was drunk and she wished he would just go to bed, and gave her the title and theme of her novel *Pure as the Lily*. It begins in Jarrow in 1933, and opens with one of Catherine's most evocative passages about the deep-down regenerative spring of life in Jarrow, which it is her purpose to identify. The scene is an allotment where Peter Walton and his son Alec find respite from the appalling conditions of life in the Depression. Alec has been out of work for eight years. Mary, Alec's teenage daughter, the lily of the title, comes away from her placement in service bringing a bag of fag-ends she has rescued from her mistress's ashtrays. 'They're gold flake, not Woodbines,' she tells Alec, as if she were giving him a box of Cuban cigars. Mary spreads laughter and happiness wherever she goes. Her ability to see the good in people and to shine the light of her own unaffected, delicate purity into the darkest corners is a trait visible in embryo in Peter, who laughs with every sentence he utters, and it is propagated too by Alec's voiceless love for his daughter. In stark contrast to the discontent and in-fighting among the unemployed dockers outside the allotment fences, Peter and Alec, with their hands in the soil and infected by Mary's high spirits, forget their problems and cultivate their own shared, family nature. The three of them seem to swell with laughter within the perimeter of this family plot. The passage, which includes a rendition of a poem by Peter, and his favourite song, 'I love a lassie . . . She's as pure as the lily in the dell,' is perfected by Catherine's use of the soft rhythms and inflections of the Geordie idiom.

The quality of their empathy, with its power to transform, permeates the whole novel. In *Lily*, Catherine deals with life as it is lived on the surface and the unalterable, primitive source capable of transforming it. Peter attempts to maintain his connection with this primitive source – beauty, truth –

through his poetry, as does his grandson, Jimmy (Mary's brother), who in turn senses it in Lally Briggs, a spirit of the North, the archetypal northern lass: a sheer expression of natural wisdom, 'the simplicity, the truth, and the depth' which Mary describes as 'welling up out of Lally's big body'.

There is absolutely nothing idealistic about this novel, firmly rooted as it is in grim realities. Purity has nothing to do with goodness as opposed to sin, for Mary gives herself out of wedlock to a man old enough to be her father. It is a moral purity only in the highest sense. It is truth, and a clue to what that means is given by her brother Jimmy, a schoolmaster, who tells his talented pupil, Fenton, that truth can be 'drained' from the 'crucible' of life by great poets. Mary is pure because she has the ability to do this not in art but in life.

Catherine is dealing here with a theme altogether bigger than anything she attempted in the 'social histories', as she has referred to her early novels. She is describing the process and the purpose of her art. To achieve this she required an antithesis to Mary, which she found in her heroine's mother, Alice.

Jealousy is Alice's driving force. She will be responsible for the horrible disfigurement of Mary's lover, Ben Tollet; she will burn her daughter-in-law, Lally, alive; and she will drive her son, Jimmy, almost insane and through drink into an early grave. It is out of this crucible that Mary drains the very essence of truth: 'love as pure as the lily in the dell; love before it was touched by hand, or marred by life; love as pure spirit,' which brings us back to Catherine's 'white light' of creative imagination, first experienced underneath the arches of Tyne Dock, its purpose clearly to transform.

Up for transformation in *Fanny McBride* are Fanny's prejudices about her favourite son Jack marrying a Protestant girl and her distaste for what she sees as her least favourite son Phil's pretentious ways – the shirts he wears, his picky attitude to food and, as I have already noted, the way he gets up when a woman enters the room. The resolution of this novel posed a particular problem for Catherine. Originally she had Fanny die. 'But when I sent it to my publisher, they phoned straight back and said, "You cannot make her die. This woman is such a marvellous character. You have got to bring her back." So I had to rewrite the end.'

It is New Year's Eve and Fanny's anxieties about whether Jack will turn up for the celebrations have grown to almost psychotic proportions. Fanny and Jack have not spoken since Jack committed the cardinal sin of marrying a Hallelujah. Emotional pain and anger rush through Fanny 'like a torrent sweeping a gorge' as it dawns on her that he does not intend to come, and, at the very moment that she is raising her hand to strike Mrs Flannagan for some appalling upstart behaviour, she suffers a stroke.

We see the next scene through Fanny's eyes. Hovering midway between life and death, she seems to leave her corporeal frame and stand looking at herself laid out as dead. She has an urge to complete the transition to the spirit world and leave behind the whole fraught business of material life. But for some reason she resists it and watches instead as Phil comes down from his bedroom and falls to his knees in front of her, sobbing and burying his head in her lap. Fanny is overcome with emotion. Then the doctor arrives, and Mary Prout. And then, at last, comes Jack – but only because he has heard that Fanny is dying. Jack doesn't cry, as Phil had done.

Then St Michael arrives in Fanny's limbo-land. Rather than rewarding Fanny with a smooth pass to heaven after all the heartache she has suffered in bringing up eleven bairns, she is amazed to hear him upbraid her for a whole load of Masses she has paid Father Owen to say in memory of her late husband. It transpires that Fanny has used them to ask God to keep McBride perpetually in purgatory so that she won't have to team up with him in eternity. (Indeed, we see that the poor man is still there, suffering.) St Michael also takes her to task for the way she has brought up her family, her stubbornness and pigheadedness and bigotry and, lastly, her inability to love her children except for one. True to form, Fanny hits back, blaming God for making her like that. But St Michael will have none of it. God only gave her the patterns; 'The making up lay with you,' he says. Then he sends her back into the real world to do better – but not without first clarifying God's position *vis-à-vis* Mrs Flannagan. He returns Fanny to the exact position she was in before she collapsed, hand raised above the provoking upstart, ready to deliver a crushing blow.

Catherine's greatest strength is her characterisation. It flows from her ability not simply to draw her characters but to become them. By the time she set about writing she was, as she said to me, capable of doing everything her characters do, and I can believe it. I once asked her whether Fanny McBride, possibly her most popular character, was based on someone she knew. 'Oh, my!' she replied. 'In my early days, in any poor quarter of Jarrow, you would see a woman in an old coat and slippers slinking along to the corner shop early in the morning for two ounces of tea, half a pound of sugar and a half pound of streaky bacon, or something along those lines . . . Oh, there were dozens of Fannys.'

Fanny is a big woman in every way – big heart, big booming voice, big sense of humour and big body, as we see when she swings her legs over the side of the bed and scratches 'the moist flesh under her great wobbling breasts'. Battered, battling Catholic grandmother, Fanny McBride stands like a colossus astride the Tyneside of Catherine's youth. She embodies her vision of Tyneside just as Fagin, scuttling vermin-like along the dark, dank corridors that separated the squalid slum dwellings of the old East End, embodies Dickens' Kafkaesque vision of the metropolis.

There is an operatic quality to Dickens' art, however, which is not present in Catherine's work. His is more of a performance: we see his most vibrant characters, but we don't always feel we have met them in real life in quite the same way. There is true social documentary in equal measure in both sets of novels, but after reading sixty or seventy of Catherine's in a relatively short space of time I found myself walking down the main street of a run-down seaside resort in the North-East wondering what was going on behind the vacant stares of the people I passed. Catherine reveals the lives of ordinary people, of lavatory attendants and rent collectors, of dustmen and labourers, of solicitors and businessmen, of doctors and housewives, and shows that no one is ordinary. Opening them to scrutiny displays heroic and tragic qualities, humour and pathos in every quarter. Ugliness, poverty, ignorance, beauty, wealth, intellect can no longer be taken as value indicators. She has levelled the landscape of appearances, overcome their divisive potential and redirected our interest elsewhere.

In *The Unbaited Trap* (1966) tall, flabby-fleshed, insipid-looking John Emmerson, a prosperous solicitor from the posh end of town, who also happens to be a eunuch, lives an un-fulfilling life with his beautiful but cold wife, Ann. All Ann asks of him is to keep up appearances, her one fear that their desolate existence together might become public knowledge. Ann's response to John's wartime wound, which has deprived him of his sexual potency, drives him into the self that he has long come to take as his own, lonely and sad. No one knows the truth about John Emmerson. The Wilcoxes, whose daughter Val is engaged to his son, Laurie Emmerson, 'just considered him a quiet, withdrawn sort of fellow'. But, as the story unfolds, John removes 'that well-bred, cultured, ready-for-anything facade' which his wife had fashioned to conceal an intolerable truth, and when thirty-year-old, warm-hearted widow Cissie Thorpe enters his life John finds himself. Their meeting – indeed, the entire plot – hinges, rather aptly considering his wife's frigidity, on the fact that Cissie does not own a fridge.

The novel is about the way people look at others: 'How could you tell by how people looked?' Laurie wonders after he has learned the truth about his father. What most people take for granted about other people is often what sets Catherine's imagination working. 'How I come to write my books . . . Well, an incident might occur, which I don't pay much heed to at first, but it sinks into my unconscious mind, which I use a lot, and years later perhaps it pops up and gives me the formation of a story or a character on which to base the story.'

The Menagerie opens with an apparently random focus on a routine greeting between a man and a woman in the bustling High Street of Fellburn – no real place, its name a cross between Hebburn and Felling, west of Jarrow, and in this novel (set in the 1950s) typical of the hundreds of pit villages on the edge of industrial Tyneside. We begin with surface rhythms, five lines of dialogue, an apparently ordinary, salutary ritual repeated on countless streets every day of the week. But in a Catherine Cookson novel such a greeting is anything but ordinary. Just a sliver beneath the surface lie the truths about the two characters which derange it. When the man moves on, he is laughing to himself, and the butt of his ridicule, Aunt Lot, one of Catherine's genius creations, turns from him with 'the air of a fine lady' – a preposterous claim, given her 'moth-eaten' shoulder cape.

Life revolves around Aunt Lot. She is the instrument of the novel's resolution. And she literally walked into

Catherine's imagination off the street. 'Aunt Lot [is] a poor young woman who is slightly off balance. It should happen one day when I was crossing the road that there before me went a figure . . . She had on a voile dress, a pair of stockings that were wrinkled round her legs, high heel shoes that were over at the sides and made her walk in an odd way. But on her shoulders was a worn-out feather cape and on her head one of the old-fashioned straw, flower-bedecked hats which were in fashion at the beginning of the century. I never saw her face, I only saw the back of her figure, and I remember the name that came into my mind from nowhere, "Poor Aunt Lot". Why I should think that name I don't know, but she remained in my mind for some time. Who was she? Where was she from? Why dressed like that? She *was* an oddity. Now it must have been years later when I wrote *The Menagerie* that there she was all ready for me, straw hat, mouldy cape, summer dress and wobbly high heels.'

Part of her imaginative perception of ordinary people is attributable to this eye for detail, but there is much more to her powers of observation than this. Early on these powers seem to have been attached to, even fostered by, her rejection and alienation from life, which brought a peculiar, creative, outsider's objectivity to her relationship with physical things. One day Catherine came home and told her mother that a neighbour called Mrs Waller had called her a 'bax . . . tard'. What did it mean? Kate had been cutting up meat for a pie on the kitchen table, and when Catherine said this Kate dropped the knife on the table in surprise. But as the knife hit the surface of the table, Catherine recalls, she at once lost interest in her own question and took no interest either in Kate's response to it. What caught her attention was that when the knife hit the table its blade tipped on to the surface and stayed there, the handle slightly raised in the air. A saying of her mother's came to her, that the blade of a good knife should never be heavier than its handle. That was the thought that filled her mind – 'This knife can't be a good knife.'

Alienation can have the psychological effect of making one look at things differently, in a detached way. In Jean-Paul Sartre's *Nausea*, a novel about alienation and the effect this has on an individual's understanding of his relationship with his environment, Antoine Roquentin, aware of an extra-ordinary change in his perceptions, decides to keep a diary, 'to neglect no nuances or little details . . . I must say how I see this table, the street, people, my packet of tobacco, since *these* are the things which have changed.' That Catherine remembers the incident with the knife so clearly suggests that a similar change had taken place in her. That her observation of the knife-blade on the surface of the table actually smothered her anxiety at being called a bastard suggests its potentiality, which in her case would be realised in her characterisation of people like Aunt Lot.

Interestingly, the feeling of aloneness which dominated her emotionally at this time, and may give a clue to her creative rapport with people and things evinced in the novels, never depressed her. 'I don't connect this aloneness with fear,' Catherine once said to me. On the contrary, it released her from fear. Detachment was in essence detachment *from* fear, though, as we shall see later in her handling of Fanny McBride, there is an intrinsic sadness to it, as if she could never quite live in our world, which she describes so well. In short, being an outsider put Catherine on a different and creative plane. As with Charles Dickens, similarly alienated and detached, Catherine's ability to focus on tiny details and invest them with significance is characteristic of her art.

In *The Fifteen Streets* the narrative builds in a little cres-cendo to a significant meeting between John O'Brien and Mary Llewellyn. It is, in the first place, a portentous meeting for little Katie O'Brien, who idolises Mary Llewellyn, her teacher, and hero-worships John, her twenty-two-year-old brother. Mary and John know each other only through what Katie has said to each of them about the other. For Katie, though not consciously for John and Mary, their meeting promises love on the scale of a Prince Charming for a beautiful princess in a fairytale. Katie is walking along the road hand-in-hand with her big brother when the chance convergence of their paths occur. Mary greets Katie. Hallo Katie. Hallo Miss Llewellyn. Mundane. What can possibly make it live up to Katie's expectations? The inspired touch is in the observation of fine detail. 'John felt Katie's fingers opening and shutting within his palm.' The sentence says it all, to us as to John, the movement of her fingers transferring Kate's expectations to her big brother, so that when John watches Mary walking away, 'bending against the wind, the coat pressed against her legs . . . he saw that she wore shoes and that her ankles were thin,' and we know that the meeting has been important for him too, that his awareness of Mary is already acute and augurs more than passing interest. Nothing is said to suggest that they will fall in love. But it is there, our little secret, Katie's and Catherine's, and now her readers' and John's too.

Reading was not a common pastime for children in the New Buildings. Catherine's appetite had been whetted by the book which the school caretaker at Simonside had lent her, and she read comics too – once she even stole one from a shop, which led to a crisis of conscience. There was the *Chatterbox* annual, the weekly *Rainbow Comic* and *Tiger Tim's Weekly*; and during those fleeting moments of security, Kate would read aloud from *Handy Andy*, *Wee McGregor* and *Tales of an Irish County Court*, and to old John during the war extracts from Sir Philip Gibbs' despatches from France. But more significant to her imaginative development, Catherine's love for words was encouraged by two mistresses at school.

In the course of four years, Catherine attended four different schools. She had been moved from Simonside early in 1913. Catherine recalls overhearing a conversation between Kate and the headmistress in which Kate said something about her being a Catholic, and as Simonside was a Protestant school this would appear to have been the reason for the move. But in fact the next school she attended, The Meases in East Jarrow, was also Protestant; and it is worth noting that Catherine also heard Kate say to the Simonside headmistress something about her real name being not McMullen but Fawcett.

Was Kate telling her that Catherine was illegitimate, and if so, why? Perhaps there was already (six months or so before the chimneypiece episode) trouble brewing with Catherine's classmates there. Later that same year, 1913, Catherine was moved from The Meases to St Bede's Infants' School in Jarrow, which was a Catholic School. Her third move, to St Peter and St Paul's Tyne Dock, came in 1916, not long after she was cruelly rejected by her friends from that birthday party. St Peter and St Paul's was also a Roman Catholic school. Stern Father Bradley, whom we have met in the guise of Father O'Malley, and kind Father O'Keefe, who is portrayed in the same novels as Father Bailey, lived in the school grounds.

These moves, one after the other, cover the period between 1913 and 1916 when Catherine's trauma took root. During this period she began her 'messages' for Kate, to the pub and to the pawn shop. During this period, too, she was molested by Kate's intended, and received the two significant rejections by her friends on the pretext of her illegitimacy. If the school moves were not occasioned by Catherine's increasing difficulties in relating to her contemporaries, the three upheavals in so short a time will certainly have done nothing to settle her emotional state. She remembers that there were frequent rows about her not wanting to go to school. She would even pretend to be ill, and was capable of making herself physically sick to support the pretence.

Almost immediately at St Peter and St Paul's there was a tussle over Catherine's rich, wavy auburn hair. The headmistress, Miss Caulfield, insisted that she plait it. Kate insisted that it remain flowing and free. Catherine was in the middle. She would arrive at school with her hair loose and return home with it plaited. The issue is recreated in *Colour Blind*, where half-caste Rosie is thrashed on her hand with a cane because one of her 'jet-black' plaits has come undone. Miss Caulfield had a cane four feet long and used it frequently on Catherine for being late and for lying to her about attending Mass on Sundays. She became terrified of the woman and suffered her more telling sarcasm badly. It was Miss Caulfield who taunted her with the nickname of 'granny'.

There were, however, three Miss Caulfields at Tyne Dock school, and while the one nearest the headmistress in age was a terror too, the Miss Caulfield who taught Catherine on the first rung of the educational ladder had earlier taught her at St Bede's, and there was a rapport between them. She, and later Miss Barrington – 'big Miss Barrington, kind Miss Barrington' – recognised that Catherine had a way with poetry. During this period she imbibed Wordsworth, Tennyson and Shakespeare. She was quick to learn and recited with a natural sympathy for rhythm. This fed Catherine's self-image, but, equally importantly, 'I learned the beauty of words, words I couldn't spell, or even understand. But there was the sound of them, the lilt of them, the pictures they conjured up in my mind.' Longfellow was a favourite poet, and it is not difficult to see why. The rhythms of his 'Song of Hiawatha' are a perfect vehicle for communicating the sense of his magical narrative incantation, and in

Catherine's novels, especially the earlier ones, 'poetic' rhythms provide a similar dimension to her prose. Incidentally, the title of her novel *The Blind Miller* pays tribute to Longfellow – 'Though the mills of God grind slowly, yet they grind exceeding small.' The same quotation had been rehearsed by Christine Winter three years earlier in *Fenwick Houses*.

The rhythmic quality, the lilt, is an important element of Catherine's prose. At the start of *Maggie Rowan*, where Catherine is among coal miners, dialect is delivered phonetically and is richly evocative of her characters' 'brotherhood' culture. Accent, rhythm and intonation capture 'the element of their origin' as poetry can capture truth. When the miners go down the pit, the Geordie becomes thicker and the usually neutral-accented pit deputy speaks in the same idiom as his men. Above ground, at home, the warmer cadences and the boisterous interchange of impudent humour (from the men) and mock-serious moralising (from the women) are revealing both of Maggie (remember, she is different and cannot understand why) and of the pitmen, their jocularity seeming manfully to conceal their plight in the pit – 'the lilliputian halls of a living hell' – and at the same time revealing their strength of character in overcoming it.

Generally in her novels, however, Catherine is sparing in her use of dialect. She writes within the Geordie idiom – she 'skelps the hunger off' her characters, she rescues their dinner lest it be 'kissened up to cork', and she has even been known to 'bugger me eyes to hell's flames' – but it is rare that she lets dialect flow. She was alive to the fact that many readers outside the North would have difficulty in understanding it. Thomas Hardy, like Catherine a writer inspired by the spirit of a culture, made the same decision. 'If a writer attempts to exhibit on paper the precise accents of a rustic speaker,' he once wrote, 'he disturbs the proper balance of a true

After tea Catherine played out in the streets with the rest of the children, but there was always something different about her, an edge that set her apart. Catherine was a bright, self-confident little girl, but being an only child with 'parents' much older than her, she was more adult than most, unskilled in the give and take of sibling play, and more self-centred. It is not difficult to see her having her say over what should be played or who should occupy centre-stage.

The day Catherine learned that Kate was her real mother and she 'had no da', she was playing shops in the street, as here using bits of broken bottle, coloured glass and china as 'boody' with which they made their pretend transactions. That day her secure childhood world was shattered beyond repair.

Kate Fawcett, Catherine's real mother. When she first saw Kate drunk, her speech slurred, her laugh raucous, her walk unsteady, Catherine was ashamed to be seen with her and the child never did accept Kate as her mother.

The Ravensworth Arms at Lamesley, where Kate, who was working behind the bar, met Alexander Davies, the man who was Catherine's real father.

Rejected by her friends and rejecting her own mother, Catherine began to play out for real the characters of the little illegitimate Annie Hannigan and the sparky little fibber Mary Ann, which many years later her novels made so famous.

The Alkali, one of Kate's watering holes. Later re-named the Zenith, the Alkali took its original appellation from its proximity to the barium chemical works, on Swinburne Street, west of the New Buildings along the old Jarrow Road. Drink was a serious problem on Tyneside, but where it was really a scourge was in those families, like the McMullens, which were already close to the breadline.

With Kate at home the onus fell on John and Jack to bring home the money. Both were dockers. When John McMullen worked, shovelling iron ore, he worked hard but for a pittance. At the end of six 10-hour shifts he would come home with only three shillings and fourpence in his pocket.

There was always a pool of labour – unpaid, uncertain of when they would be paid – hanging around the dock offices a few minutes' walk from Leam Lane.

Unemployment and under-employment were rife and John McMullen already had firsthand experience of South Shields workhouse, the austere brick building of Harton Institution, with its tall chimneys, imposing central tower, stone-breaking yard at the back and flat-faced asylum nearby. Years later Catherine would work here as a checker in the laundry.

The classroom of a Tyneside school at the time Catherine moved through four schools in as many years, the last of which, St Peter and St Paul's Tyne Dock, acquainted her with the rhythms of poetry, the beauty of words, and the terrors of hell fire. It was from then that the nightmares began.

The Tyne Dock arches, the heart of dockland which separated East Jarrow from South Shields. Here, in this dark, dismal, subterranean world, where slime dribbled in rivulets of green down the brickwork walls, the channels of Catherine's imagination were first opened.

The Jarrow tram approaching the terminus from the Tyne Dock arches – 'a full stop between East Jarrow and Tyne Dock . . . from this point Shields seemed to begin'. On the right can be seen the police box which guarded the dock gates, where Catherine used to stand – ' "Waitin' for your granda?" the policeman would say.' And just visible on the left is the public lavatory where she was shocked to hear laughing and then see a woman emerging with three men. Directly opposite the gates was the steep bank bordered on one side by public houses and on the other by part of the shipping offices, where stood the poorly clad paper boy, to whom Catherine entrusted Kate's ten shilling note and learned the meaning of honesty.

Off the steep bank ran Hudson Street, one of the streets to which Catherine would go to fetch Kate's beer and which led to the railway station (you can just see signals at the far end). It was also where the Crown cinema was ('up the top on the right'), which Catherine visited on a Saturday afternoon. Off to the left at the bottom end was Bede Street, the site of Bob Gombertz's pawn shop. Immediately to the left in the picture is Lord Nelson Street, one street up from Bede Street. To avoid the ignominy of the dockers' stares when she was on a pawn shop errand for Kate, Catherine would take the tram all the way up Hudson Street to the station, disembark, walk back down the street, taking a right turn into Lord Nelson Street, ducking down into the back lane between Nelson Street and Bede Street, and enter Gombertz's pawn shop by the rear door.

The pawn shop was a cheap and viable money lending operation for families in need. But among the lower levels, when respectability was fought for, it was hardest won, and Catherine knew instinctively that her errands to the Pawn for her mother were a humiliation of the worst kind.

London was a bigger, more terrifying place to Charles Dickens than the dockland of Catherine's experience, but just as he, an equally lonely imaginative child, was lured by 'wild visions of prodigies of wickedness, want and beggary', so Catherine's imagination was stirred by characters she saw during her everyday wanderings through Jarrow, Tyne Dock and Shields – 'Like a great sponge I'd taken it all in . . .'

An Arab procession through the streets of South Shields. South Shields was full of foreigners – Africans, Swedes, big, burly Russian sea captains, and most especially Arabs. In *The Blind Miller*, *Colour Blind* and *Katie Mulholland*, Catherine explores the racial tensions on Tyneside. But there were many other social problems which affected Catherine directly and became her purpose to resolve.

representation by unduly insisting upon the grotesque element: thus directing attention to a point of inferior interest, and diverting it from the speaker's meaning.' Catherine gave a rather pithier explanation in the Author's Note to her first novel: 'Owing to difficulty in comprehension by the uninitiated, the Tyneside dialect has not been adhered to.' Hardy's friend, the poet William Barnes, took no such decision. Many of his greatest poems, such as 'The Geäte a-Vallen to' (The Gate a-Falling to) are written in Dorset dialect and spelled phonetically, which captures beautifully the spirit of his culture, but not a very wide audience.

As we shall see, in her upstart years, which continued from her late teens through her thirties, Catherine did all she could to rid herself of the habits of a culture which had weighed her down. Even today, though her voice has 'a lilt or inflection, an inheritance from the North that adds to its charm, at least for me,' as her husband Tom has described it, she is not over-fond of the accent. I suspect this was also the case with Hardy, whose father was a builder and mother a maidservant. He rose socially and enjoyed living in his rather clinically middle-class, spick-and-span house, Max Gate, where he wrote much of his best work. It was a long way, though not geographically, from the humble thatched cottage of his birth in Upper Bockhampton. 'Never mind that his acute shyness, his increasing fame, the need to placate his snobbish first wife and other intellectual and emotional factors all led him to disassociate himself outwardly from his real past and family circumstances,' the novelist John Fowles wrote in his introduction to *Thomas Hardy's England*; 'public disassociation is not suppression.'

St Peter and St Paul's Tyne Dock had another significant impact on Catherine, relevant to her imaginative growth. At the hands of Father Bradley indoctrination in the Roman Catholic faith began in earnest. She had been introduced to

Catholicism at St Bede's, which had also given a high priority to religious instruction. But at Tyne Dock Father Bradley's stern approach acquired a sharp, Jesuit edge from visiting 'missioners', as Catherine refers to them. She cannot remember to which orders these troubleshooters from head office belonged, but it was they who brought fear and guilt on to the religious agenda, and they who invariably heard her confession. In their mouths the flames of hell were a reality, everlasting fire a destiny which could be met surprisingly easily, for example by pocketing change given in error by the beer lady or by not going to church (both of which exercise Catherine's conscience to an inordinate degree).

'Sunday was God's day. He made that for himself. And on that day you must worship him. You could miss out on Monday, Tuesday, Wednesday, Thursday, Friday, Saturday, but Sunday was a must. You must worship him by going to seven, nine or eleven o'clock mass. The penalty for disobeying was eternal hell. Hell was achieved through mortal sin and it was a mortal sin to miss Mass on a Sunday.' The eldest Miss Caulfield, who appears to have been something of a lay equivalent to these missioners, would like nothing better than to trap Catherine into admitting that she hadn't attended Sunday Mass and wouldn't think twice about relieving the Devil of his obligation to chastise her by beating Catherine with her cane. But this was as nothing to the guilt engendered by the climax of the Mass itself, when bread, according to the doctrine of Transubstantiation, literally becomes the body of Christ.

'I recall one Sunday morning, which was the only time I remember Kate or my granny going to Mass. We walked up the long freezing road to St Bede's in Jarrow, where I had my first Communion. I had a coat on. Kate had a coat on. My granny was wearing a bead cape and a bead bonnet. But the worshippers at that seven o'clock Mass in Jarrow were made up of poorly shawled women and thinly clad men, but they were saving their souls and that was all that mattered. Then there was Communion. I *hated* the taste of God on my tongue. From an early age my imagination went to work. I had a picture of thousands of nuns all over the world and all those bakeries turning out God by the billion. I knew by this thought that I was committing a mortal sin and would have to go to the priests [she actually confessed this sin to a missioner, who was suitably appalled] and put up with a penalty imposed on me to get out of purgatory.

'It was unthinkable that you should eat or drink for hours before God was placed on your tongue. I myself went out every Friday morning, which was the school's day for taking the Eucharist, cold, hungry and thirsty, longing for the time when I could take the lid off a can of tea and gollop my slice of bread and dripping. To miss this occasion was not only a mortal sin, but to come under the thunder and exposure of the dreaded headmistress. I am angry when I think of the millions of children like myself, who suffered in the same way, not in the last century or in the Dark Ages, but in this century!

'This recollection, in my case, goes far back, close to 1915, and the mental torture went on for years and years after that. The fear of hell's flames was ever constant. I married when I was thirty-three, and up to that time I still remained a Catholic, but fighting against the terrors of religion all the time. I didn't want to leave the fold, but my reason was at work, and the battle went on inside me.'

Hell was a serious threat for Catherine. Around the time that she was introduced to the confessional, Mrs Romanus from upstairs gave her a copy of *Grimm's Fairy Tales*. She lapped them up, reading the book not once but dozens of times. It was an imaginative period in which anything was possible, especially the gridirons of hell.

'From the time of my first confession I had nightmares. I dropped down through layers of *blackness*, groping for light, and woke up screaming.' Another imaginative, highly strung child, who would also become one of our greatest story-tellers, experienced similar religious terrors, but from a Protestant quarter. Robert Louis Stevenson was introduced to Calvinism by his nurse and had 'an extraordinary terror of hell implanted in me'. He too suffered the most hideous nightmares, from which he woke screaming in a frenzy of terror. His experience inspired the message of *Jekyll and Hyde*, namely that the hard law of religion is 'one of the most plentiful springs of distress', as Stevenson put it, driving the Devil underground, better to do his work. Similarly, Roman Catholicism, which became one of the most repressive influences in Catherine's life, inspired themes in many of her novels.

From the strict disciplines of Catholicism flowed misery for the 'fallen', as we have seen, and mixed marriages (Protestant to Roman Catholic) were regarded as sinful. Catherine would experience spiritual whiplash from both, and explored the latter to particular effect in *Colour Blind*, where Father O'Malley is against the marriage of Bridget McQueen, a white Roman Catholic, and Jimmy Patterson, a black Protestant. The crossing of boundary lines in marriage, be they sectarian or repressive demarcations of race or class, is a major theme in all her novels, the inner strife of the protagonists resolved spiritually by an appeal to truth over bigotry and prejudice – though often there is no happy ending in this world.

Historically, religion was as powerful as class in dividing the community and generating cruelty and hypocrisy. Catherine's first taste of this came when, in the presence of her granda, she praised the Salvation Army for not being afraid to declare their religion openly – and for not getting drunk. Kate had to drag her out to the yard for her own safety. To show how firm a grip religion had on the community, even on those of its members who did not go to church, Catherine takes us back in time and, as with all her major themes, identifies a powerful hereditary thread which bound her people.

In *Tilly Trotter* (1980), set in the nineteenth century, Catherine digs for the roots of the religious obsessions which inspired the irrational prejudices of people like her granda and finds them festering in a bed of primitive superstition. A century later, such superstition was still rife in number 10. Knives crossed on the table or when washing up were a bad omen, and the cutting of nails on a Friday was expressly forbidden. The word 'pig' carried a risk far worse than walking underneath a ladder (though there was a ban on that too), and readers of the recently published *The Obsession* may remember that Catherine, in an ironic side-swipe at this irrational fear, refers to the animal as a 'grunter', the name given it to avoid disaster at home when she was a child. A picture dropping from a wall or the sound of a cricket (or 'death beetle', as it was called) on the hearth spelled trouble, even tragedy. Extra care would be taken when such things occurred, and if, even months later, some disaster befell the household a finger would be pointed in all seriousness at some careless or chance transgression of superstitious lore.

Catherine identifies the sophistry and ignorance which mesmerises Tilly's people in the nineteenth century with those of her own people, spellbound by the psychomancy of Roman Catholicism three-quarters of a century later. Burning witches at the stake may already be a thing of the past by Tilly's time, but ignorance and fear, fertile breeding grounds for superstition, remain, and are used by Hal McGrath to pursue Tilly in the most horrifying manner. He nets her, stocks her (reclaiming the old village stocks from Tillson's barn for the purpose), fires her cottage, and finally attempts to throttle her, all with the bulk of the village behind him, convinced by McGrath that the teenager Tilly is a witch.

Evidence revolves around Pete Gladwish's dog. Used as a ratter down the pit, it is shown kindness by Tilly and that night, unaccustomed to such attentions, it displays none of its usual desire to perform. Pete beats the living daylights out of it and the dog disappears. The finger is pointed at Tilly and slanderous gossip swells in the small village community when it is revealed that Tilly is herself attached by a hereditary thread down the female side of the Trotter family to Cissy Clacket, the last witch to be buried in the parish, one hundred years earlier. Then there is the evidence of Andy Fairweather's own eyes. Hadn't he seen Tilly kicking her legs up in the vestry with Ellen Ross, the vicar's wife, 'like a pair of whores on the waterfront at Shields'? Ellen was in fact giving Tilly a quick dancing lesson. She is eventually drummed out of the village with her husband George when she saves Tilly from her persecutors by plunging a peg from the stocks into the neck of Burk Laudimer, and only narrowly escapes conviction on a charge of manslaughter.

That this same primitive sense of the supernatural was exploited by Catholicism comes across beautifully in a story Catherine tells of the first time she realised the power of prayer. The dreaded Miss Caulfield fell ill. Catherine prayed that she would die. She did – of cancer. Catherine couldn't believe it. Far from relieving her daily torture, the event threw her into a paroxysm of guilt, and she knew that her terrible sin would have to be absolved in the confessional. Her Father Confessor was so staggered that he wondered Catherine wasn't already in hell's fire, burning. 'I became a very good Catholic after that.'

Like many other people, and even as a young woman,

Catherine was unable or unwilling to allow her reason to distinguish the stories Father Bradley told her from what lay beneath them. There would appear to be a touch of irony in a writer who, through the power of her narratives, slips truths about the human condition to her readers, often without their realising it, not being able to suspend disbelief in the matter of religious stories. But the point is that more was demanded of a Roman Catholic in those days than the mere suspension of disbelief. A literal acceptance not just of the story, but also of the Roman Catholic dogma attached to it, which excluded all Protestants from joy, was fundamental. Questioning heaven and hell, as a lodger once did in the kitchen at William Black Street, was not healthy. The man earned a place in *Colour Blind* for Ted Grant, who questions 'this Adam and Garden of Eden business' and says that life in the first place was nothing but slime; and in *Fenwick Houses*, Ronnie Winter tells his mother that he's heard there's no such thing as the Garden of Eden and that we all come from apes. But these were borrowed opinions of learned men. For people like the McMullens or indeed Christine Winter, 'too busy' to read books, blind faith was the order – literally – of the day.

I spoke to Catherine about this a year or so before her eightieth birthday, after the Anglican Bishop of Durham had publicly questioned the literal truth of certain fundamental tenets of Christian dogma, and she angrily refused the Church any back-tracking in the business which had alienated her from it. 'Of course I believe everything that the Bishop is saying,' she told me. 'I was saying the same fifty years ago. It was a wonder they didn't excommunicate me. I could not accept the Transubstantiation and of course that caused the priest to have a heart attack. Today they let Protestants come into the Catholic Church . . . but at one time it was a sin for a Catholic to enter a Protestant church, a mortal sin. All these little frills on the outside make you think that everything has changed, but it hasn't. I agree with the Bishop of Durham, things he said about the Resurrection, but of course he should never have been a bishop, he should never have been a priest.' A little more than a decade later, she said to me, 'One type of person I do hate and that is a turncoat, and when men . . . God becomes a turncoat, well, you can look no further.'

For all the guilt and fear they aroused, the priests at St Peter and St Paul's did at least encourage a spiritual dimension in Catherine's life, fuelling her lifelong quest for an answer to the question: Why? More than forty years later, this seeking would lead to her discovery of 'a spirit that was an individual thing, not connected with any doctrine'. Today she is not so presumptuous as to declare herself an atheist: 'I am an agnostic. I still search, but having done so I have lost the fear of the after-life in which I lived for years.' This search became bound up with her creativity as a writer and produced some of her best work. But from the years of her life when, as 'a good Catholic', she was swept up in religion, came one of her most enchanting fictional relationships.

In the Mary Ann series, we have a delicious treatment of a child's matter-of-fact acceptance of the sanctity of the Holy Family. Mary Ann is in league with the Virgin Mary, Joseph and the infant Jesus, dashing into church, kneeling before the statuary and apologising that she can only stay a minute because she has to catch a bus, and then rabbiting on about Mrs McBride, her da and her brother, Michael. In *The Devil and Mary Ann* (1958), we even have a humorous approach to the divisions within the Church. A Protestant couple, Mr and Mrs Wilson, meet Mary Ann on a train when, for the first time, she is travelling to the Convent of the Holy Child of Bethlehem, a boarding school paid for by the Shaughnessys' benefactor, Peter Lord. Mr Wilson is alarmed at the prospect of the little girl being subjected to the terrors of hellfire by nuns, and draws an awesome picture of what will befall her, before his kindly wife stills him. Later, Mary Ann will fly to the Wilsons, demanding that they help her escape the convent because she has caught wind of things not being right at home: a Mrs Polanski is attempting to seduce her da. As in all the novels, Mary Ann is at centre stage, resolving, transforming; but in this one her time in the convent has some special delights, such as the gay-minded Sisters Alvis and Monica, and Sister Agnes Mary, who has a voice like a man's and who, to Mary Ann's astonishment, tells Sister Catherine to 'Stow it!' when her colleague reprimands her.

When Mary Ann, as supplicant, seeks a special favour from the Holy Family she sometimes observes a change of expression in the sculpted faces of Virgin and child which makes their view clear. The development of this enchanting relationship calls to mind Giovanni Guareschi's humorous series of novels about Don Camillo, the Italian parish priest with his simple but certain faith. As with Don Camillo, who conducts down-to-earth and humorously telling conversations with Christ, so with Mary Ann a deal done with the Virgin Mary invariably precipitates the action. Both narratives give ultimate credibility to the make-believe elements in ecclesiastical doctrine. Both became best-sellers. And while in reality Catherine had already renounced her faith in Christianity when she wrote these books, it is not her main purpose to reveal that here, although the reason why she did so is implicit.

Mary Ann tells stories and lives in a make-believe world upon which everyone around her depends for their salvation. The key to the art of storytelling is in making your audience believe. Mary Ann has this skill to a high degree. The Christian story, in its simplicity and spiritual depth, has proved itself one of the most convincing stories of all time. In her teens Catherine believed it wholeheartedly; she became a devout Catholic and remained true to her faith into her early thirties. It was the Church itself which shook her out of it when it insisted on blind adherence to its own special dogma – about transubstantiation, about mixed marriages, about the literal acceptance of hell and so on – which it attached to the simple story, and then faced her with an all-or-nothing choice. But no storyteller can get away with insisting on what its audience should believe. Storytelling is a far more magical process than that, as Mary Ann knows so well.

All storytellers deal in myth, clothing naked truth in such a manner as to lead their audience to it, but along their own path. Mary Ann carries her people with her on the wings of her art, and they find solutions to their problems in their own way. Catherine, perhaps because she was so devastated by the response of the Church to her, a believer (particularly when she married a Protestant), is determined in the Mary Ann series to point up the fabrication involved in telling a story, deliberately drawing attention to it with exaggerated, C.S. Lewis-style religious symbolism, for example in naming Mary Ann's saviour 'Mr Lord'. She does the same sort of thing in many of her novels, for instance in her use of the fictional village of Fellburn, with its simplistic, geographically regulated class system: Bog's End for the workers, Brampton Hill for the nobs. And even the names of her characters are often encoded; you just know that anyone called Donald is going to be nasty, anyone called Bailey is a goodie, and so on. Mary Ann, the fibber with a twinkle in her eye, is behind this, too, for she is the pure storyteller part of the writer – didn't old John once say to his granddaughter that her talent for fibbing would get her into the clink or into the money? Once, at the end of *The Lord and Mary Ann*, the author actually comes out into the open and challenges our acceptance of what has been laid before us to believe. After all the ends of her narrative have been neatly tied in a bow, she asks if we 'believe all about everything now? You don't? Well, it'll serve you right if nothing nice ever happens to you!' It is charming, disarming, but there is also the gentlest satirical nudge.

Mary Ann, the arch-storyteller, understands that lying is not just saying what isn't true but can be saying more than is true. Fabrication is an essential part of storytelling, but, as Catherine shows in much of her other work, it is not the essential part; in the end, the story is merely a vehicle. This, her missioners could never accept.

The Mary Ann novels, published at intervals, which lent balance to her less humorous early work, offer an insight into the side of Catherine from which all her stories naturally flow. But by the time she came to write them, Mary Ann was only one part of this complex woman.

CHAPTER FIVE

The Road Out

At the end of 1917 Rose died. Catherine was sleeping in the room where she passed her final moments. Dreamily she was aware of other people in the room attending her grandma, then she heard her being sick and the death rattle as she expired. No one had thought to remove the child to another bed. In the morning Catherine discovered that her gran had been laid out on the table. Rose lay there for three days, Kate occasionally putting a fresh bowl underneath to catch the blood and fluids which seeped out of her and would otherwise have messed the floor.

Rose's passing was a turning point. From this time Catherine began her 'scribbles', as she calls them. Indeed, there ensued a succession of events associated with artistic endeavour. First came the piano.

At eleven going on twelve, as the errands to the pub and the Pawn continued, she determined to do something about Kate using her. She had been sent to get a half-bottle of whiskey from a pub in Jarrow, where Kate had taken part-time work. Plucking up her courage, Catherine begged the publican and his wife to refuse to serve her. They were sympathetic. A week later, Kate lost her job. She never knew why. The piano appeared, against all reason, shortly afterwards. Was it the publican who gave Kate a reference for the hire purchase agreement? It was no ordinary instrument.

101

When it arrived and was eased into the already over-crowded front room of number 10, Catherine discovered that it had cost Kate £100. This was a huge amount of money for Kate to get tied up with on the never-never. Catherine has said that Kate bought the piano 'to show off to the neighbours'; a Mrs Tyler had one, and of course Aunt Mary had her beautiful spinet. At any rate, the piano arrived, and rather endearingly Bob the Pawn found Catherine a teacher. She took her first examination and passed with honours. But then reality dawned. Kate didn't keep up the payments and the piano went back.

The significance of the piano is that it gave Catherine something of her own to get wrapped up in. I doubt that at this early stage it was imaginatively rewarding, but there was always the promise that it would be. The piano answered a need. She was upset when it went back, but the experience took her forward. Having identified this need, she found an alternative means to fulfil it. 'It was after the loss of the piano I went in for words.'

She had already discerned beauty in words through her poetry class, and now as in school her interest focused on their imaginative, associative properties which stemmed not from their literal meaning but from their sense. Words had fascinated Catherine from the start. As a very young child unusual words didn't pass over her. For example, 'imposition' was a word she first heard in the script of the Faerie Queen concert at school (she would have been six). There was no reason for Catherine to store it in memory, but she did. Perhaps it sounded interesting; most likely her attention was caught by the intonation which the character (a house-wife) used to articulate its sense – 'a thorough im-po-sition!' – in this case about the outrageous price of a duck. Financial hardship being central to the McMullens' anxieties at home, this may have struck a chord. Perhaps, as the housewife in the play is so disdainful of the duck seller, the hook might have been this disdain, an emotion prevalent enough in her experience at the lower end of the social spectrum. Years later a neighbour used the word, again disdainfully, after Kate had insisted Catherine charge her three shillings and sixpence for processing a particularly large load of laundry. Her mind turned at once to the Faerie Queen.

On one level, her keen interest in words was simply part of Catherine's eagerness to learn. But our ability to draw sense from words beyond their literal meaning – their power to seduce by appealing to the imagination as well as to reason – is what first led her, at eleven or twelve years of age, to cook up stories of her own. She would get an *idea* from a word which would then set her mind whirling with a story as she walked to the pub with the Grey Hen.

In *The Menagerie*, when Larry Broadhurst kisses Pam Turnbull, long after she had jilted him almost at the altar, Larry's mind turns, of all things, to the word 'penumbra'. Pam had used it once during their earlier life together. It had bothered Larry then: he hadn't known what it meant, but didn't let on for fear that upstart Pam would think him bovine. In effect, the word signified the gaping cultural gulf between them, and now, at the moment of their reconciliation, he remembers it again because he fears (and is right to fear) that their reunion won't last.

The novel is about upstart Pam's inability to connect with her roots. That Larry remembers the word has nothing to do with its meaning, everything to do with the idea that it represents in his mind of their irreconcilable differences. And we shouldn't feel sad for Larry, for his sense of the word is what matters; what it triggers serves him well. At the end, he is urged by Jessie, who is everything Pam is not, to write a novel 'about Aunt Lot and everything . . . it's a way of life.' We have no doubt that he will.

This period of Catherine's life, when her imagination was growing, coincided with the First World War. After Rose died and Jack was killed in action in September 1918, there were just three McMullens left at number 10: old John, Kate and Catherine. By this time the chores of going for the beer and to the pawn shop had been added to. Kate was washing for a woman in Croft Terrace, a quiet, 'swanky' part of Jarrow, and Catherine was the gofer. So heavy were the loads of laundry that she could manage only a few paces at a time before having to put her burden down on the pavement and take a breather. Anyone could have seen that all these trips were taking their toll on the girl.

In addition, on Saturdays, Catherine was 'doing' for their neighbours the Flannagans, scrubbing out their scullery and washing down their stairs. Then there was the daily trip to Tyne Dock, a mile each way, to and from school; and she had begun to take it on herself to go to the piles of used cinders by the tram sheds to the west of the New Buildings to search with real destitutes for usable pieces of coal for the fire. Kate had never asked her to do this, and old John would not have been seen dead doing it, though occasionally he would help her back with her pickings. That Catherine chose to go scavenging in this way was sign enough that she was now part of the whole depressing ethos, and it was exhausting her.

She had first experienced the odd, tired feeling, not just tired but 'funny tired', around the age of nine when at St Bede's. Now it was her regular companion. But Kate, despite her sympathy for Uncle Alec when he was ill, had no time for Catherine's infirmity. Kate worked hard and drank hard. Frailty had no place in her vocabulary. The integrity of the poor was bound up with this ethic. You worked until you dropped. Stamina, or gumption, was prized; sensitivity was a luxury no one in Kate's position could afford. She put the pains in Catherine's limbs down to growing up. She may have thought her daughter was malingering; or, since it was below Kate to go to the Pawn, it may have been that she didn't want to face having to take on this particular chore. Whichever way she looked at it, there was nothing to be gained by cossetting Catherine in sympathy.

In 1919, after Catherine had turned thirteen, there came the fourth major upset in her young life. She fell in the school playground and injured her hip. She was brought home and put to bed. But she didn't get up. Kate insisted she must. The accident had occurred towards the end of the year, and in Christmas week Kate sent her on a 'message' for three bottles of beer from the pub – this is the occasion, which I have already described, when Catherine pressed Kate's ten-shilling note in the hand of the paper boy and fortunately he returned with the beer and Kate's change. Catherine had protested that her leg was hurting. Kate would have none of it: 'You went out to play snowballs yesterday. Well, if you go out to play snowballs you can go a message. Get yourself away.' The pain was what caused her to enlist the paper boy's help. 'That I wasn't shamming about my leg was demonstrated early in the next year,' Catherine told me. 'Again it was snowing heavily. But she would have none of my pleas that my leg was painful. I could hardly walk. I was going to school and that was about it. To walk to school generally took me about fifteen minutes, that is if I hurried. This morning it must have taken well over an hour. I remember opening the door of the classroom, going in and that was that, I had passed out. That was my last day at school. I was carried back to a strange doctor, who said I must be taken home and my leg kept up. I lay on the saddle in the kitchen.

'That night I must have become unconscious again because

I remember hearing my granda's voice, "If she gets past three o'clock she'll survive." Then I was conscious of Kate's face above me and I turned mine away from the smell of whiskey. I must have woken some time later in this blackness, there was no light in the kitchen. I was shivering, and I was in awful pain, when I cried out. My cry must have disturbed her drunken sleep because she came to the foot of the saddle and she said, "Stop that and get yourself to sleep." That incident kept as alive in my mind as that with the paper boy, but this with bitterness. I was to learn that hate and bitterness were two emotions that can wipe out love.'

Catherine did not begin to recover until the spring of 1920. She remembers the day she got out of bed with extraordinary clarity, as she does all the critical moments in her imaginative development. Her first steps took her to the kitchen window. Looking out, she saw the yard door on to the back lane was open. As she stood there, two of her playmates, Florrie Harding and Janie Robson, happened to pass by the open doorway. It was as if she was looking at her life from another world. She knew that she would never play with them again. Something had happened inside her. There was a complete cut-off. Her rejection by and of her friends had earlier led to the feeling of aloneness which I have described. But now, at this moment, aloneness became complete detachment, a kind of disinterested neutrality, a simultaneously depressing and enlightening transition, 'an all-knowing, desolate life, a negative life that told me there was nothing of value, nothing worth striving for'.

At the start of *Fanny McBride* there is a clue to part of what Catherine felt. Fanny is alone, deserted by her family. She lies in bed looking at the ceiling, calculating the passage of time by the position of a shaft of light from the sun in relation to a discoloured patch above her on the ceiling, reputed to be a bloodstain left after the murder of a woman upstairs. The stain is her sundial, fixed, stationary, redolent only of what has been. There is a future, but only outside, in the movement of the sun. Fanny lies still, like a prisoner in a cell, as if her story has come to an end on the very first page of the novel.

Catherine told me that this scene came to her during a trip she made to the North-East after she had moved to Hastings. 'Dr Murray Anderson of South Shields was one of my first friends here when I used to come back. I used to stay at his home when I came to give talks, and he would get up in the middle of the night if any of the old girls were dying, and he would go to comfort them. I thought that was simply marvellous. He told me that one of the saddest things was on visiting day, to go into the ward in the hospital and see patients sitting there, just staring into space with no visitors, even though some of them had big families.'

There is something of Fanny's mood in the depressive aspect of Catherine's own 'cut-off' in 1920, but there was also a mature understanding which translated it into a 'moment of realisation'. This didn't defeat her bleak moods, but it did play a large part in her subsequent momentous decision not to return to school. Catherine had at last decided to take control. For the first time, *she* would take responsibility for her own life and be accountable only to herself.

She told herself that she only knew how to do two things: she could write and she could do housework. First she took a job as a daily for a woman in Simonside Terrace and developed a classic crush, 'a girlish passion' as she called it, for the woman's eldest son. Fortunately, the fellow didn't take to his role in the classic serving-girl romance, and before long Catherine left and turned to an occupation more suited to her new spirit of self-motivation.

She took one sixpenny lesson in pen-painting and discovered that she had a talent. She began painting decorative motifs on cushions, tray-cloths and mantel borders, and set up a club to market her wares. 'I sat at a table under the window in the kitchen for eight to ten hours a day filling in a pattern of a basket of flowers on a satin cushion cover with oil paints applied with the nib of a pen, five days a week. Saturday was given over to collecting the club money for the said cushions; part of the Sunday I would spend making the articles.' There were clubs for everything in those days; they worked on the principle that people could afford small amounts from the weekly wage to put towards little luxuries. The enterprise was a success and with it came her first taste of self-respect. One result was that she began to sort out her life at home. She informed Kate that she would no longer be taking the Grey Hen for the beer, and it was during this period – 1920 to 1923 – that she first faced up to her mother when Kate went to strike her once again on the ear.

This new spirit took her life in another direction too. 'From when I was about fifteen [in 1921], I was courted, as the word was, by three pit lads, and may I state emphatically they were all gentlemen!' These innocent relationships were sometimes conducted within the St Peter and St Paul's church social scene, which revolved around dances on a Saturday night. 'Me first lad,' Catherine once confided, 'a fellow called Micky Moran, was a pitman who spent all his spare time decorating the church, you know these stencils that go round the church – all the crosses, all the way round . . . Granda used to call him "the spare priest". I was about sixteen at the time. We'd go to dances in the schoolroom after we had played whist [today it would be called a youth club]. Then there was Kit Gannon, he was also a miner, and Todd Lawson, he became one of the leading footballers – a Newcastle footballer! They were all miners from mining families. Although there were very few miners in the New

Buildings – they were mostly working in the shipyards or on the trams and things like that – in my teens my friends were from mining families. That is how I know so much about what went on in their homes.'

What Catherine found in their homes was warmth, something quite other than the fleeting moments of security between battles in her own home. She portrays such a scene in *Tilly Trotter*. Tilly, alone and with no place to live after the Trotter cottage has been burned down, finds work in the Sopwith mine and a roof over her head with the Drew family, who are everything Catherine would have liked her family to be – warm, caring, rich in spirit in spite of their poverty. What Tilly saw in the sea of faces before her when she first visited for Sunday tea was a revelation. Sunday, with the mine closed, was the one day on which Biddy Drew could count on her whole family to be round her in the kitchen. There was laughter, but behind it a real closeness, a happiness which Tilly sees comes from deep within. It answers a crying need in Tilly, not for sex with boy or man, but for someone to be kind to her.

Catherine was changing, blossoming. The little illegitimate child, Annie Hannigan, persecuted by her friends and driven into her lavatory sanctuary in the backyard because she had no da, was on the wane, and the sparky little fibber Mary Ann, cutting deals with the Virgin Mary to make things right at home, was retreating into the shadows of her psyche. Neither would ever completely leave her – they are as much part of her complex make-up today as all her autobiographically inspired fictional creations – but from Catherine's teens other aspects come to the fore.

There was something different about Tilly Trotter, just as everyone said there was something different about Catherine. A few who met Tilly – like farmer Brentwood and young Steve McGrath – see promise in that difference; others, a threat or challenge. Tilly is a beanpole of a girl, 'like a yard of pump water, as straight as a die', but the difference told in her eyes, 'the strangest eyes . . . so clear and deep', and she was a girl who could 'read and write as good as the parson hisself'. Sex is available, but Tilly isn't. She is just not interested. What she needs is warmth. Steve, a year younger than her at sixteen, a lad to whom she owes more for her survival to date than anyone, is put off by Tilly time and again. As it happens, Steve, whose extraordinary act of faith transports his affections across three books – the entire Tilly Trotter trilogy – will, in the very final pages of *Tilly Trotter Widowed* (1982), be rewarded for his patience.

There is something of the teenager Mary Walton of *Pure as the Lily* about her, too; and something of Alec Walton, Mary's father, in the way John McMullen enjoyed this period of Catherine's innocent teens. Catherine was coming into her own; the pen-painting and her new social life were positive developments. John was proud of the way she was going, and deep down felt the same love for her as Alec did for Mary.

Fifteen-year-old Christine Winter of *Fenwick Houses* reflects another facet of Catherine at this time, particularly in her relationships with boys. Don Dowling informs Christine that she is going to be his girl, they'll get married when she's older. Christine says she 'ain't', he's more like a brother to her. She is carefree, and wants nothing earnest to impinge on her life. She likes to be told by her friend Molly that she is pretty, but doesn't want a lad getting serious over her. Molly is a tonic, a real friend, with a laughing, down-to-earth personality. Even her outrageous bad language sparks laughter in Christine and binds them more tightly together. It was during this period that Catherine too found a friend and confidante in Lily Maguire, the first real girl friend of her own age that she ever had. They would go off together on their bikes into the countryside. There were no bad times with Lily Maguire any more than when Christine and Molly were together; only plans for the future and laughter.

Christine's friend Molly is part of Fellburn, an embodied spirit of the place. She will probably stay there and marry a pitman, though she has plans to do better than that. When Christine finally agrees to go to the church social with Don (in the company of her brother, Ronnie), she insists that the two boys forget their differences. Then all three of them are like kids again, and Christine doesn't mind when both take her by the hand and run down the hill towards the bridge and the schoolroom, where the dance is to be held. All is innocence, all is fun. That is what Christine wants. 'Enjoy yersel' when you're young,' says neighbour Mr Patterson, lolling by the wall as he watches them going down . . . 'Life flees. We're nowt but feathers in the fire.'

And yet, in spite of their common determination not to get seriously involved with a man, each of these three girls – Tilly, Mary and Christine – is hurt when a man gets under her skin. For Tilly it is farmer Simon Brentwood, an older man. For as long as Tilly can remember there has been a spark between the two of them, and she idolises Simon – until the day she comes across him with Lady Agnes in a barn, their limbs working like windmills in a storm. For Mary Walton it is also an older man: Ben Tollet, a shopkeeper for whom Mary works. He takes advantage of her, although Mary had already fallen for him, and she becomes pregnant. Mary's father, Alec, feeling much the same about Ben's advances as old John did when a shopkeeper once demanded a kiss from Catherine in exchange for her purchase, beats Ben up. For Christine in *Fenwick Houses*, it is her gentleman friend, Martin. Martin comes from outside Christine's class, just as Catherine's father came from outside Kate's. He may be only middle class, but he is a world away from any of the boys Christine knows. Christine's progression from school-room dances with pitmen to Martin, and his subsequent using of her, which tore Christine apart, bears some comparison with Catherine's experience.

In her teens Catherine yearned for her real father and needed what no young pitman could give her emotionally. 'From the time I was fourteen I had sat every Sunday at the eleven o'clock Mass behind a tall, handsome, very well-dressed man, and, as a child, I longed that such a man could be my father... Anyway, this man never spoke to me. He came out of church before me and walked straight away, passing little groups of people chatting together, of which I'd be one.

'Then one Sunday he stopped and spoke to me. He said, "We walk part of the same way home." I was dumb. We walked to the Tyne Dock gates. He went one way to Eldon Street, where he lived nearby, I went the other way through the famous Tyne Dock arches, past the little street where I'd been born, up the Jarrow Road, on to the open stretch of the Jarrow slacks, where the tide lapped the bank and the season-ing timbers bobbed up and down. And so into the kitchen of 10 William Black Street. And I hadn't touched the ground. I had been borne on the white light of wings. *He* had spoken to me! After all these years I had admired this wonderful being, and he had spoken to me.'

The man was eleven years older than Catherine. The story of their ensuing relationship, which Catherine has never spoken about before, so hurt her that it precipitated her departure from the North, and we will return to it a year or so into the affair, when she is twenty and he is thirty-one.

As Catherine says, her teens were marked by a strong desire to find her father – 'It was the beginning of a period when I began secretly to search for him, first of all by asking questions of my Aunt Mary, because Kate only once ever brought him to the fore until she was in the last years of her life.' Aunt Mary gave Catherine what she wanted to hear, and it couldn't have come at a worse moment.

Catherine was galvanising her strengths. It was a positive, if, with the pen-painting, an exhausting period in which Mary chose to tell Catherine that her father had been a well-spoken, well-dressed man of distinction, with his kid gloves, top hat and silver-mounted walking stick. This revelation threw Catherine completely off course, adding just the kind of vanity to her mounting self-confidence – 'a false sense of superiority', as she has put it – that would immediately distance her from her new-found friends. Years later Lily Maguire, her first close female friend, would recall that the moment in their friendship that stuck most vividly in her mind was Catherine telling her that, as she saw it, Lily would end up marrying a miner, while she would marry a rich man from a better class.

What Aunt Mary had done was to catch Catherine at the most susceptible moment in her swing from utter depression to self-belief. Suddenly everything seemed to fall into place. Her father must be the reason why she had had such difficulty fitting in. She wasn't like the rest of her friends in the New Buildings. She was better than them. This did her inferiority complex a power of good; unfortunately, like everything else that Mary promoted, it amounted to a veneer which, whether true or false, would do little to help Catherine find the warmth and acceptance she so desperately desired.

Then, a year later, in 1923, Kate married David McDermott, the seaman who had been introduced to her by Jack all those years before. He was a quiet man, and Catherine seems to have got on well with him. He liked a drink, but was away at sea for months at a time. Kate probably felt that the timing was right for marriage: she was forty-one, and Catherine at seventeen was making her own way. But it was another upset in the status quo at home which exacerbated Catherine's sensations of aloneness.

Tensions were certainly running high in number 10 and Kate now had a drinking partner when David was at home. One day the atmosphere became so highly charged that Catherine screamed at her mother that she was getting out once and for all. The strain of Catherine's long days pen-painting, nose to paper, day in, day out in front of the kitchen window, unrelieved by any great show of profit, was, after more than three years, beginning to tell, and when one day she found herself too weak to contest Kate in some raging argument, Dr McHaffie was summoned. He diagnosed her exhaustion as a symptom of anaemia caused by lead poisoning from the paints she was using. Anaemia, a lack of red cells in the bloodstream, is also a symptom of hereditary haemorrhagic telangiectasia; but at this time there was no reason for Dr McHaffie to suspect that Catherine had contracted so rare a vascular disease.

Catherine wound up the club and registered with an employment agency, which found her a job as a companion–maid in a big house in swanky Harton Village. Psychologically it was a bad move. Having been elevated in her own mind by Mary's revelations, she now found herself below stairs, at someone else's beck and call. She discovered that 'companion–maid' was a euphemism for servant. Washing, cleaning, cooking and serving, she worked from six in the morning until nine at night, when she flopped exhausted into bed. She stood this for only a fortnight.

It was around this time that Catherine met Councillor Bill McAnany at one of the regular whist drives and dances at Tyne Dock schoolrooms. Behind the scenes Father Bradley had asked McAnany whether he might not be able to do something for her, and on 22 October 1924, at eighteen years of age, Catherine began working as a laundry checker . . . in South Shields workhouse.

At first things went well. The matron in charge was a bit of a tartar, but very good at her job, and Catherine threw herself into work, her own situation put into perspective by the real destitutes, 'the weeping women and grim-faced men [who] had watched their last sticks of furniture being carried out by the bums,' as she wrote in *Colour Blind*.

From her late teens she had become increasingly aware of the depths of degradation unemployment could bring to a town. 'All about me were men standing in groups, thin men, lost men, men who sat on smouldering tips, picking cinders all night in order to fill a barrow to be pushed to either Shields or Jarrow, hoping to sell the contents for a shilling. Men who had lost hope.' Now, in the workhouse, when on part duty in the evenings, she was admitting families – 'the men to one side, the women to the other, the children to the nurses' home or the nursery, or an old couple knowing they'd have to spend the rest of their lives in the workhouse. Shields workhouse in those days was not far removed from the Dickensian era.' Individuals like Mrs Henagen – the woman's name and the pain and degradations of this place whisper to us across the years through Catherine's novels – aroused her compassion. Confined in a wheelchair, in the foul-smelling atmosphere of the infirm ward – the stench of urine particularly repulsed Catherine – Mrs Henagen was only thirty years old but looked twice that, prematurely aged by despair.

Catherine arrived at the workhouse a strong Catholic, regularly stopping off at St Peter and St Paul's on her way to visit her family, drawing comfort from the peace and quiet of the darkened church, lit only by the red Sanctuary light. She believed that being a checker in the workhouse laundry was what God intended for her at this point, but none the less felt driven by ambition, an urge to move forward, although at this stage she could not identify a goal or purpose to aim for.

She knew she could write. She had started her scribblings at the age of eleven, and in 1922, at sixteen, she had written a 16,000 word story about God entering the world as Christ on the second floor of a tenement building. She called it 'On The Second Floor'. She even managed to persuade Lily Maguire's sister, Maisie, to copy it out in calligraphic text for the grand sum of two shillings and sixpence, before submitting it to the *South Shields Gazette*. Not for one moment did she think that 16,000 words might be a little too long for inclusion in a newspaper, and she was mortified when it was returned, obviously unread, by the next post.

Rejection was no stranger to her, but now, at the workhouse, 'I definitely found out what it meant.' Among the staff, who ranged through all the social levels from the bottom rung up to lower middle class, there was an acute awareness of who was who and of the place of each in the pecking order. Here Catherine's upstart pretensions, her commitment to attain the 'norm' that her father represented, were never going to win her friends. 'There were eighteen staff in my department and within no time they knew of my history and of the drunken family from which I came, and there I was in the workhouse nursery with a whole lot of illegitimate children.'

Catherine's selective image of herself as vested with genes from her father which set her apart from the hoi polloi might have militated against compassion or seen her disdainfully marking time at the workhouse, but in fact the opposite was true. She proved her commitment to rising above her situation through sheer hard work, drawing on just the kind of gumption which enabled one of her best-known heroines,

Katie Mulholland, against all odds to establish an empire barely a stone's throw away. In her relationships with the other staff she set the same high, indeed perfectionist, standard which marked her attitude to work, and this did little to warm her fellow workers to her. On one occasion when a female member of staff was talking smuttily at the dinner table, Catherine reprimanded her in front of everyone, even threatening to report the woman to matron. It was not the best way for the new girl to settle in. But Catherine wasn't playing at her part, nor was it primness which inspired the reprimand but her increasingly ruthless integrity.

'She is quite just, and she can be awfully kind, but she looks to the end of things and doesn't care a rush for any one, but sticks to what she wants herself. I tell you, 'Tild, I used to hate her, but I don't now; I respect Katherine, she is so perfectly *true*.' The quotation is one that Catherine may recognise, but it is unlikely that many readers will. It comes from a novel by Elinor Glyn called *The Career of Katherine Bush*, which she read around this time, and it gives a good idea of what drove the real Catherine, if not quite so true a record of how this new persona was received by her colleagues.

Her outburst at table earned her the nickname of 'bloody St Catherine' and began a long period of persecution at her colleagues' hands. She was made an outcast – or rather, she had made herself one and was unable to retrieve the situation. Whenever she came into a room, all talking and laughing would be suppressed. She'd return to her bedroom to find that the others had stripped it or made her an apple-pie bed, folding the bottom sheet up midway down the bed so her feet were caught up in it when she got in.

The campaign against her drove her back inside herself and she began once more to put pen to paper. She sent a play she had written about rivalry between the house and hospital sides of the workhouse to a writers' correspondence school, only to receive another rejection note strongly advising her not to take up a literary career. Rejection was coming from all sides; but it served only to steel her resolve. She had been bred on strife; later she would write that strife became 'a kind of yeast' which led to an awareness of an extraordinary strength within her.

Determined to move forward, she got hold of a copy of *The Naval Book*, a book on nursing for naval trainees, and became intrigued by the anatomy of the human body. Father Bradley had told her that she wasn't sufficiently well educated to become a nurse. This was her response. She also took to reading *T. P. and Cassell's Weekly*, a new literary periodical (it was founded in 1923), always taking care to hide it from her colleagues lest they thought she was over-reaching herself.

Quite distinct from and far more significant than these attempts to educate herself was what she describes as her cultural ambition: 'I did not think of the word "education", the word prominent in my mind being "culture". I knew that ladies had to have culture, and culture had something to do with the arts.' She was giving herself the finishing school which, if she had been born a Larkin – like the little girl in the New Buildings who went to boarding school and thence to France – would have been her due. She bought a second-hand violin and took lessons at a shilling a time. But soon she and those within earshot (her playing inspired matron's dog to a regular howling accompaniment) agreed that it wasn't for her. Next she took lessons in French, but her accent failed to come up to her tutor's expectations. So, 'in some despair I took up physical culture [martial arts – she actually learned how to wield Indian clubs], this with the hope of getting rid of my puppy fat and of developing a beautiful body.'

All this was fertile ground for her colleagues' derision, and rather than be defeated by it she decided to play the clown to their provocation. For example, she deliberately acted up one day when she heard her persecutors sniggering from behind closed doors as she practised her clubs, making a fool of herself in the hope that it would defuse their antagonism. We are reminded of the incident in the pawn shop when she poked fun at herself at being the daughter of 'a nigger'. There's the same self-effacement, the same attempt to transform pathos with humour. Here it shows us just how much she would have loved to gain acceptance by her persecutors.

Catherine will have been aware that in her society, with its many different social gradations and subtly defined sub-levels, anyone who attempted to cross a social demarcation line would very likely be vilified as an upstart. But though her alienation depressed her she would not give up her attempts to improve herself. This remained her central goal. In any case, Catherine could see nothing intrinsically wrong with what she was doing. In her experience, everyone, if not actually trying to rise in the world, would have liked to. Even old John McMullen, who professed to mistrust anyone who, by work or learning, had risen in the world – they had sided with the enemy! – was deeply chuffed when Arne Fuller, an old friend of his who had made good, invited him for a drink. He didn't go, but he bored everyone with the story for months afterwards, truly proud that Arne had asked him.

Among Catherine's detractors were those who, like her Aunt Mary, enjoyed the social in-fighting and posturing for its own sake and made constant attempts at 'refeenment'. They, and others like Kate, who despised the two Richardson girls in the New Buildings for their posh accent but would have liked to talk that way herself, were slaves to Mrs

Malaprop. To Catherine these were the real upstarts. She would lampoon them in *A Grand Man*, where Mrs Flannagan sends a note to school saying that her daughter, Sarah, cannot attend because she has an 'illustrated' throat.

Weren't such half-hearted attempts at social superiority worse than her honest and open commitment to making a better life for herself? Upstarts and snobs litter Catherine's fiction, but the snobs generally come off worse. An upstart may be a snob too and, like Aunt Mary, behave condescendingly to those on a lower social level. But not all upstarts were snobs and Catherine certainly wasn't. Her self-improvement strategy was something she was doing for herself. Catherine had made a mistake in publicly reprimanding the woman at the dining table for her smutty talk, but this wasn't snobbish behaviour.

Anne Thornton in *The Girl* is a snob and, like most snobs, cruel with it. The novel's title reflects her snobbery, for she insists on calling Hannah Boyle, her ward and the daughter of a Newcastle whore, 'the girl'. In *The Wingless Bird*, Charles Farrier's mother is a snob, aghast when her son indicates his intention to marry shop-girl Agnes Conway. When she and her husband refuse to attend their wedding, Catherine kills them off in a road accident. In *The Devil and Mary Ann*, Beatrice, the merciless convent girl who mocks Jarrow and Mary Ann's ma and da, calls Mary Ann a sow's ear and forges a rude piece of poetry about Sister Alvis in Mary Ann's handwriting, is also a snob.

Snobs exist at all levels of society other than the lowest. Upstarts exist at all levels of society except the highest, though they may rise to the highest level by being an upstart. There have always been snobs, but upstarts have only existed since money replaced heredity as a measure of class. Snobbery aside, upstarts were simply people rising in a world that was changing in the direction of accommodating them, people availing themselves of the new and still slim opportunities that for centuries had been denied them. The word is meaningless to Americans, who do not have our social history, and it is interesting that Catherine, whose novels turn to a high degree on the anachronisms of the English class system, found it difficult at first to conquer that market.

The Golden Age of Agriculture, when labourers knew their place and lived largely off the land, was long gone. The world had already changed dramatically over the past half-century, and it was still changing. Now that money was part of the equation, the old loyalties between labourer and hereditary landowner, which had existed for centuries, had been eroded. Since the Industrial Revolution the money men in the City of London had taken control of working men's lives. The working-class myth, which attached pride and dignity to the position of the workers (and suggested that rising out of it was a betrayal), suited the money men, for it fostered company loyalty, but they were not about to succour it at their own expense. Nor did it seem to Catherine that there was much real working-class solidarity in any case. In fact, the only example reflected in industrial action came during ten days in the middle of May 1926, with the General Strike. Through inter-union conflict and squabbles over demarcation lines (between boilermakers and shipwrights, for example) the unions failed consistently to present a unified front, or to convince the majority of workers to join them. In the words of Mr Hetherington to Katie's brother Joe in *Katie Mulholland* (1967), 'it's every man jack for himself.' Catherine's persecutors were deluded if they saw her efforts to rise above her class as betrayal, because in reality the values they felt had been betrayed belonged to a world which had long gone.

In *Tilly Trotter* and *Katie Mulholland* we see the great change from an agricultural to an industrial society taking place, and along with it an increased freedom of movement – for the mercantile and commercial classes, at least.

Coal provided the fuel of revolution, and the various industries returned the favour in their own ways, the railways by decreasing the cost of moving it, iron and steel by shaping the ships that carried it to foreign lands, glass by using otherwise unsaleable coal in its manufacturing process and the chemical industry by its use of brine, a nuisance in the pits but invaluable in the manufacture of alkali; and in its turn the chemical industry provided essential ingredients for the manufacture of pottery, paper, soap and textiles. If you were an entrepreneurial spirit and wanted to get on, you tried to get into coal.

When we meet George Rosier in *Tilly Trotter* in the 1830s he is merely a mine manager of the Sopwith Coal Mine, owned by landowner Mark Sopwith. Sopwith, like all the other hereditary landowners in a region once noted for its agricultural strength, is now concentrating on mining the mineral that lies beneath his land. Rosier, as any other entrepreneurial spirit would have done, seeks a share in a mine. When he appears in *Katie Mulholland* he has clawed his way into the industry and begun to cement a profitable relationship with Palmer's shipyard in Jarrow, which was at the epicentre of the industrial revolution. Rosier's son Bernard is eighteen when, on a June day in 1852, he stands with his father in Palmer's and watches the launching of the *John Bowes*. This ship, the first profitable iron collier, could do in five days what 'would have taken two sailing colliers a month to accomplish'. It was a turning point in the revolution – and, incidentally, the reason why our Queen Mother, a Bowes-Lyon, has such close links with Tyneside and is one of Catherine's foremost fans.

Others of Catherine's new gentry, such as the Mallens and Edmund Lagrange in *The Glass Virgin*, also rose from the merchant classes. By the mid-nineteenth century the remarkable surge of economic activity in a variety of industries had changed the power structure of Britain completely and set in motion a social revolution in which, as a woman, Catherine was a pioneering participant. In *The Upstart*, she shows one aspect of the social confusion which resulted from this great change, when the old values still existed alongside the new.

By 1898, when the novel opens, money has long been the principal measure of class, and there is utter confusion when the *nouveau riche* tradesman-turned-businessman Samuel Fairbrother comes into contact with a below stairs set-up which hasn't changed for a hundred years. Butler Roger Maitland is appalled when his new master, the owner of a chain of shoemaking shops, associates him with the kitchen staff. Loud-mouthed Fairbrother has bought his thirty-four-roomed house, stone, mortar, servants, lock, stock and barrel, the last owner having fallen on hard times. His ethic is work, work, work, and, having never had a favour offered him on a plate, he cannot see why life for his servants should be any different. He and Maitland look at each other across a gaping cultural divide.

At the outset, both are uneasy, and Fairbrother and his wife Alice display all the symptoms of a couple totally at sea in their new environment. Maitland offers his resignation, but is persuaded to stay. It is inconceivable that the house can be run without his experience. But there is no easy solution, and the Fairbrothers (they have eight children) display all the symptoms of the discomfort that goes with rising from one social level to another – recrimination, anger, hypocrisy – which erupt into family feuds. We watch Maitland, a quiet catalyst in this extraordinary experiment, tactfully educate Fairbrother in his new role as master, while maintaining a kind of classless integrity behind his butler's mask which will, in the course of the novel, put him firmly in control.

When Catherine searched history for the reasons behind the anachronisms, hypocrisies and absurdities of the English class system from which she, and all her people, suffered, she found confusion, envy and exploitation at their roots. In the end she prefers a kind of existential solution to the class problem. It is the characters who take responsibility for their own lives and eschew or overcome the pettifogging prejudices and hypocrisies of society who achieve fulfilment. Her novels cover a period of change from the rise of the mercantile class at the expense of the landed gentry in the eighteenth and nineteenth centuries, when money replaced heredity as the means to position in society (e.g. *Katie Mulholland*, *The Glass Virgin*), through the 1930s, when financial disaster brought a desperate call for workers' rights (*The Blind Miller*), to modern days, when class problems are borne in the psyche of her people, however deeply they may be buried in history, and a psychological adjustment is required to overcome them. The best novel in these terms in undoubtedly *The Round Tower* (1968), which won the Winifred Holtby Memorial Prize from the Royal Society of Literature.

It is set in the late 1960s and early 1970s in Fellburn, with its posh Brampton Hill and its Bog's End slum, this time focusing us on Affleck and Tate's engineering works. The chairman of the company, Jonathan Ratcliffe, one of the *nouveaux riches*, lives in Bower House on Brampton Hill. The drawing office of Affleck and Tate is managed by Arthur Brett, who lives next door at The Larches and is a man with a good deal less ambition than his boss. Ratcliffe's one irritation is that Brett owns six acres of land leading down to the river which he has never cultivated. It is a beautiful spot, but it takes Brett every last penny simply to maintain. Ratcliffe, hungry to enhance his own property, has tried in vain to get Brett to part with the land. But to Brett it is worth more than money; it is a symbol of something which Ratcliffe, for all his new-found wealth, will never have.

They are very different men. The Larches is brimming with antiques, many of them inherited by Brett from his grandfather, who set up home there in 1892. There is continuity in Brett's life, even a hint of breeding, and he fancies that he has an aesthetic appreciation. But for all this, Brett is a mouse of a man. He has none of Ratcliffe's guts, and his wife Irene sees eye to eye with him about very little. Yet, in his weakness, Brett needs Irene, while at the same time hating himself for 'visiting the corpse long after love is dead', as he puts it indelicately. When a thing of true beauty (Ratcliffe's daughter, Vanessa) falls into his hands, Brett shows his true colours by devouring and then rejecting her in favour of the sick, safe world he knows. Afterwards, faced with the truth about himself, Brett realises that there is only one course left open to him. But even his suicide is not courageous.

In welcome contrast to the Ratcliffes and the Bretts are the Cottons who live on Ryder's Row, a short row of houses among the goods sheds at the foot of the railway embankment, fronting on to the main Newcastle Road. The Cottons are attached to the Ratcliffes through Emily, who has served them for years when no one else would suffer their regime. Emily is worked to a standstill. She has a son, Angus, and a daughter, Rose. Angus is a balanced young man, hardworking, open, kind. He and Vanessa have grown up in parallel worlds which would never have touched had it not been for Emily's position in the Ratcliffe household. Seen through the innocent eyes of Angus and Vanessa, as children, the social gulf between the families does not seem so wide. But when they grow up, Brett's wife Irene, who shares Jonathan and Jane Ratcliffe's snobbishness, is in turn suspicious of and disgusted by their friendship, which continues harmlessly enough up to the point when Brett makes Vanessa pregnant and Angus stands accused.

This is the cultural stew in which Catherine brews her novel. Class attitudes and envies are skilfully played of course, but if readers expect a romantic resolution they will be disappointed, even though Angus and Vanessa do come together. Angus is in love with Van, as he calls her – he always has been; but the closer they become as adults, the more unsure is Van. On one occasion she is even repulsed by Angus's ignorance and crudity, which she sees as deeply ingrained in him, as deeply as his loyalty to his mother Emily, which binds the family together but which Van suspects runs deeper than his love for her can ever go.

On the one hand, Catherine gives us the Cotton family, homogenous, caring; on the other, the veneer of the Ratcliffes. But she repels any facile judgement between the two. For a moment even the closeness of the Cotton family, the very core of the working-class myth, seems to tip over into claustrophobia, as Emily's favourite bit of poetry (from Longfellow, of course) suggests:

> *I have you fast in my fortress,*
> *And will not let you depart,*
> *But put you down into the dungeon*
> *In the round tower of my heart.*
>
> *And there will I keep you for ever,*
> *Yes, for ever and a day,*
> *Till the walls shall crumble to ruin,*
> *And moulder in dust away.*

Catherine is engaged in drawing a realistic picture. Van, for all her rejection of her snobbish family, realises that she *is* coming to the Cottons from a foreign place, emotionally as well as materially, intellectually as well as socially.

When Van takes up residence on Ryder's Row, she descends into a deep depression. Like the ribbons round the maypole, her thoughts become entangled and her nerves wrought up. She is incapable of sorting out what she feels from what she thinks, and though she doesn't in fact commit suicide, she discovers, as Catherine was to do, that thirty aspirins in a glass of water take a long time to dissolve.

Angus's success in his haulage business does nothing to help the situation, particularly as he uses his money to buy The Larches – Brett's old house, where he raped Vanessa – on Brampton Hill. What Angus won't realise is that dressing for the part is not enough. Money cannot solve social problems which have become psychological problems.

Casting off the inherited ideology of an English class system which has become part of the nation's psyche is an ideal to which it is easy to assent, but as difficult for Angus and Van to achieve in their case as it will be for Catherine in her own. Angus and Van will not find peace of mind until they build a house of their own, within, and the walls which confine them in their separate worlds 'crumble to ruin, and moulder in dust away'.

Catherine's escape from the fortress which confined her took colossal inner strength, more even than it took Katie Mulholland to carve out her empire, though the source of their strength is, of course, the same. 'My characters are strong,' Catherine once said to me, 'they always come through. But that is because they are me . . . I am capable of anything. Doubt is the only obstacle. But I had to have something to cling on to.' Ironically, it was Catherine's persecutors who supplied her with it.

She was reading large quantities of books at this time. 'I was twenty and a reader of novels, particularly those of Ethel M. Dell, Charles Garvis, Warwick Deeping, Ouida, Arnold Bennett and such like.' These are storytellers, writers with the power of getting their readers to turn pages. Ouida was the pseudonym of Marie Louise de la Ramée, who lived from 1839 to 1908. Her mother was English, but her father, Louis Ramée, was a teacher of French, his mother tongue. Ouida wrote forty-five novels, her popularity achieved from flamboyant, emotionally charged narratives, as in *Under Two Flags* and *Moths*. Warwick Deeping was another immensely popular, prolific novelist, whose best-known work, *Sorrell and Son*, was published a year after Catherine entered the workhouse. It turned, significantly in the context of Catherine's own life, on a father's determination to provide his son with a private education which would protect him from class prejudice.

Arnold Bennett was an even more significant figure for Catherine. The son of a potter and pawnshop owner from near Hanley, since 1910 part of the Borough of Stoke-on-Trent, Bennett, at twenty-two (in 1889) had escaped his working-class environment, where there was 'an atmosphere of grim sticking to it, of never being beaten by circumstance', and went on to make his name by writing about it.

Then came Elinor Glyn, though not by Catherine's choice. Glyn was a novelist forbidden to Catherine by the Catholic Church. 'Well, what could you expect when she wrote about naked women lying on bear skins?' Catherine chided her colleagues for reading Glyn, which was why one day she found a copy of *The Career of Katherine Bush* placed in her room by her persecutors. It was a masterly temptation, for the novel tells of a secretary girl's determination to rise in the world. Catherine took it up and couldn't put it down. They had read her right, but they could have had no idea just what effect it would have. 'I read this book,' she recalls, 'and I can say it was from this time that my life changed, and utterly.'

Elinor Glyn lived from 1864 until 1943, and many of her works – often sensationally romantic – were adapted

128

for the big screen in the silent film era. The scene for which she became infamous, and to which Catherine refers – a scene of great passion (in fact on a tiger not a bear skin) – was featured in Glyn's most sensational novel of all. *Three Weeks* was published in 1907 and described as a *succès de scandale*.

The Career of Katherine Bush tells the tale of a girl who becomes secretary to Lady Garribardine, who has a friend who discovers that Katherine is highly intelligent and falls in love with her. At first Katherine's mistress is incensed, because the girl is common and this man belongs to the aristocracy; but then, rather than spoiling the match, Lady Garribardine decides to educate Katherine in the ways of the world, and directs her to Lord Chesterfield's *Letters to his Son*.

Catherine told me how, on reading this, she simply flew down to the South Shields library and devoured the first volume of Chesterfield's *Letters*. 'Over the years I have come to think that Elinor Glyn was put on this earth mainly to write that book in order to show an ignorant North Country girl the path she must take.' In Chesterfield Catherine found 'a mentor, a friend; and the fact that I was in the same boat as his son drew me closer to him.' She had found her 'something to cling on to'. For it was Chesterfield who showed her a way forward and gave her the confidence to take it.

Philip Dormer Stanhope, the Fourth Earl of Chesterfield, was born on 22 September 1694 to a man ruined by privilege. As Catherine put it, 'Chesterfield's father, the Third Earl, was a rake, a kind of man who apparently never grew up.' He shunned his wife, who died when she was thirty-three after bearing him nine sons (of whom Philip was the second), and went off to France. Their son, the Fourth Earl, Catherine's mentor, was brought up by his grandmother,

Gertrude Pierrepont, the Marchioness of Halifax, and she set him on the path to success. She saw to it that he had a good education, certainly, but equally importantly she taught him what in those days were known as the 'graces' and might today be called social skills or style. He went to Cambridge University and by nineteen was learned, witty, a great orator, a gambler known for his 'high play', and, in spite of a fairly hideous appearance, popular with the ladies.

Chesterfield entered Parliament in 1715 but after a highly successful maiden speech was challenged by a member of the Opposition, who pointed out that he was not yet twenty-one and therefore too young to represent his constituency. Chesterfield stepped down until he came of age, whiling away the time as Gentleman of the Bed Chamber to the Prince of Wales. When in due course he became an active politician he did well, although he might have done better had he not delighted in putting down those who were at one time or another favourites of the King or Queen. He became Ambassador to The Hague, then Lord Lieutenant of Ireland, where, through tact and good judgement, he achieved much in a very short space of time. Finally, he became Secretary of State at the Foreign Office, before retiring at fifty-three with rheumatic gout and increasing deafness.

During his time as Ambassador to The Hague, Chesterfield conceived a son with a woman called Madelena Elizabeth du Bouchet. The boy, also named Philip, was born in 1732. Chesterfield saw to it that he was well educated. He sent him to Westminster School, thence to the universities of Lausanne and Leipsic, and finally on the extended European tour to France, Germany, Switzerland and Italy under the protection of a full-time tutor and with introductions to the best society in all the European capitals.

The *Letters* written by the Fourth Earl to his illegitimate son began when Philip was seven – the age at which

Catherine was told of her illegitimacy by her playmate. They continued during the boy's Grand Tour – he nearly always addressed him 'Dear Boy' – and through his political career (he was twice elected to Parliament) and his diplomatic appointments in Hamburg, Ratisbon and Dresden, until his untimely death at the age of thirty-six. In a symbolic sense, these letters – patronly, sometimes avuncular in tone, and full of advice – affirm a connection between father and son that Philip's illegitimacy called into question. They are an attempt by Chesterfield to rest a finger on the roulette wheel of fate, which had spun the boy a poor return at birth. They concern education in the narrow sense very little, though they do show how to go about getting it. Indeed, they are at their best when Chesterfield seeks to supplement Philip's academic education with wise words from a man of the world.

When they first appeared in book form in 1774, one year after Lord Chesterfield's death, they were an instant success: five editions appeared before the end of the year. This initial enthusiasm was due not to Chesterfield's reputation as a man of deep genius (which he was not) or to his political success, but rather to the public perception of him as a man of social ingenuity and wit, and to his 'perfect knowledge of mankind'. For historians, the letters offer an extraordinary insight into the habits of the day, the temper of the Age of Reason. Their interest for Catherine, however, was that they provided her with a step-by-step strategy for rising in the world. Nevertheless, the traditional English prejudice against success found a harsh voice in some critics of the eighteenth and nineteenth centuries, who seized upon Chesterfield's philosophy of self-interest and the frankness with which he expressed it. Echoes of this dissent call into question how Catherine could deliver herself up to a tutor who has been described as having 'the mien of a posture-maker, the skin-deep graciousness of a French Maréchal ... a calculating adventurer who cuts unpretentious worthies to toady to society magnates, who affects the supercilious air of a shallow dandy and cherishes the heart of a frog'.

'In my young days,' admits Lady Garribardine in Elinor Glyn's novel, '[the *Letters*] were considered highly immoral and pernicious by most of the canting Victorian hypocrites – when, of course, every one of the world knew that Chesterfield's advice on all points was the most sensible and sagacious that could be given, but hypocrisy had risen to a colossal height in the 'sixties and 'seventies.'

What Lady Garribardine is suggesting is that Chesterfield's detractors are as out of touch with the ways of the world as Catherine's colleagues at the workhouse were – or preferred to be seen to be. Yet there is a certain cynicism in Chesterfield which does seem at odds with Catherine's deep moral sense. He urged his son to 'pry into the recesses of others' hearts and heads', to 'bait your hook to catch them', to 'flatter people behind their backs, in the presence of those who will not fail to repeat, or even amplify, the praise to the party concerned', to 'preserve the *appearances* of Religion and Morality'; he states that 'without some dissimulation no business can be carried on at all,' and holds that 'a man of the world must, like the chameleon, be able to take every different hue.'

But Chesterfield answered Catherine's needs in various ways. To begin with, his son was illegitimate and it was as if he were speaking to Catherine directly. Then there was her belief that her real father was, like Philip's, a gentleman, and her need, in her increasing isolation, for a father figure to advise her. The main key to her allegiance, however, is that he appeased her nagging sense of inferiority. And the self-denigration process which had begun in the back streets of East Jarrow by the Richardsons' chimneypiece required appeasement. Chesterfield describes his servants as 'my

equals in nature . . . only my inferiors in fortune'. Catherine
uses this quotation more than once in her novels, and on
many occasions her characters benefit from patrons who
espouse the idea it expresses. For example, in *The Black
Velvet Gown* Percival Miller, when educating the children of
miner's widow Riah Millican, brings Chesterfield on to the
syllabus and quotes him exactly on class equality. In *The
Devil and Mary Ann*, when Mary Ann has begun her school-
ing, paid for by Mr Lord, he writes to her as if he were
Chesterfield. His letters begin 'My dear child' and are
couched in exactly the same style as Chesterfield's. To her
father, Mike, he says of Mary Ann that at times he finds her
'more than my equal, even my superior'.

Contrary to what Chesterfield's critics said of him – most
famously Samuel Johnson, who declared that Chesterfield
taught 'the morals of a whore and the manners of a dancing-
master' – moral virtue is in fact a key concept in the *Letters*.
'For God's sake,' he writes to his son, 'be scrupulously jealous
of the purity of your moral character,' and while he recommends dissimulation in business – 'not straightway laying
all your trump cards on the table' – he distinguishes it from
simulation, which is deceit.

Chesterfield's advice always flows from first-hand personal experience. He is ethically scrupulous simply because
he has learned that deceit doesn't work: 'If in negotiations
you are looked upon as a liar, and a trickster, no confidence
will be placed in you, nothing will be communicated to you,
and you will be in the situation of a man who has been burnt
in the cheek; and who, from that mark, cannot afterwards
get an honest livelihood if he would, but must continue a
thief.'

He recommends the chameleon as model for the aspiring
diplomat – 'to adapt your conversation to the people you are
conversing with' – as common sense. 'Baiting your hook'

may be a provocative expression, but it turns on a realistic assessment of the political jungle which his son intended to explore, not on an espousal of slyness or cunning. It is not Chesterfield's purpose to train his son in the role of reformer, but rather to encourage him to derive his morality from experience: 'We must take things as they are, we cannot make them what we would, nor often what they should be.' How near that comes to Catherine's 'Necessity, through time and circumstance, made life.'

What emerges from the *Letters* is that while moral rectitude is essential, it is justified as indisputably by how things actually go on in the world as by any precepts of religion: 'There is nothing so delicate as your moral character, and nothing which it is your interest so much to preserve pure. Should you be suspected of injustice, malignity, perfidy, lying, etc., all the parts and knowledge in the world will never procure you esteem, friendship or respect.'

In short, Chesterfield proves moral values at the altar of reason, not religion. On this reading, Chesterfield's eighteenth-century critics – devotees of reason to a man – failed to grasp the nettle of their age and were stung by their own hypocrisy. For Catherine, dire warnings of hellfire from the Catholic Church had engendered only fear and guilt. Here was a man who understood the world and gave morality new roots in wisdom derived from experience. What was there to fear in that?

Nevertheless, useful as he was at this stage in Catherine's life in getting her up and out of her situation, Chesterfield could not divert her from the path to breakdown. Indeed, it could be said that he encouraged her along it. 'Chesterfield is often spoken of as "artificial",' wrote Roger Coxon, 'and in the broadest sense that he scorned the primitive.' Since Freud, we tend to think of 'natural' as meaning an absence of phoniness, but Chesterfield, writing long before Freud, believed that artifice could be so completely absorbed that it *became* natural. At the workhouse Catherine went along with this view, but 'when the mirror of breakdown was held up to me [and] I saw myself as I really was ... a fugitive from my ain folk', she threw off the 'pseudo-lady covering the real me, and I knew if I was ever going to write a word that anybody would want to read, I'd have to strip her off and be myself.'

In her novels Catherine digs far deeper than her mentor and with great insight embraces the primitive. She puts humanity on the slab and wields her scalpel to cut away man's pseudo-self, in particular his hypocrisies over class, race and religion. There is no joy for the upstart who leaves his true self behind, or for the bigoted in society; they are society's prisoners and gaolers.

In *A Dinner of Herbs*, Willy Harding is a cowhand on the Roystan farm. His benevolent master, Sir Reginald, who could have been a disciple of Chesterfield, takes it upon himself to open up 'a new world' for Willy. But it is only because Willy refuses to let his 'education' at Sir Reginald's hands uproot him out of his true nature that he finds fulfilment. In *The Menagerie*, when Pam Turnbull is considering whether to return to her home-town boyfriend, Larry Broadhurst, her rich husband Ron tells her that she will miss not only the material things he can give her, but the social and intellectual bonuses. Pam admits to Larry that if she had been left to herself, 'to grow up being myself', she and Larry could have been happy. Part of her wants 'to live ordinary, and part of me never can now'. She, unlike Willy Harding, does not remain true to her nature, and Larry, pushed and pulled out of his own true nature by his love for Pam, narrowly escapes the mental breakdown which befell Catherine.

The Invitation (1970) is a wonderfully comic illustration

of what happens to upstarts who lose sight of their true selves. Set in fictional Fellburn, with Brampton Hill and Bog's End mapping its social topography, this is a novel about the way social mountaineering frays the ropes which, at bottom, connect us to our nature. Maggie Gallacher is another of the rumbustious, half-comic characters at which Catherine excels. She and her husband have risen in the world, not just to Brampton Hill, but to the very pinnacle of respectability in a supra-district known appropriately as The Rise. Just how far they have come is shown on the first page of the novel, when they receive an invitation from the Duke of Moorshire, described as 'the mountain peak' of their striving.

Unlike her husband, Maggie still has her feet firmly on the ground, as firmly at least as the painful corn on one of her feet will allow. She has enjoyed their rise but, much to her husband's chagrin, is still capable of delivering a 'body-shaking, mouth-stretching' brand of laughter that is more characteristic of a slum dweller in Bog's End. It is Rodney who has changed.

Maggie's excitement over the four weeks leading up to the party, a musical evening, is tangible. Her preparations have been exhaustive, right down to rehearsing for the high point of the evening, shaking hands with the Duke. Come the day, Maggie stuffs her ample form into a blue velvet gown and yields her corn, still raw from last night's encounter with a safety razor, to the heel of a pink slipper.

Maggie's corn becomes a symbol of her situation. She has managed to shave off only its hard-skinned exterior, though she knows only too well that it (like Maggie herself, if she is to succeed in her new social environment) must be pulled up by the roots. Rodney, however, takes in her fine appearance with a comment about what money can buy, and slips into his dinner jacket with minimum fuss, as if partying with the Duke were a weekly occurrence.

Catherine's description of the party is a triumph of comic affectation seen through Maggie's eyes, the response of her corn to the heel of her slipper reflecting precisely the misery which she suffers at the hands of Rodney, who is clearly embarrassed by her every word and deed. Only once during the evening does Maggie find a soul-mate: a man called Bailey, who agrees with her that the music is awful. Rodney ensures that the association is short-lived.

The real party piece is Maggie's determination to meet the Duke. He hadn't been on hand when they arrived – his brother had been taken ill and he had had to excuse himself. And when he does arrive and starts mingling with his guests, Maggie seems always to be just out of reach. Rodney, of course, manages to have an audience with him when he is off getting Maggie a plate of food (lest her sweet sherry go to her head and crown his embarrassment). Then, at last, at the end of the party, guests line up in couples to shake hands with the Duke, and it seems inevitable that Maggie will achieve her heart's desire. Gradually she and Rodney shuffle towards the great man until there is only one couple between the Gallachers and him – whereupon, against all precedent, the Duke wheels around the couple he is receiving and walks them away down the steps towards the sunken garden. Maggie lets out a ripple of indignation and when a woman standing nearby admonishes her, she rocks back on her heels and lets all pretence go with a loud 'BUGGER THE DUKE!' As all eyes turn towards her and the head of the Duke stops bobbing down the steps and turns, Rodney whisks her away to the car.

In September 1927 Catherine was promoted to assistant laundress at the workhouse, but four months later when the position of laundress fell vacant and she applied for it, she was passed over. It was not quite the final rejection, but, added to the rest, it led her, armed with Chesterfield, to the single biggest decision in her life to date.

'My answer to the question why I left the North is there were many reasons, all tangled and representing one word – rejection. I had been rejected by the man who had fathered me. I think Kate rejected me from when I was born because she went through hell . . . I think I rejected her when I was seven and learned that she wasn't just Our Kate, a relation, she was my mother. I knew I was different from the time I ever began to think because I was illegitimate, a bastard. When I was eighteen and went into the workhouse as a laundry checker I definitely found out what rejection meant . . . There I was, this tall, good-looking girl, who dared to act the lady and was aiming to educate herself by learning the fiddle, taking French lessons and studying anatomy and physiology because she intended to be a nurse. Who did she think she was?! And then the great surprise, just look who she was courting now!'

The handsome, well-dressed man, eleven years her senior, whom she had idolised as a girl of fourteen, wishing he could have been her father, had finally, five years later, walked her part way home from church.

'From then on, every Saturday night he would take me to the pictures. On a Sunday morning we would go to eleven o'clock Mass. Sometimes he would walk part of the way up the Jarrow Road with me. That was added wonder. In the evening we went to Benediction and after we walked up into the country, and this pattern went on for a whole year, and never once did that man kiss me, and never once did he accept an invitation to be my partner at any of the three staff dances, headed by the master and matron, which were great events in our life. And my heart did not question. It was too full of adoration. I may say that only once did he ever take me into a public place except for a coffee after the pictures. And this was to a dance in Shields. That was before he got to know my history and that of my family.

'One night he was waiting with me for the Jarrow tram. It was sleeting badly and we had taken shelter, of all places, round the corner of this little street where I had been born, next to a public house. (Oh, I had to be born next to a public house! And within ten yards of the actual dock wall.) And as he stood waiting for a tram he bent and kissed me. I was down with wonder. And then he told me why he had been so reticent. He had been getting over a love affair. He had discovered, just before he was about to marry, that his future wife was subject to epileptic fits . . .'

Catherine felt more than a bit used – 'he knew I was deeply in love with him, but I was sympathetic, and I thought things would change from that. He would now accept the invitations, not only to the dances, but to other functions. But no. Not once during the following year did he ever deem to accompany me to a public place.'

They had arrived at this watershed in their relationship at the very site of her lowly birth, which, directly or indirectly, had dogged her ever since. And now she became convinced that it was all happening again. 'The excuses were many and of all kinds. And what I suffered from the main part of the staff was unimaginable . . . their laughter, their covert remarks and sneers, their even betting on when he would turn up this time. Yet he took me to the gates of the workhouse every Sunday night and he stood for a few minutes like a number of other couples around us. During those two years I never had a partner at all the dances and functions. But I danced because there was a tall young fellow who worked as a mental assistant and he was a very good Charleston dancer and I was grateful to him because he would always ask me to dance.

'How many nights I cried my eyes out, asking the question: Why? Why?

'Then came the climax. It was my twenty-first birthday. Kate couldn't give me a party in our kitchen. But my Aunt Mary at the top of the street had made her three rooms into a very nice comfortable home and her front room was well furnished. It even had a spinet piano in it. I invited eight of my associates, four of them real friends, they all brought their boyfriends. Mary had a very nice tea set out and we waited – and we waited – and we waited – and the main guest never turned up. Oh, there was some laughter and gossip . . . Well, the next week a letter said he was sorry, but he had been taking the money to pay an insurance claim and had lost it and he was very upset. He thought our friendship should stop because he would have to save up to repay the money that had been lost.

'There had been one time when we had talked of marriage. He was being moved to Durham. But he said it was too much to ask of me to leave my post and also my home – my *home*! – at any rate, yet.

'Not being a fool, my eyes had been opening slowly and I realised the character of this "gentleman" with a beautiful face, marred by a very small mouth.

'Coming to my real self at last I wrote him a letter that should have burnt his fingers as he held it. I was due for my holidays and decided to go to Ireland to see my stepfather's sister, who was blind. Kate sent me a letter from him and it was to say that he had been to a priest and told him that he had made use of me over the past two years, not sexually, oh no, but as a salve to ease his hurt feelings. And the priest had said that he had done me a great wrong and he had to ask my forgiveness.

'After I read the letter I took up one sheet of paper and I wrote across it three words – I wrote not in a straight line, but right across the page three words, GO TO HELL! I did not see him for many months after, and it was coming out of the pictures. He begged me to become friends with him again because he missed me so much. I laughed in his face. But he kept on and I lost the last bus home. There was only now what they called the drunk bus – the 207 from Shields market to Jarrow. This was always full of men who had just come off the ferry. The pubs in South Shields closed half an hour earlier than those in North Shields, and the men still able to stand on their feet got on the ferry, went over the river for a last drink, came back and got on the bus. And it was into this bus that I had to be pulled by them – on to the platform – while my late suitor was still begging me to write to him. The bus started and he walked along with it for a while and there I stood with those drunken arms around me, looking down at him, the man who had rejected me. And I felt in a way that I had won, but only in a way.

'The drunks were very merry and they kept shouting to each other, "She's not going to write to the lad!" And different voices, "Why isn't she going to write to the lad?" "The poor fellow's bad!" "The poor fellow's sick!"

'The bus stopped at the bottom of William Black Street. I got off to the cries of the merry drunks, saying, "You be a good lass and write to the fella. Now go on now!" I walked up the dark street to the house that had always been my home and as I did so, the smile left my face and from deep within me there came a cry and it said, "I'll show him! I'll show him!"

'Of course, I knew that I had been rejected not only for myself but because I was illegitimate, I came from a notorious family. It wouldn't do him any good in the insurance business to be linked up with such people.

'That was the end of my courting days, so to speak. The fellow from the mental block began to ask me out. This caused a great furore, a different kind of furore, in the mess-room. The staff came back to me in a horde. Didn't I know he was engaged to be married? No, I didn't. So the next time he asked me I put the question to him. No, of course he wasn't. Not any more. He had once been engaged to this girl but that was broken off ages ago. One Sunday dinner I was home for the weekend and was drying up the dishes with Kate in the scullery and there was a knock at the door.

'It was my dancing partner. He had come, he had actually come to ask me to marry him, with a special licence. I laughed. He was the last person on God's earth I would have married. The most intelligent part about him was his feet. When I went back into the scullery and told Kate we leant together for a moment. It was a rare moment, we laughed again. And then I went back into the front room and he asked me if I would write a letter for him. He wanted to get into the Halifax police. I did this for him and he went away, very disappointed. A week passed and then the staff were in their glory, most of them, with the exception of my few friends, they were in their glory! My boss even came to me and slapped down on to my desk a newspaper cutting. It was to say that a wedding had taken place on Saturday last and that his wife had given birth on the Sunday. I couldn't believe it. But it was true. And the staff had the time of their lives. The Great Lady had had a second rejection. I knew that I could stand no more of this and so I began looking up employment in my line as far away from the North as I could possibly find ... And I was away from the North. The last I remembered of it was standing up in the train as it came out of the tunnel at Tyne Dock, making for Newcastle on my journey South, where I was to remain for forty-six years. And I said that day ... on looking out of the window, I saw in the distance the little church in Simonside, the school where I had gone until I was nearly eight, and farther beyond, the outline of East Jarrow and 10 William Black Street, and I cried to it, "I am never, *never* coming back!" '

CHAPTER SIX

⚬⚬⚬

Girl From the North Country

'When I left the North my first job was in a workhouse in Essex, not far from Manningtree. I was stuck there for nine months and I realised that I hated the country. Suddenly this girl who had come from this industrial area, where even at night time you heard the horns of the ships and the background noises of the goods trains, found herself in the midst of desolate countryside. In fact it wasn't desolate, I was. The land was mainly farmland; it was like a different country and I was so lonely.'

Catherine had answered an advertisement for a laundress at Tendring workhouse and began work there in May 1929 at a salary of £130 a year. The coincidence of Catherine's first placement after Tyneside in the country of her future husband's birth, which at this time she was in no position to appreciate, carries a faint irony. The placid, endlessly flat Essex countryside was in diametric opposition to the raw, emotive landscape of Catherine's birth, and she hated it. She even identifies the difference between herself and her husband with reference to it: 'Up here I know that I am in my own country, not flat like the fens that Tom likes so much. They leave me cold; they just leave me cold. This countryside is raw, and it is with me and I feel it . . . Up here the seasons are rougher than those in the south, and I imbibed them for twenty-two to twenty-three years right on the river and

145

there was a harshness.' To Catherine, Essex was like a great, silent vacuum; but only seven years later Tom would show her that fulfilment might lie in his quietly considering nature, shaped by the spirit of this place. Catherine acknowledged this by gracing the at first sight featureless East Anglian landscape with the only novel of hers set outside the North.

Tom, who was something of a sportsman (boxing, football and cricket were his strengths), loved boats, and later, when she was an established writer, they bought a boat and two or three times a year they explored the Cambridge fenland rivers. *The Fen Tiger* (1963), written under the pseudonym of Catherine Marchant (a name she never liked, dreamt up by her advisers after a women's magazine tempted them with an offer too good to refuse), reveals none of her antipathy to the landscape. The fens are also Graham Swift country – 'flat, with an unrelieved and monotonous flatness . . .' where you 'shut one eye and fall prey to fruitless meditations on the laws of perspective', as he wrote in his novel *Waterland* (1983). A new perspective was the one thing Catherine needed by the time Tom came into her life.

For Catherine, as for Swift in his novel, it is the deepdown character of the fen people, bedded in their watery land, which inspired her. Swift's hero, one of the 'water people' who have lived there for centuries, has a strong sense of his roots in the place. Catherine's novel speaks of a similar awareness, of a time when these people, who lived by spearing fish among the reeds, defended their domain against those who would drain it, and their spirit out of them.

An earlier book, *Slinky Jane* (1959), may also owe some debt to these fenland visits. In Catherine's fictitious village of Battenbun, eels are known as Slinky Janes. The catching of them and their habits had been described to her by an old fisherman of the fens. The confusion out of which she weaves her narrative turns on the appearance of a strangely alluring woman in this isolated place at the very moment that a Slinky Jane appears in a pond, where never an eel had been found before. But Battenbun is not in the fens; the action has been removed to Northumberland.

Unhappy with her position at Tendring, after seven months Catherine applied successfully for a position in Hastings, Sussex, and, as she told me, 'arrived there on the twenty-ninth of January 1930, to take up the post of laundry manageress of the workhouse and general hospital laundry with the enormous wage of three pounds six shillings a week – and in 1930 that was indeed an enormous wage, especially for a woman'.

Whatever she thought of Essex, she could have chosen no place in England more unlike Tyneside than Hastings in 1930. 'The workhouse inmates could be considered to be on a picnic compared to those in South Shields,' and other than the salt-laden wind from the sea there was nothing about the town which bore any resemblance to South Shields.

'The finest, purest sea breeze on the coast – acknowledged to be so – excellent bathing – fine hard sand – deep water ten yards from the shore – no mud – no weeds – no slimy rocks – Never was there a place more palpably designed by Nature for the retreat of the invalid – the very spot which thousands seemed in need of.'

Mr Parker's enthusiasm for this southern coastline in Jane Austen's unfinished novel *Sanditon*, written more than a century earlier, characterises the Sussex shore perfectly. Moreover, by the time Catherine arrived Mr Parker's dream of creating a fashionable resort and retirement retreat out of the little village of Sanditon, with clean stone terraces and crescents of fine houses and hotels, had long been realised in nearby Hastings. This middle-class recreational resort and

The Girl from Leam Lane

rest home for the genteel and elderly was a million miles away from the Tyneside of Catherine's experience, with its arches dripping slime in 'rivulets of green' and its sea of mud, the Jarrow Slacks, polluted with chemicals from the barium works, and its sad groups of unemployed workers waiting at the dock gates to be taken on.

However, to begin with she enjoyed working at the Hastings Institution. It was very hard work, but she wanted, needed, to work hard. In the same year that she arrived an Irish girl called Annie Smyth joined the staff as an orderly. Annie had a mentally deficient daughter called Maisie, and was clearly in need of support. Catherine befriended her. She got on well with the matron, too. In *Maggie Rowan*, Catherine gives us an insight into her relationship with her matron bosses and an explanation, too, as to why the Shields workhouse had refused Catherine the position of top dog. At fourteen years of age, Maggie had gone to work at Mrs Thornton's laundry, washing the clothes of the Brampton Hill toffs, whom she so wanted to join. Maggie was the perfect employee, she was a perfectionist – it became a mania with her. Mrs Thornton, like Catherine's matrons, valued her, took Maggie under her matronly wing, but didn't dare let her have real power. 'Once Maggie felt power she would be like the beggar on horseback . . . she'd ride to hell.'

Catherine was a stickler. She wasn't doing the job at the Hastings Institution just for her weekly wage. She did the job because it needed to be done, and no stone went unturned. Nor had she forgotten the promise of a big house of her own, which she had made to herself all those years before. Her weekly earnings at the Institution were made up of three pounds in salary and six shillings which she was paid instead of taking her dinner there. Virtually starving herself, she lived on the six shillings, spent eight shillings and sixpence on her flat rental and put most of the rest into an endowment policy with Sun Life of Canada.

To begin with Catherine had lived in the Institution, but she had soon found a flat and filled its one room with a great load of furniture: not just any furniture, but what would be regarded today as real antiques. You could pick up such things for a song in and around Hastings in 1930 – indeed, until some time after the Second World War when the antiques trade took off, America beckoned, and prices soared. It may only have been a one-room flat, but it was Catherine's first real place of her own, away from Kate and old John, and she started on it as she meant to go on. However lowly, this was the first realisation of her 'picture on the wall' of a better life than she had known.

In April of the same year, on Maundy Thursday, old John McMullen died. It is not difficult to imagine how bleak life must have seemed to Catherine's step-grandfather at number 10, once she had gone. What had he left to live for? The only sadness Catherine has ever described at her leaving the North was John's farewell. He was a difficult man and no relation at all, yet the love he felt for Catherine, his 'voiceless love' as she describes it, has meant a great deal to her in recent years.

At the time, however, Catherine was engrossed in making her own life. The one thing she didn't want was for the North and all it held for her to impinge upon it. She didn't go to John's funeral, but she sent Kate twenty pounds to cover the cost. Later she learned that the funeral director had received half of this sum; the rest was presumably spent by Kate on drink.

It didn't escape Catherine that the Hastings people were as different from her people as the town was from East Jarrow. At times she must have wondered whether they offered a kind of parody of what Chesterfield had in mind for her. Once, years later, when she had begun to be noticed as a writer, Catherine was walking along the London Road in neighbouring St Leonards when she saw approaching her a woman who must have been to this area what Fanny McBride was to Tyneside. She was a county type, dressed in 'tweeds, brogues, a Henry Heath hat and a collar and tie', and was pointing her finger at Catherine as she marched towards her. Catherine was startled, but convinced herself that the woman must be pointing at someone behind her. Then the woman came to halt – 'her finger still pointing' – and relieved Catherine of any doubt as to whom she was after with an 'Ah! Mrs Cookson! The regional writer!' In her high-falutin voice, she informed Catherine that she had read her books and demanded to know why she insisted on writing about that awful Tyneside, when here, on her doorstep, was a far more attractive proposition.

The idea that Catherine should base a novel on the area was imparted more by way of a command than a suggestion and Catherine was too staggered by the onslaught to respond meaningfully. But typically she took it as a challenge and actually set about tackling the place, searching for its soul among the few fishermen left from older days, people she felt might lead her to the spirit of the place. But it didn't work; she found she couldn't write about it with any strength at all.

In her inaugural Hastings years, following the upheavals in her social life up North, Catherine discovered she was quite a draw to these southerners. She had arrived determined to put all thoughts of love or marriage behind her. Work was her prime motivation. But she was young (twenty-four in 1930) and attractive, and these qualities together with the no-nonsense self-discipline which now characterised her extrovert personality – though it never completely eradicated the softness at the centre – made for a formidable combination, which, for reasons she couldn't fathom but which may well have had to do with their own lack of spine, held a particular attraction for married men. 'It would appear that I was only attractive to married men,' she told me.

In *Colour Blind* the same fate befalls Rose-Angela when she grows into a young woman, and she, too, wonders what it is about her which attracts them. Was it her voice, 'so like her father's'? Was it her face? Was it the quietness in Rosie which did it for these men, particularly married men?

No doubt Catherine will have enjoyed the balance which male company and appreciation brought to her toil at the workhouse. No doubt, too, when the work was done, she lit up in company and lit company up, as she still does today. But her strength of character still cloaked a painful vulnerability, born of her alienation and rejections and a yearning to be loved, which could so easily be abused. And it was, by one after the other.

Perhaps these men took her independent spirit, unusual in a woman at the time, as a licence to exempt them from serious or long-term commitment. She had no intention of being a married man's mistress, however, and when she discovered their situation she saw them off. One especially embarrassing occasion actually involved the intervention of the man's parents. He was the Sun Life insurance agent and, though not yet wed, was engaged to be married. Catherine had had no idea that there was another woman on the scene. When his parents discovered what was going on they came to Catherine, begging her to let him go. She couldn't believe it.

Inevitably these various relationships were coloured by her attitude to sex. The lesson learned about sex before marriage, about what happened to people like Kate, was not forgotten now that she was leading an independent life down in Hastings. When one man jilted her after she refused to let him make love to her, it brought to the surface the agony of this repressive restraint, preached from the pulpit of the Fathar's chair by the fireside in number 10. But this was only one part of her problem with sex. Another was her religious faith, which remained strong.

It is important in understanding Catherine at this time, and throughout the years leading up to her nervous breakdown in 1945, to realise just what her faith meant to her. During her teens and the years when she was working at the Harton Institution in Shields, it was everything to her. On one occasion, during her fraught relationship with the man who precipitated her departure from the North, she had even considered becoming a nun. She had gone to Father Bradley and discussed the possibility. He had told her to think again, and Kate had told her that the nuns had enough problems without her adding to them.

In the 1930s, after she arrived in Hastings, she was still bound to her faith in Catholicism, though increasingly only by the fear so effectively instilled in her as a child, a fear which, even today, makes her describe Catholicism as 'this great dominating, fear-filled religion, a religion that has kept people bound to it by terror of the hereafter'. Times have changed, and Catholicism now reaches out to its people in a different way; but for those brought up on it by the Jesuit-style 'missioners', there can be no change. 'What is it now? The remnants of a fable, and what a fable. There is hardly a tenet left that hasn't been twisted and turned or eliminated altogether ... I can't stand turncoats. And if anyone was a turncoat in politics or religion, it is the Catholic Church. Faith? I ask you, faith in what?' Twice between 1932 and 1940 Catherine would give up her faith, and twice she would return to it, until finally she came to the mental and spiritual crisis which tore her apart.

It is important to realise that sex and religion were connected in her mind. One of the many sources of guilt which had given her so much unrest in her innocent teenage years was her imagining that Father Bradley knew well enough what she thought about in bed at night, her knees still cold from the lino on which, last thing at night, she would kneel to say her prayers. But at the core of her deep-down disquiet about sex lay her illegitimate birth and the fear that had been drummed into her that she would go the same way as Kate. As she saw it, her illegitimacy was the source of all her problems, including her friends' rejection of her, and it still gnawed like a canker inside. Looking back on a career of more than fifty years in which Catherine has sold more books and reached more people than any other living writer, it is easy to see that there were other things that made her different from her contemporaries in the New Buildings and in the Harton Institution. But as Catherine saw it at the time, being a bastard was the big difference which made her an outsider, and she hid her shame from everyone, driving her obsession underground, better to do its work.

Sex before marriage was off the agenda, and no insurance agent from Hastings, or any of his ilk, was about to convince her otherwise. The extraordinary thing – positively unfair in the circumstances – was that during the period between arriving in Hastings in 1930 and meeting her future husband, Tom, six years later, Catherine developed a reputation as something of a loose woman. 'I knew I had a name, and the unfairness of it caused me to cry at nights, for I was a reluctant virgin. I was warm-hearted and wanting love, but determined, however hungry I was for it, not to go the way of my mother.'

Long after she had mortgaged her endowment policy and

bought her fifteen-room dream house (just three years after she had arrived in Hastings), she was able to laugh a little about this. A doctor let it be known that he suspected she had bought the house with money earnt between the sheets. Catherine enjoyed telling him barefaced that indeed there had been a time when she had made regular trips to London and Paris to seek out her select clientele. He had retreated rather swiftly with his tail between his legs.

This period of disquiet and longing saw the development inside Catherine of a character who was to become one of her most popular heroines. Anna Brigmore – *Miss* Brigmore, as she was known to anyone but her closest friends – is of course the governess of Thomas Mallen's nieces, Barbara and Constance, who are ten and seven years old at the start of *The Mallen Streak*, the first novel in Catherine's biggest-selling trilogy. Miss Brigmore comes from a middle-class family fallen on hard times. Her father had used money from his clients in the bank where he worked to keep his family's standard of living high. Miss Brigmore had, therefore, entered service of necessity. She was well educated, strict but fair, a stickler, the 'embodiment of high moral principles, but happily flawed', as Catherine's first agent, John Smith, once referred to her.

Miss Brigmore's unhappiness was that her early upbringing had made it impossible for her to find 'bodily expression' with any man who might normally be regarded as suitable for a governess. She yearns for love, and finally Thomas Mallen puts her out of her misery – her 'years of virginity, her personal torment'. We learn of this through Barbara, who hears Miss Brigmore moaning in her room and finds her in bed with Thomas, his hand fondling her naked breast. Miss Brigmore's relationship with Thomas is touchingly real. They remain very close; indeed, Anna takes control of Thomas's destiny when he loses the family estate.

The force behind Catherine's 'personal torment' was not, of course, Miss Brigmore's antipathy to consorting with members of staff on the Mallen estate, but, as I have said, the repressive regime of her childhood and her obsession with her illegitimacy. But it is quite conceivable that, in time, she would have got over these obstacles: for increasingly, in the first two years of her time in Hastings, she was becoming independent of her past life. What ensured that she did not was an appeal from Kate, in 1932, to be allowed to come down to Hastings to visit her daughter.

Catherine couldn't say no. Kate assured her that since John's death she had beaten her drinking habit. But still Catherine was on tenterhooks before her arrival. She knew that Kate would want to meet her colleagues and friends at the workhouse, and Catherine feared that all the good work she (with Chesterfield's help) had done to cover up her 'disgrace' of a background would be undone in a trice.

In the event, the opposite was true. Kate was free of drink and on her best behaviour. She went down a storm at the workhouse. Only the matron, whom Catherine had told about Kate and her own determination to shake free of her, took Catherine aside afterwards and told her what she wanted to hear – that it was obvious that Catherine and her mother were poles apart. It was an interesting comment on Catherine's relationship with her boss and suggests that the matron knew how to ensure she got the best out of her workhorse.

The staff lower down the hierarchy warmed to Kate's unaffected humour and down-to-earth chat, and when Kate, Catherine and Annie Smyth repaired to the flat, it must have seemed quite natural to Annie to ask Kate (who, now that John was dead and her husband David was away at sea for months at a time, was alone at number 10) why she didn't come and live in Hastings permanently. I can hear the deafening silence that will have followed, Kate turning to Catherine, Catherine's cheer that all had gone so swimmingly well suddenly frozen with dread that Kate's 'recovery' might be tested on a permanent basis.

That was how it happened. That was how Catherine's short-lived independence disappeared almost overnight. Indeed that, indirectly, was what set her on the road to breakdown, whatever the underlying causes. For Kate did come to live. Embarrassment forced Catherine into formalising Annie's invitation, and later that same year, 1932, Catherine found herself on the way to the railway station to collect her mother. She arrived five minutes late to find Kate sitting on her cases in the forecourt, blind drunk.

'Because I was five minutes late she went for me immediately. I was absolutely horrified to see that she was well gone along the old road. I cried to God, Why? Why have I done this? Straightway I knew that my new life was shattered.'

In preparation for Kate's coming Catherine had moved out of her one-room apartment and taken a much larger flat in an old building on the seafront with sufficient rooms for Kate to take in paying guests. The northern landlady, used to squeezing three or four lodgers into the one bedroom of number 10 along with Jack, was about to be released upon unsuspecting visitors to middle-class Hastings. In fact, nothing much came of Catherine's idea at first, because Kate spent most of her time down the road at a bar called The Hole in the Wall, almost permanently drunk.

Alcoholism is never completely beaten. Like Catherine's nervous breakdown, dark shadows of which haunt her to this day, Kate's alcoholism could only ever be consigned to the background of her personality by a great effort of will, and when now the craving reappeared after a short break, it seemed to gain a vicious vigour from guilt or whatever else she was feeling deep down, which no alcohol could ever cure.

Kate was fifty. Unlike Catherine, she wasn't in Hastings to build a new future. The move, which pulled her up by the roots from the only life she had known, would never have been easy. Kate Fawcett *was* her environment; she wasn't separate from it in the way many well-travelled southerners are. You couldn't distinguish the two. In Hastings she was a fish out of water. Also, from the moment she arrived drunk, and probably before, her daughter regretted her coming, and Kate would have known this. It was a recipe for difficulties even without the drink; but *with* drink, it was a recipe for guilt, bitterness, violence and, as it turned out, total disaster.

Catherine soon realised that she had to get Kate away, away from pubs like The Hole in the Wall, and hastened her search for a house of her own on the outskirts of the town. One day, as she sifted through the properties for sale, she spotted a notice for a house called The Hurst, which the estate agent described as 'fifteen-roomed gentleman's residence'. He must have been a good agent or a lucky one, for the house in question was something of a problem to sell and he had alighted on a description which was bound to make Catherine sit up.

Anyone experienced in house-buying would have avoided The Hurst like the plague. It was riddled with woodworm and rot. Its multiple roofs, one giving over on to the other, with gulleys between, promised huge maintenance bills. The prospect of heating the rambling place would have put most people off. But to Catherine these were just practical problems – and weren't they replacing the floor and installing a new sewer system? More to the point, didn't it have a butler's pantry and a wine cellar and a spacious drawing room with floor-to-ceiling windows which let on to a large garden? It really was the house of Catherine's dreams. And she knew exactly what she would do with it.

She decided that she would take in guests to help pay for the work it needed or maybe turn it into a nursing home of sorts. Of course it would take hard work to put it right, but she wasn't afraid of hard work and where else could she find a property so splendid at a price she could afford? Above all, it was a house she could love, a square of ground that Catherine could call her own; and it remains a great source of pride to this day. 'I bought it in 1933 when I was twenty-seven years of age, without the help of any man, but through the savings of years and my endowment policy. I mortgaged the policy and bought this gentleman's residence.'

The relationship between Catherine and The Hurst lasted twenty-one years. Tom impinged upon it from 1937, when he moved in, in the first instance, as a paying guest. When finally, in 1954, they gave up the struggle with it – for it was a struggle from the first day the rains came and washed through those roofs – 'it had eaten up my energy and every penny poor Tom and I were earning.'

The Hurst, or something like it – a grand manor house situated not in Sussex but in the North, not far from Gateshead – is of course Beatrice Steel's folly in *The Obsession*. Pine Hurst, as it is called, arouses an all-consuming passion in Beatrice and nothing will deflect her indulgence of it. The house becomes 'her child', and her desire for it is driven by a conviction that she alone in the Steele family has inherited from her father traits which give her a feeling for land, and specifically for the house. When Beatrice's mother and then her father die, and it is revealed that her father has gambled away all the family's money, the real risk of losing Pine Hurst turns Beatrice's obsession into a psychosis. It is an interesting autobiographical parallel, but not one which helps to explain Catherine's own nervous breakdown, as we shall see.

Catherine and Kate moved into The Hurst in 1933, and since someone was needed on the ground, as it were, while Catherine was earning the money to keep them, and she couldn't depend on Kate, Annie and her mentally deficient daughter moved in too. Catherine was now working a sixteen-hour day. When she came home from the workhouse she began work on The Hurst. And when she had made the house habitable, she began taking in guests – which began a whole set of other problems. Guests came, but rarely returned. 'My mother (now really on the bottle every day) and her monstrous practical joking ensured this. Added to this, when expecting the guests to pay, I was often told that my mother had already subbed half of it. How low can one fall! After two terrible rows I had been placated by my stepfather [David McDermott, who was home on leave], a quiet man, to overlook her lapses. Then later, when her domination and drink drove me almost to suicide, I knew in one way or another there must be an end to it.'

Kate's practical joking had to be seen to be believed – 'she would do all kinds of things, like smearing jam on the doorknobs.' She was out of control. This was also the period during which Kate mixed her explosive cocktail from four bottles of spirits, and, as I have described, Catherine narrowly missed being hit by David McDermott's hobnailed boots. On another occasion a French couple arrived and were treated to one of Kate's pies. 'Kate was a very good pastry cook, not much when it came to sophisticated cuisine, but pies were her forte.' She could be really artistic, creating delicate little foliage effects on the crust. Now, the French like their food, and although pies are hardly a staple of French cuisine, Catherine would have been confident of their reaction to what was being laid before them, as they sat around the dining room table at The Hurst. It fell to the head of the table to take a knife to the pastry. Gently she eased the blade into the crust before separating the section. All eyes upon her, she plunged a spoon into the depths of the dish. But as the spoon re-emerged it carried with it not a soup of succulent beef, but a pan scourer and a mousetrap. Catherine died inside.

The evening had gone so well. Her guests were an educated couple and had been talking to Catherine about various French writers, whose work she hadn't read but, as ever, was very keen to learn about. Perhaps it was this strand of conversation, and the rapport between Catherine and the French woman in particular, which had set Kate off on her bizarre recipe. Catherine was still bent on improving herself, and Kate and Voltaire did not make for a happy mix, particularly since at this stage, as Catherine admits, her desire for learning carried with it a degree of affectation. The pricking of the bubble of her daughter's apparent pretentiousness may have brought Kate its own reward, but Catherine was furious.

Mother and daughter had different allegiances. Kate *was* her Northern culture, instinctual, primitive. It was this kind of thinking about Kate which years later would have one of cousin Sarah's boys telling Catherine that she wasn't fit to wipe his Aunt Kate's shoes. Catherine, on the other hand, was dressing herself up in her 'new-natural' culture, fortified by Chesterfield and her own determination to break new ground. The problem wasn't simply a case of Kate being gross (which, owing to the drink, she was), but that her daughter's development and abhorrence of her drinking was alienating her. Kate was a dominant creature, she didn't take kindly to this; and eventually, inevitably, she went too far.

Kate had always needed to dominate. Even in the wake of

Rose's death there had been a crescendo of argument and violence with old John to settle who was the dominant partner. But now Catherine was not about to defer in her own house to this drunken parody. One dinnertime, this time on the losing end but refusing to lie down, Kate rose from her chair and let out a scream that would have made Edvard Munch double-take. Catherine's civilised guests were astonished. Kate then took to the stairs and from the landing let out yet more blood-curdling wails. It was a terrifying sign of how deep within herself Kate had joined battle with her daughter.

Afterwards, just as inevitably, Catherine's guests had been understanding. They had a relation, they said, capable of much the same; Catherine shouldn't mind on their account. Whether or not what they said had been true, it was hopelessly inadequate. Civilised, sweet, but there was really nothing more to be said. It was the end.

Subsequently Kate agreed to Catherine's suggestion that she move back to the flat, the lease to which Catherine had not yet managed to sell. Kate saw this not as defeat but as a chance to show her daughter that she could make it on her own. Her one stipulation was that Catherine refit the apartment so that it would take six guests.

For some months their paths didn't cross. Then Catherine heard that somehow Kate had managed to lease for five years a large terraced house. 'One day I received a note from her asking me to go and see her. At that time I allowed myself only one hour a week in order to take a fencing lesson. On my way there I called on her and I immediately recognised that she was well away. She asked if I would meet her new guest, who was a grammar school master. I said, "No!" I was in a hurry and I must go. She preceded me along the passage and threw open the door of the sitting room. "This is my daughter, Mr Cookson!" I saw a young man rise from the table where he had been writing. He said, "How do you do?" Why I should answer him as I did I will never know. For I said, "Do you fence?" It was a moment before he said . . . "No." And on this I turned on my heel and walked out.

Tom Cookson was twenty-four when they met, Catherine thirty; the year was 1936. He was an Oxford graduate, his subject Mathematics. He had been teaching at Hastings Grammar School since September that year. Catherine believes that the reason Kate sent for her was that she wanted to show her off to this educated man. But whatever her reason, Kate certainly never dreamt that she was matchmaking on an amorous level. Tom was a studious young man, Catherine was older than him with, as far as the world could see, a forceful, extrovert personality. It was an unlikely love match, and had Kate even contemplated it, she would have dismissed the possibility that such a quiet, shy man as Tom would dare to take her daughter away from her. But that is just what Tom did.

Two nights after their abruptly curtailed first meeting, he showed up uninvited at The Hurst and asked Catherine to accompany him to the cinema. Catherine was as surprised as Kate would have been. There was she, a busy woman some years his senior with a personality capable of dealing with anyone from down-and-outs to mental patients on a daily basis, with a guest house (which now included the occasional epileptic patient) to maintain and run, being asked to the pictures by 'this boyish fellow'. But when Tom issued his invitation in his polite, unassuming fashion, Catherine was even more amazed at her response. She said simply, 'Yes, I would. Thank you.'

They went to the pictures and afterwards walked the two miles home, whereupon Catherine invited Tom in and they sat either side of the fire in the study and talked, and talked.

By the time the hall clock struck twelve they had been sitting talking for almost two hours. 'What happened then I can't explain. Whether it was he who leant towards me or I towards him I'll never know. But we kissed. I knew in that moment it was right.'

When Kate learned what had happened she was dumbfounded. She and Annie laughed their heads off at Catherine 'and this twenty-four-year-old boy'. Tom represented something which neither Kate nor Annie could understand. Then, to their horror, these two dependants sensed that something important was being hatched. This wasn't just a passing flirtation. All Catherine's development, which Kate took as posturing, was being brought to ground in Tom, who gave Catherine sturdy roots on which she could graft her 'new-nature'.

Certainly there was physical attraction. Tom was captivated by Catherine's voice – 'something strange to my ear . . . vibrant with life. I had heard nothing like it before.' There was also 'a lilt or inflection, an inheritance from the North', which completely slayed him. Catherine also admits that she found Tom 'attractive looking', but more than this, in Tom, Catherine glimpsed her own fulfilment. 'This man was someone I knew I'd been waiting for all my life. He had a mind which was not only brilliant in his work but which met my searches.' In Tom, Catherine had, at last, found someone with whom she could share the things that preoccupied her.

Tom recalls being amazed at the vigour of Catherine's commitment to her 'fight against superstition, bigotry and intolerance' – her fight not against her people's exploitation by their capitalist bosses, which was the common cry in the 1930s (Tom and Catherine's first meeting coincided to the month, October 1936, with the Jarrow Crusade), but against the ignorance, prejudices and hypocrisies which she had suffered firsthand, and which she perceived kept her people in strait-jackets self-sewn. At the time, she was reading two authors who seemed to back her in this fight. When Tom first arrived at Kate's lodgings in the late summer of 1936, Catherine had been away in Paris, visiting the French woman to whom Kate had served her mousetrap pie. The woman had introduced Catherine to the writings of Voltaire, a leading figure in the Enlightenment, the eighteenth-century movement towards freedom from superstition and intolerance. Shortly before Catherine met Tom, she had been reading *Candide*, which had particular relevance to her doubts about Catholicism. She had also made the acquaintance of Socrates through reading Plato's *Apologia* (it is not too difficult to appreciate why Tom's amazement was threaded with admiration that this 'person who had left school at fourteen' was so obviously 'consumed with a desire for learning'). Plato describes the accusation of Socrates by Meletus, the leatherseller, for corrupting young boys' minds in the way he was educating them. What struck Catherine was Socrates' integrity – his refusal to budge from his position when he stood accused, even though he was to drink the poisoned cup: 'Like Christ, Socrates never wrote a line; like Christ, when they brought him before them, he stuck to his convictions.' She was inspired too by Plato's idea that there is this spring of knowledge – out there are concepts which have a real existence, distinct from the material world, and on which we draw – a spring of knowledge 'into which we can all dip . . .', as she put it to me recently. With her deepening doubts about Catholicism she warmed to these philosophical ideas: 'I felt I could follow Socrates,' she said to me, 'I felt I could follow him without fear.' At the age of twenty she had coined a phrase, ' "I learn each day by gaining a greater knowledge of my ignorance." I thought I was very clever . Now I discovered that Socrates had said similar words to his judges in the fifth century BC.' Excited by the idea that she might tap into this spring of knowledge, she saw that with Tom, she had the makings of a dialogue. The quest she was undertaking need never more be a lone quest.

In return Catherine gave Tom a new confidence. 'I knew not only did I need him, but he needed me even more.' Tom was 'quiet', shy and reticent. But this kind, quiet man had not been overawed by Catherine's abruptness when they first met, he had pursued her. He jokes now that he can't imagine where he found the courage to do so, but he knows that he found it in Catherine.

Integrity was the point at which Tom, the academic, and Catherine, with her firsthand knowledge of life, met intellectually; the shared value to which their lives had led them, albeit along two very different paths. It encouraged their perception of each other as two sides of the same coin. I don't believe Catherine expected ever to meet anyone who would contrast and complement her at one and the same time, or even that she could have created a character who could perform such a role, before she met Tom. Catherine and Tom were at opposite poles, and yet precisely because each was the antithesis of the other, they knew almost at once that they were made for each other, for 'in the channels where the intangible but real life runs, we were one, and we recognised this.'

Theirs was a dovetail attraction. She discovered in Tom the beauty of love as a two-way process, giving as well as taking. Above all, Catherine needed to give. Not since hanging on to her grandma's skirts as a child had she known real love. There is nothing simple about working out this strongest kind of love, and today Catherine recalls many arguments, mostly about who was in command – 'In the end we decided it was better to be second mates ... He is the flesh below the hide.' There is a lovely irony in Catherine's first salvo, 'Do you fence?', for though Tom claimed not to, they proceeded to fence together for years, and their long union, and especially Catherine's work, benefited from their fencing. When Catherine says, as she often does, that Tom has been the only one who has been of any help to her in her work, she means it, not because her agent and editors and publishers don't help, but because Tom's help has been at a fundamental level, at the level at which the very shape of her writing has been formed. In the end, all her novels are about creating harmony out of disharmony, unity out of disunity, finding serenity through love.

When Kate saw all this going on it became clear to her that neither she nor Annie could any longer count on Catherine as the fulcrum of their lives, and the two women teamed up to make sure the match didn't happen. Their laughter turned to ridicule and malice; they even resorted to opening Tom's mail in search of anything that might turn Catherine against him. 'I could write a book about what happened during the next two years,' said Catherine, 'and eventually they did part us for a time . . . In all Kate's stages of drinking I think this was the lowest.'

Readers of Catherine's novel *Hamilton* may remember the awful slyness of the Stickle family who inveigle themselves into Maisie Carter's house after her mother commits suicide. Their purpose, to drain Maisie of her inheritance, is obviously different from Kate's and Annie's, but the parasitic pressure they exert on their quarry bears the hallmarks of the period in Catherine's life when she was 'feeding' Kate and Annie in an emotional and material way and they were draining her. They (like the Stickles) fancied they controlled her, rather like some members of an orchestra fancy they exercise control over their conductor, but the need is greater on their side. Neither Kate nor Annie could survive without

Catherine; deep down they knew that, and they responded with as much venom as did Maisie's persecutor, Howard Stickle.

What resolved matters for Catherine and Tom was that Kate found that she couldn't make it on her own. One day a letter arrived at The Hurst in which Kate hoisted a white flag. She would return to the North if Catherine would free her from her lease commitment on her house. Catherine agreed, though the deal wiped her out at the bank. Kate had lost; in fact, very soon she was to lose everything. In February the following year (1938), her husband David McDermott's body would be found in the Tyne. He had been blown from the quayside on his way back to his ship, weighted down into his watery grave by bottles recovered from his pockets.

Tom, meanwhile, had taken off for Austria, where he was to spend the school summer holidays. In theory, he was due to return to lodge with Kate from the beginning of the new school year in September 1937. Now that she was giving up her guest house, Kate suggested that since it was all over between him and her daughter, perhaps Catherine would let him lodge at The Hurst. On the day, a Saturday, that Tom walked through the front door of The Hurst, 'we knew immediately we were one again.'

Annie, however, was still running the place with the help of a cook called Mrs Webster. Incredibly, when Tom returned, the same old animosity started all over again. This time Catherine acted; but it wasn't an easy decision. What would become of Annie? What would become of their business at The Hurst when Annie wasn't around to manage it? Catherine couldn't be at the Institution and run The Hurst at the same time. Nevertheless, she moved decisively and dispassionately. She mortgaged The Hurst and, so that Annie could set herself up in business, bought her a house (which would be signed over to her shortly after the war). Then Catherine sold some land which had belonged to this property, taking half the amount to recoup some of the cost of the house and giving the rest to Annie. At the point of Annie's departure there were seven guests in The Hurst. Annie took three of them, leaving Catherine with 'two mental patients, a penniless army captain and Tom, and no money in the bank'.

The following year, in August 1939, Catherine gave in her notice at the workhouse, returned to run The Hurst full-time and despatched Mrs Webster to help Annie. It was a bold move on the eve of war, which was declared with Germany the following month – whereupon The Hurst was requisitioned as a home for the blind, with Catherine in charge.

All this time, indeed since before she arrived in Hastings in 1930, she had suffered bleeding from the nose (another symptom of telangiectasia), and no doctor had found a cure. The battle with Kate and Annie had taken its toll emotionally on a body weakened by this trying, tiring illness. Now, under treatment by a doctor for her 'nerves', she had to cope with twelve blind male evacuees from the East End of London and it was hard, unrewarding work.

Then one day Catherine received a letter, which brought news of the evacuation of the grammar school to St Albans in Hertfordshire, an event which threatened to split her and Tom up again. On opening the letter she made an immediate decision. Tom was already over the threshold on his way to school when she ran out of the front door after him and called out to him that they should marry on the following Saturday. Tom came back to her, took her hand and then turned and ran for joy down the road to school.

For two or three years before this, Catherine had been seeing the parish priest in an attempt to resolve her increasing doubts about Catholicism. The priest would come to The

Hurst, play the piano, stay to tea and then wonder at Catherine's reservations about the Church when clearly it made for such a jolly time. Now, when she asked him to marry them, he told her that he wouldn't unless Tom became a Roman Catholic too. Tom was a Christian, a member of the Church of England; his father had been a verger in Essex. But that wasn't enough. He was a Protestant, she was a Catholic. The priest wanted Tom to turn. Tom, for whom integrity was all, would not. Together he and Catherine put it to the priest that they would be married in a Register Office. In the face of this possibility, the priest compromised and Tom signed a document saying that he would bring up their children in the Catholic faith.

They married on 1 June 1940, nine months into the Second World War and two weeks or so before Catherine's thirty-fourth birthday. 'I had married a Protestant. Perhaps we were married in a Catholic church, but under protest, which was all done very suddenly because Tom's school was under orders of evacuation, and I couldn't be left behind. The priest threw the ceremony at us. There were only eight people present and it was only on the promise that I would get him to turn.'

The priest's attitude of disapproval towards the marriage and the atmosphere at the ceremony distressed Catherine, confirming her doubts about allegiance to a Church which could alienate a Christian in such a way. But the deed was done and the papers signed. Now, surely, she need have no doubts as to her identity – Tom had made her a Cookson and for that alone she was proud. Within a month they left Hastings and travelled to St Albans, where they took a flat in Victoria Street, across the road from the library.

In an extraordinary quirk of fate, with the bitter taste of the wedding ceremony still fresh, she and Tom immediately received another dose of religious mania. 'I took Tom on our first Sunday morning there to Mass. There was a young priest on the altar, and when he stood up to give the sermon, he said the theme of it was "Hell's flames". He went on to state that hell was no figment of the imagination. His actual words were: "Hell is a burning fire, where we will be sat on gridirons for ever more. And get that into your head . . . This is no fable or imagination!" How I kept my seat and kept Tom there I don't know. He was a man recently down from Oxford, and I had brought him to listen to this ignorant pig of a priest, spouting the very topic I had been fighting against for years. We never went back.'

A short time later Catherine discovered she was pregnant. It was not to be an easy pregnancy. Someone had got word to her that Kate was very ill; it was a false alarm 'from a false friend'. Catherine would have to cross London, which nightly was being battered in the Blitz. The trip north, in the wartime blackout, proved a very exhausting experience, and re-opened old wounds. She recalls, 'My mother was very surprised to see us. She had nothing but a sniffly cold. At this time I was five months' pregnant, added to which I was having regular nosebleeds.' The flow of blood was so bad that it drenched the pillow on their bed.

Then, on 7 December 1940, their first child, the spitting image of Tom, was born, three months prematurely, dead. Catherine and Tom were absolutely overcome with grief. It was a tragedy for which neither was prepared, 'particularly so because our child, not having lived, could not be buried in sacred ground. It was buried with an old woman from the local workhouse in a common grave'.

This was the first of a series of emotional traumas which must have made Catherine feel that her whole life was cursed. Over the next four years, between the end of 1940 and the summer of 1945, she lost three more babies. What she, as a mother, felt at such a loss was one thing. What she felt on Tom's behalf was even worse. Her marriage, far from resolving any problems, seemed only to be dragging Tom down into her old vortex of pain. These four terrible losses underpinned the persecution of herself which brought her to breakdown in the same year that she lost her fourth child. Catherine was strong. Strife was her 'yeast', the culture in which her achievements had been grown. But this was not the same. In this it was not just her alone.

She began having nightmares in which a judgemental, black-robed priest appeared. These terrifying dreams dredged up from her past the voice of the 'missioner', her Father Confessor who consigned her to hell for admitting that she didn't like the taste of God on her tongue. She began to imagine that her and Tom's tragedy was the result of her questioning her faith. She was floundering in the same mire of superstition as her people.

As always when she is at a low ebb, Catherine decided to work her way out of it. With the happy chance of the City Library within walking distance, she decided to undertake a programme of self-education. She drew up a list of books which ranged over English literature from Chaucer to the 1920s, and the verve with which she went about it astonished her husband. 'As in everything she tackles,' Tom remembers, 'she persevered working through that colossal list.'

In Catherine's historical novel *Tilly Trotter*, education of the working classes is recommended as a cure for superstition. The idea is that by showing people how to think for themselves, education enables them to escape the control of others and to *be* themselves. Descartes' self-evident intuition, 'I think, therefore I am,' lies at the heart of it. The French philosopher and mathematician was one of the seventeenth-century precursors of the Enlightenment which Catherine had been studying.

In *The Black Velvet Gown*, another novel set in the

nineteenth century, Catherine explores a number of related themes – the fear among those in power in society that education of the working classes would diminish their control over them, the rich promise which working-class people were convinced education held out to them, and the success and failure of education in delivering that promise.

Miner Seth Millican takes it upon himself to learn to read, despite his boss's disapproval. Further, he teaches his wife, Maria (known as Riah), two sons (Davey and Johnny) and two daughters (Biddy and Maggie) to read and write, so that they will never need to earn a living down the pit. But when Seth dies during a cholera epidemic, and his family find work and lodging at Moor House, the home of an impoverished gentleman (Percival Miller), Riah interests Tol Briston, a worker on the big estate nearby called The Heights, in learning to read, and Tol's sister, Annie, accuses her of unsettling Tol. What will education do for Tol other than make him aware of the hopelessness of his lot in life?

When Percival Miller overhears the row between Annie and Riah, he announces a proposal to further the education of Riah's children with two hours' tuition a morning. Daughter Biddy turns out to have a large appetite for learning, but it doesn't improve her station in life. At the end of it all she is only able to secure a place in the laundry at The Heights, the lowest position in the servant hierarchy. For Riah herself, education stands between her and her growing attraction to Miller. Education is all he ever thinks about, other than Riah's son, Davey, who takes to Miller's curriculum about as eagerly as a horse to brine and, realising that he is becoming the special object of Miller's attentions, responds by taking a scythe to him.

Education is no all-purpose panacea, and may be a dangerous tool. The educator concocts his own prescription to cure ignorance, and, as Miller admits to Riah, his motives are not wholly altruistic. He is educating her children not only 'for their own good' but to give himself 'some kind of an aim'.

Up at The Heights, where *grande dame* Mrs Diana Gullmington rules the roost, Biddy's learning is causing a sensation of disapproval. When, in a game of forfeits in the servants' hall, she recites a poem by Shelley, family members who come to watch are alternately dumbfounded and hostile. Afterwards, a friend of the family called Laurence (the son of Diana's sister-in-law, Grace Gullmington) counsels Diana's teenage grandchildren, Paul and Lucy, not to mention Biddy's performance to their parents, fearing their disapproval of literacy among the lower orders. As it is, Biddy is threatened with dismissal and her books with burning, and Paul and Lucy's hostility turns into an open vendetta. One Sunday, when Biddy is working in the laundry, Paul and Lucy burst in and taunt her for studying French and Latin. Biddy flares up and points out their provincial accents, whereupon Lucy slashes Biddy across the face with her riding crop and ends up in a tub of washing before Biddy is trussed up by her wrists on a drying rack with linen torn from the sheets, raised so that only her toes touch the ground. Biddy is found later, unconscious but still alive.

Behind all these shenanigans runs a serious dialogue between Laurence and Grandmama Diana Gullmington. We learn of 'great stirrings' outside the closed world of The Heights – strikes, riots which soldiers have been brought in to quell, merchant ships subjected to naval guardianship, even the murder of a mine deputy, a historical reference to the murder of Nicholas Fairles in 1832, a particularly gruesome business where the principal got clean away but which caused enormous class tension at the time. Education is seen as spelling the end of the old social order by

Grandmama, who, as I have already mentioned, sees the placing of human beings in a social order as God's work and as implying that reason has no place in the life of a servant. Laurence, on the other hand, takes the progressive view: he is for people using their own minds.

England remained so far behind Europe in the matter of educating its people that even in the late nineteenth century it was criticised for deliberately withholding education from the working classes in order to keep them in their place and their expectations low. Technical training was permitted only because 'this kind of learning would not encourage workmen to be dissatisfied with the station in life into which they had been called by a wise providence,' as S.J. Curtis wrote in his *History of Education in Britain*.

Implicit in *The Black Velvet Gown*, however, is the message that education does not guarantee success in the world, at least not in nineteenth-century England. Nor would Catherine's problems a century later be solved by her programme of education in the flat in St Albans. If there is a final conclusion to the debate in the novels it is in favour of intuition and knowledge grounded in experience – 'wisdom without learning', which is what Dr Rodney Prince divines in uneducated Kate Hannigan and is the source of her allure. Once again, it is an autobiographical conclusion. It would be Catherine's own experience as a writer that the channels of creativity can be blocked by too much rational analysis. She would watch, for example, as her flesh-and-blood northern characters 'wilted under Tommy Cookson's correct but stilted English' when he gave her a course in syntax and grammar. In the early twentieth-century Tyneside novels Catherine alerts us to the categorical difference between intellect and imagination, between reason (capable of dissecting things into infinity) and intuition (capable of reaching a truth with a marvellous economy).

As a child Catherine was enthralled when a lodger arrived carrying a set of Shakespeare and put the books on a chest in the bedroom of number 10, but it was the romance of the Sonnets which captured her imagination. She recalls another lodger, too, a huge, bearded sea captain with a laugh as deep as the swelling ocean and a smell of mothballs and brine, who told her not to believe in heaven or hell because they, like everything else – even the sky and the sea – are only imagination. For her own personal fulfilment she would need to return to the imaginativeness of her youth. This would be an uncomfortable process and, perhaps sensing this, she turned, for the first time in ten years, to Chesterfield for support.

As with all his other advice, with that on learning there is a discernible profit motive. For Chesterfield, knowledge operates like a deposit to be drawn on at a later time: 'Let me most earnestly recommend you to hoard up, while you can, a great stock of knowledge,' he writes to his son, 'for though, during the dissipation of your youth, you may not have occasion to spend much of it, yet, you may depend upon it, that a time will come when you will want it to maintain you.' Ideas, concepts, quotations become valuable property stored in the lumber room of the head, a stock list, much as the seventeenth-century novelist Daniel Defoe has Robinson Crusoe make inventories of his possessions for the purpose of survival. In 1941 Catherine was still cast away on her desert island, and with Chesterfield as her Man Friday she set about increasing her intellectual stock in the hope that it would help her find a way off it.

Chesterfield's advice was useful in one respect at least. The *Letters* encouraged her to form her own judgements on what she was reading. 'Use and assert your own reason,' he urges Philip. 'Reflect, examine and analyse everything in order to form a sound and mature judgement. Great learning, if not accompanied with sound judgement, frequently carried us into error, pride and pedantry.' Catherine rumbled those writers who lost her in a fog of verbiage. 'That I myself write plain English,' she says, 'is all due to this man.'

While in St Albans she also began work on a book of rhymes for children and paid a visit to the local art school in search of an illustrator. The art teacher told her that none of their students was up to such a commission and suggested that she might like to learn to draw. She tried, only to discover that she couldn't draw children, a telling enough comment on recent wounds. She returned to the school and informed the teacher that she had enjoyed the class but had decided that instead of children she would draw stone. He must have wondered what on earth he had taken on. But Catherine found herself in perfect sympathy with this primitive material. As anyone who has seen her drawings of St Albans Abbey and Hereford Cathedral will appreciate, she does indeed have an extraordinary ability to make stone look like stone. Three-dimensional, rich in texture, it is alive to the senses, tempting us to see these artworks as a rehearsal in techniques which, in a different medium, would bring her fame, once she had learned how to redraw herself with equal honesty.

Eight months after the loss of their first child, in August 1941, Tom enlisted in the RAF and together they moved to Leicester for his training.

Catherine had not been to church in more than a year and her mind was besieged by strangely oppressive fears as her faith fell away from her like flaking skin. The Church's doctrine on mixed marriage, its adherence to stories of hellfire and its strategy of maintaining allegiance through fear and guilt infuriated her. But she could not let religion go. Transubstantiation now seemed not just misguided but even repulsive to her. It is a first precept of the Catholic Church that in the Mass the bread and wine literally turn into the flesh and blood of Jesus Christ. Try to accept this, truly accept it, and you can begin to see where her problem lay. People who pay lip service to their religion and worry, for example, if the church is cold, or who go there without truly believing the dogma or because attendance is a mark of social respectability, will find it a challenge to understand the fears which beset Catherine at this time. But in the stormy sea of Catherine's self-doubts which her childhood had bequeathed her, her faith had been the one certainty. Its erosion cleared the way for self-doubt to gain the upper hand and in just four years her fears would become so unbearable that something had to give.

In Leicester, where she rented digs while Tom was away at training camp, she decided to do something about it. 'One Sunday morning I made myself go to Mass and I came out of that place so angry I could have exploded . . . The climax came when I was leaving. There were double doors and when I closed one I saw this large notice there and it was headed "On Mixed Marriage". It went on to say that mixed marriage was not recognised by God and the only hope the Catholic part of it had was if they turned their partner into a Catholic, if they brought their partner into the Church. This was what I must work at every day, because the Catholic party was living in sin, and knew only too well the outcome of that! I was so furious . . .'

But still she couldn't let it go. She couldn't just turn her back on it and laugh. This was where reality lay: if it didn't, then there was nothing. 'The fight went on within me. I lit candles to Our Lady, who I understood to be the mother of God . . . and I bought a number of Masses. Oh yes, you had to pay for having a Mass said . . .'

Later that same year, 1941, Tom was moved to Cranwell in Lincolnshire and Catherine discovered she was pregnant again. This time she suffered a miscarriage. Then, in 1942, Tom was posted to RAF Madley in Herefordshire and together they took digs in Hereford, where, once more, Catherine turned her hand to drawing. Here she lost her third baby and was advised not to become pregnant again.

This posed a problem. It was a sin against God to practise contraception, to prevent life – another ticket to damnation. She knew she would have to take her problem to a priest. The priest didn't tell her to exercise celibacy; he told her to leave the sinning to her man. What kind of hypocrisy was that? How could the priest suggest such a thing? He had struck at the very heart of her doubts. He was dodging the issue because the doctrines of his church were at odds with life, real life.

Catherine's problem with religion was that she had been brought up in a rigidly, even ruthlessly, disciplined Church, some of whose doctrines she had doubted from the start, which had filled her with guilt. But religion had answered a need in her, a fundamental spiritual need, which would never leave her. Now that the disciplines and doctrines were suspect, what did that mean for the validity of the spiritual answers which that same Church had given her? These priests were reducing the whole thing to a child's game. Leave the decision to your man. Let him go to hell. Why didn't they all grow up and get to the heart of the matter?

Deep down, what she was after was truth. Catherine had once before been cheated in a matter of love, love for two people whom she had known and believed in as her mother and father. But parental love was as nothing to this love, the very essence of feeling, which she had discovered in her relationship with the Holy Family, and in particular with Christ's mother, the Virgin Mary, through whom she had always dealt. Mingling with her feelings of outrage was a kind of aggression, little stabs of aggression. She was not a child any more, but what they were doing to her was tempting her to lose faith altogether, to lose faith in those whom she had loved and had loved her. Like the first time, it was the negation of all that had been true.

CHAPTER SEVEN

⚭⚭

Catharsis

The years since 1932, when Kate had arrived in Hastings to live, had been a nightmare of drink, recrimination, argument, fights and hard physical work. Work getting Kate organised, work (from 1933) getting The Hurst into some sort of shape, work making it turn a profit as guest-house-cum-home, and through the whole period long hours of toil each day at the Hastings Institution, which, until Catherine's resignation in July 1939, formed the backbone on which all other work was ribbed.

Tom has said that, for his wife, work is the essence of being, it galvanises her energies. But those energies had been wasted by illness: 'I had been losing blood practically every day since I was eighteen.' They had been wasted by the extraordinary campaign waged by Kate and Annie over Tom, and by the terrible loss of three babies in the three years that she and Tom had been married. They had been wasted, too, by the battles raging within her, not only about religion, but about herself – 'my illegitimacy was hitting me harder than at any other time.' She was being torn apart by her two sides, which she identified with Kate and her unknown father. Sublimating the first, her nightmare side (Kate), she could apprehend her other side, her 'new nature' which promised an alternative destiny, a fulfilment longed for and prepared for by reading and following the strategy of refinement devised by Lord Chesterfield. And yet, despite all her feverish doing – drawing, painting, educating herself – that side of her seemed to be leading nowhere. Only Kate remained real: an awful, negative reality. Fulfilment on almost any level was denied her. Tom alone provided succour, 'the strange delight of knowing that she was wanted', as she would write in *Kate Hannigan*.

Her life was going round and round like a fairground carousel, Tom holding her tight round the waist lest she fall off. Every so often people popped up in front of her, offering false avenues of escape. 'I recall there was a very civilised priest in Hereford and he talked to me so quietly and nicely, and strangely we became friends. But it was no good.' A printer who liked her drawings of St Albans Abbey and Hereford Cathedral suggested she turn her hand to postcards. Another printer agreed that her drawings showed talent; why didn't she illustrate Arthur Mee's *Kings' England*? Catherine took up both offers, but the postcards made her only a halfpenny each, and the illustrations for Arthur Mee's *Kings' England*, sized one inch by one and a half inches, kept her eye to a magnifying glass all day long and rewarded her with a cheque for five pounds and conjunctivitis. A kindly, talented painter called André van der Meersch offered her lessons in perspective (which she might have used in her life as well as in her art), but he was an old man and died. No one, it seemed, could stop the endless, sickening motion of the less-than-merry-go-round, which was leading in ever-decreasing circles, closer and closer to the grinding engine-house of her mind.

Physically, odd things had begun to happen. She became thin and wasted; the veins in one leg became inflamed (she had contracted phlebitis); her anxieties lost any reference to specific preoccupations – religion, illegitimacy – and stared back at her in the mirror of her mind with merciless intent, confining her to bed, even paralysing her legs. Then one day she fell; and for a full two weeks she stayed in bed, staring at the ceiling. Catherine's fears had got her where they wanted her, alone in her lonely room, Tom away at the RAF camp, her unsympathetic landlady pacing the floor below. And they set about their business with surgical precision.

Things that had happened in her past had left such an accumulation of marks upon the landscape of her life that the thin social veneer with which she had tried so hard to smooth it over now inched away from its surface, revealing the marks and sores. Resentments became putrid, foetid, like little germ factories building into one massive boil, self-pity, hate, aggression as dreadful, nameless terrors swimming together to spawn its angry head.

She lay helpless, bound to her bed like the timbers in the Jarrow Slacks, prone in the mud, one of a row of skeletons unearthed in the graveyard of her mind. Then she sank, wallowing, choking in the black mire, and knew for the first time that there was no escape. Trapped beneath the surface of the mire she looked about her at a madman's world of twisted, grotesque creatures, sprawled at all angles, weirdly suggesting motion but horribly still. She gazed into the face of a man whom she had known as a child, a man who sold coal but who had no legs, and she saw her own horror in that man's face – it was misty, the face had gone, but the feeling remained. Her feeling turned to rage, rage against Nature, rage against God, rage against Kate.

These are images culled from the novels, from *Kate Hannigan*, *The Blind Miller*, *The Fifteen Streets* and *Feathers in the Fire*. Catherine said to me once, 'Strange, isn't it, that I have never written about my breakdown.' But it is all there. Confined in her room in Hereford, she too dreamed fantastic dreams in which she was wallowing among strange, faceless, reptilian monsters which transformed themselves into hands.

Many of her novels explore mental stress, but none comes as close to offering us a glimpse of the author's spiralling descent into hell than *The Garment* (1962). Driven to the point of breakdown by her husband, Donald, Grace Rouse begins her final descent when she shows herself vulnerable to every nuance in her husband's slyly destructive treatment of her. What was once sickening in his behaviour towards her now appears sinister. But everyone else is won over by Donald's jolly exterior, giving no credence to Grace's apparently paranoid version of events. The agony of the insane is that their version is true and yet no one but they can see it. Madness is not a blameless world, it is a world in which the madman is not allowed to place blame. A doctor friend warns Grace that if she continues to bottle up her anxieties they will come to a head in her brain like a boil. It is the same image Catherine uses to describe her own breakdown.

One morning in August, a silly scene with Grace's son, Stephen, results in some insolent behaviour, condoned by Donald, which in Grace's troubled mind seems to complete a picture, a jigsaw of truly paranoid impressions that her children have entered Donald's conspiracy and are united against her. Then, that afternoon, Donald suggests re-employing the gardener, Andrew MacIntyre, into whose arms he had previously driven Grace. Alienated, alone, she sees this as Donald trumpeting his control over her lover and slamming the door on her one avenue of escape. It is Donald's final manipulation, and all hell breaks loose.

In breakdown there is no pretence. All the face, all the gentility which guards against truth in a civilised world melts away in the heat of pure rage. It is, in a way, a cleansing. The boil bursts and all the putrid, foetid resentment of a lifetime pours out. Ever since Catherine can remember, whether it is her disgust as a child at Kate shoplifting a part-bale of

The laundry at Harton workhouse in 1923, a year before Catherine, at eighteen, replaced the checker – the woman farthest left of the four who are wearing smart Sunday uniforms.

Catherine's own problems were put into a fresh perspective by her employment as a laundry checker in the workhouse. Among the women confined within the foul-smelling atmosphere of the infirm ward (shown here) were characters prematurely aged by despair.

Catherine aged about twenty. Through her teens, the child characters of Annie Hannigan and Mary Ann had retreated into the shadows of her psyche and others, like Tilly Trotter, Mary Walton (of *Pure as the Lily*) and Christine Winter (of *Fenwick Houses*), come to the fore. Now, like them, in spite of a determination not to get seriously involved with men, she fell deeply in love with a man much older than herself and was hurt so badly that the pain drove her from the North.

Banter between local girls and sailors in Shields harbour. One unhappy consequence of Catherine's illegitimacy was a repressive attitude to sex at home, where restraint was preached from the pulpit of the Fathar's chair lest Catherine go the same way as Kate.

Catherine's period of employment from 1924 to 1929 at the workhouse in South Shields gave her an opportunity to do something positive about the depths of degradation which, she was all too aware, unemployment could bring to a town. Here, and at Hastings workhouse from 1930 to 1939, she developed the extraordinary appetite for work which her husband would describe as the essence of her being.

After the bitter break-up of her first real love affair, Catherine arrived in Hastings with all thoughts of love or marriage behind her. But she was young and attractive, and the no-nonsense self-discipline which characterised her extrovert personality made for a formidable combination which, for reasons she couldn't fathom, held a particular attraction for married men.

This period of disquiet and longing – 'I was warm-hearted and wanting love, but determined, however hungry I was for it, not to go the way of my mother' – saw the development inside Catherine of a character who was to become one of her most popular heroines, Anna Brigmore of the *Mallen* trilogy.

The Hurst, the fifteen-roomed house which Catherine had promised herself as a young child living in conditions which precluded it as anything other than fantasy existence. But for Catherine The Hurst was never merely a dream. She bought it in 1933, at twenty-seven years of age, long before she became a published writer.

Catherine standing in front of The Hurst, a house she could love, a square of ground she could call her own. The relationship between Catherine and The Hurst (its ultimate potential explored in *The Obsession*) lasted twenty-one years, by which time it had drained her energies and all that she and her husband were earning.

Undaunted by the problems of refurbishment and maintenance Catherine was taken with the grandeur of The Hurst, its butler's pantry, the wine cellar, the spacious drawing room with floor to ceiling windows looking out on to a large garden with tennis court. But she came to it with Kate, pictured centre of group on Catherine's left, who saw to it that her daughter's passion for the house would not run smoothly.

When Catherine first met Tom she had been on her way to a fencing lesson. She is seen here third from left. Little did she know that she would need all her defensive skills to ensure their love a safe passage. Tom, straight out of Oxford and six years Catherine's junior, was not someone whom Kate found it easy to accept as her son-in-law.

Tom and Catherine married on 1 June 1940. 'I had married a Protestant. Perhaps we were married in a Catholic church, but under protest . . . The priest threw the ceremony at us. There were only eight people present and it was only on the promise that I would get Tom to turn.'

flannelette or a fear so strong in adulthood that it makes her sick lest she go out and take the life of a child, Catherine must cleanse herself of it. She literally vomits her fear away. Alienation, nausea, repulsion, purification compose a major theme of the novels. Nervous breakdown is the ultimate evacuation, not of the stomach or bowels, but of the mind, in her case an involuntary purging of all the filth of her childhood experience. Potentially, it is a cathartic experience; but, as with a boil that bursts, healing is neither instant nor guaranteed. Putrefaction may set in.

In *The Obsession*, nervous breakdown turns Beatrice Steele into an animal, prowling around the house, whispering, scratching at locked doors with her nails like a crazed dog. In *The Garment*, Grace Rouse yells out, screaming mouthfuls of saliva and abuse, goading, terrifying. Kate is one object of her abuse – she is screamed by name. At first I made no connection with the minor character in the novel, Kate Shawcross, clergyman Donald's admirer. Read it as I did and the autobiographical content of Grace's awful purgation is alarmingly clear. In any case, it includes other elements which have a transparent autobiographical reference – for example, her resentment about fetching the coke, or her slipping into a Geordie accent as she spews out her oaths. All pretence is over as she bares her claws and the real fury begins. It is a terrifying scene, brought to a close by Dr Cooper with his syringe, Donald nursing his torn and bleeding face at the end of the bed, Grace cursing him into oblivion.

Catherine, at her own request, was admitted to St Mary's Hospital, Burghill, north-west of Hereford, for a period of psychiatric treatment, which included ECT – electroconvulsive therapy, the electric current once so powerfully administered that it lifted her off the table. In 1945 such places were not what they are today, and Catherine's experience resonates with images of cold stone stairs, of waiting her turn for treatment on heavy wooden forms, of the glare of arc lights, of the effort afterwards of lifting her legs (made unnaturally heavy by the current) back along the corridors to her bed, of the smell of urine in the wards, recalling the desolation and misery of the infirm wards at Harton and the bitter memory of the urinals opposite the dock gates from which that woman had emerged, laughing, arm-in-arm with three men. In *The Blind Miller* Catherine gives Sarah Bradley the same experience in prison, where the smell of urine permeates the air.

Each night Tom would ride fourteen miles on his bicycle to visit her, this after riding fifteen miles back and forth to the camp and their digs. After five weeks Catherine was allowed out for a day.

'I recall that the nice priest from Hereford saw me and cried out, "What on earth are you doing here?" '

CHAPTER EIGHT

⚮⚮⚮

Birth of Inspiration

Catherine walked out of the mental hospital with one thought in her mind: to get back to The Hurst. As a voluntary patient she was free to do so, and she arrived home on her own, determined to get the house back into shape and to work, work, work, so as to divert her energies from fearful introspection and aggression. It was June 1945. She lived alone there for nine months, fighting her battle out, Tom unable to join her until his demob in the spring of 1946.

Upon opening the front door for the first time in five years, she was struck by the most appalling smell and must have wondered whether it was some kind of nightmarish imagining from the depths of breakdown. For the smell which pervaded the place was the smell of urine. There was a mixture of relief and revulsion when she discovered that there was a full chamberpot in each bedroom. 'The home had been occupied only during the last few months by an officer's wife, who had used it as a guest house for other officers.'

The whole place required a complete overhaul. 'I worked in that freezing barracks mostly dressed in two dressing gowns, a huge pair of eskimo boots and a big woollen scarf around my head. It had no central heating of any kind, only one large fireplace in the drawing room and a number of smaller ones in other rooms. It was after the war and we were still on a coal ration of a ton a year. So I spent at least an hour a day sawing old trees down and sawing them up to keep some kind of warmth in one room. This was besides cleaning the place, cooking, washing by hand (there were no machines of any kind, not even a wringer) and writing in every spare minute.'

This nine-month period on her own was probably the most demanding time of her life, for on top of her mental trauma, she suffered the loss of her fourth baby, again by miscarriage. She pinned up a chart in the kitchen to record each day how she was doing. The lowest point of the graph marked the day when she prepared for suicide. She planned to take all her pills, made all the necessary preparations, and then at the last minute, thinking of Tom, flushed them down the lavatory. Momentarily she felt better. She found herself on her own, with no medicines to cling on to, and it felt good. She took it as a sign of the way she must take: no dependence, no props, her future was up to herself.

In this troubled, hermit existence, she turned to writing, 'the locked shelter in which once you get the door open you can live', a safe place to be herself – like Annie Hannigan's 'little square house' sanctuary in the backyard, or like the 'hiding place' for which Reginald Farrier yearns in *The Wingless Bird*: returning from the trenches in the First World War, emotionally shot to pieces, he appeals to his brother's widow Agnes Conway to provide it, with a quotation from Psalm 32: 'Thou art my hiding place; thou shalt preserve me from trouble; thou shalt compass me about with songs of deliverance.' Catherine, though, was not reading psalms any more.

She began by writing plays. 'But after having written the third play I questioned myself as to what I really knew about the characters.' They were cardboard, two-dimensional, mostly plucked from the upper middle class and living the kind of existence which Chesterfield might have known at first hand, but which was largely foreign to Catherine's experience.

Turning away from the plays, she embarked on a different project. The idea was to write a series of short stories. The first she called 'She Had No Da'. It was about a girl from the North who had no father and whose playmates destroyed her little world by telling her that the man she thought was her father was not. This, she could see, worked better. Again, it was a sign. She had brought her writing back to herself, and it worked. But still she was sick with anxiety every minute of every day, when she was not sublimating it in physical exertion or writing. Her chart showed that Catherine had known only one day free from fear in the first year she was back at The Hurst. But occasionally she did experience moments of relief. Catherine describes one such moment in a collection of recordings issued on tape towards the end of 1996, which includes a song called 'Falling Leaves'. She was sitting at a baby grand piano in the drawing room during a break from her gruelling, self-imposed, fourteen-hour working day. Tall windows looked out on to the lawn, bordered by trees and an old rhododendron hedge. As she was staring mournfully out at the garden, a gust of wind stirred the trees and set free a fall of leaves, which floated past the window, caught in a ray of clean, clear autumn sunlight. Instantly Catherine was infused with a feeling of sheer joy, 'as swift in passing as the leaves themselves'. Fleeting moments such as this offered an exquisite peace that was new and seemed to awaken something inside her. She composed the song 'Falling Leaves' there and then at the piano. It was another sign. The moment of joy was distinct from anything she had ever felt from Catholicism, and it was instantly creative.

When Tom returned he encouraged her writing, and she

decided to join the Writers' Circle in Hastings, which met in a room above the public library. Here members had to read their work out loud to the rest of the Circle. Catherine's nerves were so bad that when her turn came she had to stay seated, giving the excuse that she suffered from rheumatism. After each reading there would be a discussion, in which other members offered criticism and pointers for future work. She found that the stories she took, from her intended volume, were often well received. She gained confidence from this and enjoyed analysing and commenting on others' work, the experience underpinning and informing her solitary efforts.

Before Tom's return Catherine had counted the hours and the minutes until she could hold him in her arms again. But now that he was back she was once more a schoolmaster's wife, a role which carried with it certain obligations. For example, she was expected to attend school functions, some of which interrupted the strict schedule to which she kept, and at times she resented this. Also, these events took her out of the house into potentially discriminatory company. She had always felt she had to dress up in her best bib and tucker, and thrust and parry wittily among the masters and their wives to maintain her (and especially Tom's) standing. This was one of the areas where Chesterfield had served her well in the past, but now, since her breakdown, there was always the danger that her nervous disorder would without warning crack the facade. In *The Obsession* Catherine uses Beatrice Steele to explain the awful unpredictability of her state of mind. Walking down a street, Beatrice suddenly experiences 'that tired feeling' which invariably preceded an attack. With it comes a feeling of dread: 'Oh, my God! Not here!'

One day Catherine was walking down Queen's Road in Hastings on her way to a masters' and boys' cricket match at the grammar school. Stopping at the Fifty Shilling Tailor's, where she had to cross the road to reach the cricket field, her eyes fell on a brick lying in the gutter. It was one of a number left there by men working nearby. She eyed the brick, a rough, particularly pink brick. Then she turned to the Fifty Shilling Tailor's and eyed its shopfront window, a large, particularly smooth expanse of plate glass. The desire to hurl the brick through the window was so strong, and Catherine hovered on the edge of indecision for so long, that one of the workmen noticed something was up.

'D'you want to take it home with you, missis?' he asked her.

She told him that no, she didn't want to take it home, but she could think of another use for it. Fortunately, the workman had defused the situation. Catherine walked quietly across the road and took her place among the schoolmasters, charming them with ironic remarks about cricket and the performance of her husband on the field, all the time wondering inside at the kind of creature she had become.

Going out into the town terrified Catherine for another reason, too. The emotional pain of four miscarriages had left her with an aversion to babies and a terrible, uncontrollable urge which threatened to take her at any time. 'I am a kind person, I wouldn't hurt a fly,' Catherine said to me, 'so how could this kind, caring, loving individual have the terrible desire to pick up a baby from a pram outside a shop and run off with it, worse still, to take hold of that baby and dash it to the ground?'

After her fourth miscarriage it was ten or fifteen years before Catherine could hold a child in her arms, and during this time she underwent three operations on her womb. Even people close to her failed to understand what her losses meant to her. I recall Catherine telling me of a visit one Christmas by Tom's parents. There had been a baby in the visiting party and they had tried to get Catherine to hold it. She had declined, making light of it, and so they had pressed her again, and again, and when she continued to refuse they had become upset. It was some time – long after the holiday was over – before she was forgiven for her apparent coldness.

In Tom and Catherine's childless life together there have been some compensations. 'I've lost four babies but I've brought up more babies than in an orphanage,' she said to me recently. 'There were always boys at Loreto [the house to which they moved after selling The Hurst in 1954]. One came every day for his lunch and he stayed two years! Another came when he was sixteen and he didn't leave until he was twenty.' This was down to Tom, who was no run-of-the-mill schoolmaster. Not only did he take a personal interest in the future of the boys in his charge, staying on late at school to give extra tuition or to oversee some extra-curricular activity (he was rarely home before eight), but he was also at pains in his relationship with his pupils never to milk the privilege of authority he held over them. Mature mutual respect was what Tom Cookson aimed at, and it was a winning strategy. The first knock at the front door of Loreto after they moved in 'was a doctor, whose three sons went to the grammar school. One of the boys Tom had taken under his wing and patiently prepared him, as no one else would have done, for university. There stood the man with this great hamper, holding a really hot four-course dinner. What could be a better start than that?'

It is unlikely that Catherine's extraordinary literary output could have been maintained had her time been taken up with a large family clinging to her skirts. But her novels cannot be said to have filled the vacuum. 'I can honestly say that I don't get any real satisfaction from any of them. It is very odd. The only thing I get satisfaction from is the urgent desire to write and write and write. I see my brain as an old machine that requires daily oiling and the only way I can keep it going is to oil it with words.'

Their dogs, however, did help. First came Bill, who is celebrated in a couple of the novels. In *The Menagerie*, Willie Macintyre has a dog called Bill, a bull terrier. Newcastle United and bull terriers are Willie's life, and his love for Bill is down to his perception that the dog shares the character of his favourite football team. Willie had had another bull terrier when he was a boy, but it had developed mange – bull terriers, we learn, are born with it in their blood. Catherine actually caught mange from her Bill, a Staffordshire, brindled bull terrier, and had a particularly nasty time getting rid of the disease: Tom had to paint her, head to foot, in a kind of sheep dip solution. In *Fanny McBride*, Corny, Fanny's grandson, has a dog, an unfortunate mixture with a bull terrier's massive chest and a whippet's slimline hindquarters. He is a light brushstroke in Catherine's picture of personal identity and inherited traits which preoccupies her in so many of the novels. But for the real Bill's identity we must turn to *Hamilton* (1983), a richly comic novel and the first of a trilogy (*Goodbye Hamilton* and *Harold* followed in 1984 and 1985 respectively).

Elsewhere Catherine describes Bill as 'our child, a tearaway, a bad lad – but a loving lad', and his appearance in *Hamilton* gives us a graphic and accurate description of the way Bill on his lead would pull Catherine off her feet and whisk her through Hastings in his slipstream. Again, she records in the novel the memorable occasion when Bill slipped his collar and she raced after him up roads and down alleyways in the sedate town, to the amazement of onlookers, eventually to discover him at the butcher's where he is 'rewarded' with a bone.

Bill was a rascal and Catherine loved him. When he died in Tom's arms at nine years old, both she and Tom were devastated. After Bill came golden labrador Simon, and after he died, again in Tom's arms, they had a poodle called Sandy, who appears in *Goodbye Hamilton*. Years ago, not long after we first met, I was a bit surprised to come across a photograph of Sandy sitting with Catherine and Tom in their garden. Catherine hadn't exactly come across to me as a poodle sort of person. But Sandy was a child to them, as Bill had been. Poodles, she will tell you, are not dogs at all; they are children who never grow up. While Sandy was with them, Catherine became a patron of the Newcastle Dog Shelter and fell for another poodle, a hopelessly unkempt and rejected bitch called Sue. They took her in and spruced her up, and the dogs so took to one another that the Cookson home was never more replete with doggie love.

If the joy which these dogs gave them is a measure of Tom and Catherine's capacity for love of children then it is a sad measure too of the tragedy which denied them their own and goes some way towards helping us to understand the pain of their loss, which hastened Catherine's breakdown in the 1940s and spawned her terrible urge to harm babies, and on many an occasion sent her rushing home to vomit and fling herself on her bed to beat the urge out of herself.

Catherine's unravelling of this tortured period of her life is so honest, so absolutely public and open, that one feels those dealing with cases of involuntary shoplifting, baby-snatching and the like would do well to take note. Today a principal reason for spelling out the terrors of her nervous breakdown is the obligation she feels to her faithful readers. If even one of those millions feels, as a result, that they are not alone in their particular hell, her harrowing revelations will have been worthwhile. She may say that she has no satisfaction in writing the novels other than meeting the dictates of her urge to write, but it is for Catherine the height of success 'if in the process of writing I say something worthwhile, something that might make someone laugh or cry or think – most of all I hope it makes someone think, and often I have letters that tell me that they do . . .'

Catherine's breakdown, fraught with her loss of faith in God and precipitated by the death of her babies, was the culmination of an identity crisis which had led, with Aunt Mary's assistance, to her upstart years, to Lord Chesterfield, to hiding behind a veneer with which she felt able to face the world and hoped to rise in it.

Catherine's recovery was inextricably bound up with her writing. At the end of the 1946 she embarked on her first novel, *Kate Hannigan*, which reflects fundamental changes in her way of thinking about herself. As I have already noted, in the early novels Catherine puts humanity on the slab and wields her scalpel to cut away hypocrisy, envy, bigotry, pretension and superstition. But before she could do this she had to set about herself with similar precision.

Discarding her plays with their wooden, upper-class characters was the first cut. It was a cut into pretension, into her dear Lord Chesterfield, or at least into the veneer that covered her true self and which Catherine's reading of him had fashioned. With this cut Catherine learned the most painful lesson of her nervous breakdown – that if she was ever going to write anything worthwhile, she would have to 'strip off the pseudo-lady' and be *herself*. Her road to recovery was to be something of an existential odyssey: this cut meant that she had to come to terms with who she was, the fact that she was Kate's daughter, Kate's illegitimate daughter, the fact that she was a product of the environment which contained her drunken granda, the Pawn, the beer, the cinder tips.

At the same time, Catherine never lost sight of her alienation from the society of her birth. For whatever reason – her father, her artistic nature – she was, like Meursault, the hero of Albert Camus' classic existentialist novel *The Outsider*, 'wandering on the outskirts of life, solitary...'. This was an important creative stance for her as a writer and there never was a desire to go back to the North.

It was a creative position achieved by another writer with a good deal less searching, because he realised from the start what set him apart from his people. D.H. Lawrence left his home in Eastwood, a mining village eight miles from Nottingham, in 1910, two decades before Catherine left her working-class roots on Tyneside. A few years later he gave the following words to Ursula Brangwen in his novel *The Rainbow*: 'I have no allocated place in the world of things, I do not belong to Beldover [Eastwood] nor to Nottingham nor to England nor to this world, but they none of them exist. I am trammelled and entangled in them, but they are all unreal. I must break out of it, like a nut from its shell which is an unreality.' Like Lawrence, Catherine in 'escaping' from Tyneside was fleeing not so much from a place as from the unreality of her existence in it. She was out of place in it, and the more she tried to be accepted the more out of place she had become. Now she only truly belonged in her imagination. Her escape was from unreality into 'the channels where the intangible but real life runs'.

Her understanding of this was assisted by a complete overhaul in her spiritual life. One bad day in 1948 she threw her head back and challenged her fears head-on, sending 'to blazes and bloody damnation ... God, dogma, the Catholic Church, the Devil, hell, people, opinions, laws, illegitimacy... and fear. Bugger them all!' As she says, 'It was a brave show,' but really splitting away from the last 'thing she had to cling on to' wasn't easily effected.

Those few inexplicable moments of joy when she had known exquisite peace and creativity had been interspersed with awesome moments which brought an ecstatic but at the same time frightening insight into things, breaking them up into energies, intensities, drives, as if there were 'a power passing through and interlacing all things'. This fearful awareness has never left her. Recently she told me of an experience, which incidentally sourced two locations in *The Mallen Streak*, but which at the time reduced her to a block of fear. 'Tom must be tired of the times we have brought the car from Hexham to Langley from the "top" as we call it, and I have said that it is the most beautiful sight that I have ever seen. As you approach the dam you're on a hill and you look across and you see that you're surrounded by hills, and Langley seems to be in this valley. And all the way – everywhere you look – there are hills coming down, all the way round, coming down to this valley. Up here I know that I am in my country. This is my kind of country, not soft like the downs but rugged hills broken up into soft parts, an expanse of sheer mystery. The Tor in *Feathers in the Fire* was set just at the back here.

'But I first became afraid of hills up here when one day Tom took me across Scap Fell. We were travelling by car from Hastings to my cousins in Birtley in Durham because I had been asked again and again to give a talk to a group of Women's Institutes.

'Before, when visiting the North to seek out localities for my stories, and also to give talks, I had travelled by train, but this time, there we were in the car and Tom, as always, took the longest way round in order that we could see the beautiful scenery of Northumberland. I found myself heading for what I didn't know then was the great, great expanse of Alston moors. At different times in my life I knew when I had been any place that had a deep fall to the side I had the most strange feeling, sometimes touching on terror. But what I experienced that day went past terror. Tom drove over the hills up, up, into this space that went on for eternity. The heights and everything about it found me crouched on the floor of the car beside the seat. I was shaking with terror from head to foot. All I could gasp was, "Get out of this! Get out of this!" On and on he went, aiming to get out of it, of course, by reaching the end of it. At one time he stopped the car and said, "Look, try, try to sit up and look about you. It's the most magnificent sight."

'I couldn't answer, my heart was racing so fast. My pulse was racing so fast that it is a great wonder to me now that I didn't have a heart attack then.

' "Just lift your head," he begged, "or look through the windscreen. Just lift your head."

'I managed to raise my head from my huddled, crouched position and look through the windscreen and there I was confronted by a fly moving slowly, slowly upwards. I followed it. I followed its progress until I realised it wasn't a fly, it was a car in the far, far distance, mounting the rise, and I let out a scream and once more my head was buried.

'So on and on he drove until we ran down into some sort of a village, and he dragged me out of my cramped position and I sat on the footboard and was sick. "I'll never forgive you," I said, "for doing this to me."

'He got out the map and he said, "Well, we can't go back. We've got to go on. It isn't very far now. We've just got to go up that bank and then we'll be all right."

'We went up that bank and then I died another death because dropping straight down from the edge of the car was this great, great fall and it was studded with trees. I later used that definite part where one brother murders the other by throwing him down this hill. [Readers of *The Mallen Streak* will recognise this as the cliff where Thomas Mallen's illegitimate son, Donald, a dark, brooding character given to long silences and bursts of temper, is killed by his consumptive half-brother, Matthew.]

'All I remember next was Tom saying, "It's all right now, it's all right. We're on a flat part. There's nothing to fear at all. It's all flat." He stopped the car and I got out and again sat on the footboard. There was nothing surrounding us for miles except about twenty yards from the road there stood the wreck of an old house. I understood, after, it had once been an inn where the men driving the ponies down from Scotland to Yorkshire and Lancashire stopped and rested and had a drink. But now it only showed a broken roof, a door hanging on its hinges. The walls were standing, but the window frames and every piece of wood seemed to have been stripped from it. I stared at it and the sight of it fell into my subconscious and lay there working until I thought up the story of *The Mallen Streak* and this dirty filthy wreck of a house became the setting for the conception of a child between two of the main characters in the book [Matthew and Donald's fiancée, Constance Mallen].

'There are many characters in the book, but these two were important. They were trying to shelter from a terrible storm with their horses and it is here that they expressed their love for each other . . . I described the house, the filthy condition and their coming together, all as if I had thought it up on the day of terror on the fells of Northumberland.'

Sensitised by her nervous breakdown Catherine had become so acutely aware that it was almost inevitable, given her obsessive propensity for action, for doing, that if she could draw on this power, which she perceived interlacing people as well as things, it would transform her writing. Years later she described it to me, using a kind of imagery which comes from a dream she had at this creative time of flying up a telegraph pole, looking along the conductor wires and flying to the next before sliding back down.

'There can be no God in the way religions describe, but there is a power out there. There is something. I myself have touched that something. Call it spirit or soul or what have you; it might be only a means of electricity ... I have for some time looked upon it as a great cable of electric wires that run round the world and through us, and you can tap your own wire, you can plug into it ...'

When she and Tom moved to their second home, Loreto, they found themselves with a bit of woodland. When taking a break from her writing, Catherine would sometimes walk in among the trees. She knew that if she stopped and leant for a moment against the big bole of an oak she would feel her tensions slipping away into it. Putting this together with her description of the spirit in things, I was reminded of D.H. Lawrence's description of the same power, which appears in *Fantasia and the Unconscious*: 'I come so well to understand tree-worship,' he wrote. 'All the old Aryans worshipped the tree. My ancestors. The tree of life. The tree of knowledge ... This marvellous vast individual without a face, without lips or eyes or heart ... Here am I between his toes like a pea-bug, and him noiselessly over-reaching me, and I feel this great blood-jet surging. And he has no eyes. But he turns two ways: he thrusts himself tremendously down to the middle earth, where dead men sink in darkness, in the damp, dense undersoil; and he turns himself about in high air ... A huge, plunging, tremendous *soul* ...'

In *Sons and Lovers*, Lawrence refers to the same magnificent power when Paul Morel, who represents Lawrence himself, is lying on the ground next to Clara Dawes, a married woman with whom he is having an affair. The grass stems close to their eyes are 'curving and strong with life in the dark'. It is in the grass, it is in the peewit calling, it is in the warmth of Clara's breathing and in her eyes – 'life *wild at the source* staring into his life, stranger to him, yet meeting him'. Recognising this makes Paul afraid, as it did Catherine, but there is also a kind of satisfaction. It gave them 'rest within themselves... to know their own nothingness, to know the tremendous living flood which carried them always'.

The second time Catherine became aware of the creative potential of this force was when she was faced by her publishers with rejection following publication of her first novel in 1950: 'I was already practically through the sequel, *Annie Hannigan*. This, in my opinion, was even better than *Kate Hannigan*. But I got a letter from Murray Thompson [her publisher] to say that they would take this book but it wasn't as good, in their opinion, as the first. They would do what they could with it. That inflamed me, those words. I know now why there were doubts about it because I was still expressing my feelings about the Catholic Church. What was more, I was also going into the mind of a young man, thinking about his sex life and arising thoughts concerning it. Hearing it now, his thoughts were quite poetic, but Mr Thompson must have thought they were a bit way out. That is the only thing that I can think made him question the book.

'Anyway, I remember crying my eyes out and getting on the phone and saying, "I won't have it accepted on those conditions. Send it back!" I think it was one of the bravest things an author has ever done, specially when starting out as ignorant as I was of how difficult it was to get a book published. I can see myself coming out of the little cubbyhole under the stairs where the phone was and going into the drawing room. I was terribly upset, not only that I was not going to let them publish the book, but I knew that I hadn't another story in my mind. There was me, who was never without an idea, never without a story to tell to someone, yet my mind was utterly blank. I thought I was finished. I sat in the cold, icy drawing room. I remember Tom had just gone to school. There was no one to talk to. I tried to think of what I would do next, but my mind was an utter blank. Never before that, and definitely never since, has my mind known such a void. I felt I had nothing more to say, I had nothing more to talk about. I had no more tales to tell. And then I became angry inside. Why, why, now that I had written those two books, was I empty of an idea for a story – or for anything else, for that matter?

'Why I did next what I did, I will never know. But quite suddenly, and this might sound quite sentimental and dramatic, I threw my head back and looked up at the ceiling – don't forget that at this point I had rejected God, oh, definitely. God with the Catholic Church had been thrown out of the window. And I'd said so openly. I had yelled at God that I was finished with belief in the great fable that his followers had established and I would fear no more – brave words when I was full of fear about everything . . . . Anyway, as I said, I threw my head back and looked up at the ceiling and cried aloud, "If there's anything there, give me a story!" Now, was there anything more sentimental or highly dramatic than that? . . . and stupid!

'Believe this or not, I sat back in the chair and there came to me, within the following hour when I was almost frozen stiff with cold, the whole story of *The Fifteen Streets*, right from the opening to the very last words. Every character, every incident and definitely the background. It was all there. I won't say I couldn't believe it. I just accepted it. I knew here was a complete story and I must get it down straight away. I went from there into the dining room, where I usually did my writing on the table, and with my frozen fingers I wrote the title, "The Fifteen Streets". From that moment until months later when I finished that story, I can say with truth I never altered a character, an incident, or anything else in the whole plan. I worked on it practically night and day. I worked on it through bleedings and flu and desperate tiredness, but I got everything down as it had been given to me when I asked for it on that particular morning.

'Strange to say, that book is alive today and has started the career of many actors. This very week it has been performed in a little village hall, one of many village halls that has produced it as a play. I had to smile when one day I received a cheque for one pound two and something which was the profit from a show of *The Fifteen Streets*.

'Well, that mightn't have been a miracle, but it came from somewhere, from some spirit deep within me, that is below the subconscious. Perhaps it was the first time that I recognised that I had a spirit that was an individual thing, not connected with any doctrine. It came from somewhere, but certainly not from the religious picture of the Omnipotent.

'I do believe that this same spirit is in every one of us; it is how we use it that matters. But you have to be able to recognise it first.'

Camus writes in an afterword to *The Outsider* that his hero 'is driven by a tenacious and therefore profound passion, the passion for an absolute and for truth . . . a truth born of living and feeling, but without which no triumph over self or over the world will ever be possible.' Back at The Hurst in the 1940s, still struggling to write anything worthwhile, Catherine had come to the same uncompromising conclusion. But it wasn't only the veneer of the 'pseudo-lady' and the pretentious superficiality of the characters in her plays which she felt bound to change. She knew that she couldn't write as well as the poets to whom Miss Barrington had introduced her and she feared that she would never make a living from writing because of what she calls her syntactical naivety. Deep down she feared that although she could appreciate the beauty of words she didn't have the education to organise them in the syntactical framework which she thought would broadcast their sense.

As far as the mechanics of language were concerned she saw Tom as everything she wasn't. His scholarship in Latin and Mathematics gave him a scientific, analytical approach. He could describe the job done by commas, colons, semi-colons, verbs, adjectives and adverbs, and he knew the grammatical rules which were a mystery to her. So it was that she would 'tell Tom the story in order to set it in my mind. I would then put it down in longhand, then reassess and correct it, after which he would go over it.' It was a reasonable idea, but it produced 'grammatically correct sentences, which made my characters gutless . . . And I fought him. Oh yes, I fought him to do the thing in my own way because I knew my way was right.'

One can't help but feel sorry for Tom in these battles he was made to fight, but eventually he saw how important it was for him to lose them. It was all part of the loosening of the bonds, a further freeing of the creative channels. It was crucial to the flow, sometimes torrent, of Catherine's imagination that her characters didn't have to leap barriers of stilted English. If she had deserted what linguistically was bred in the bone she would have been as lost as a writer as if she had deserted her people.

More than a century earlier, the Northamptonshire poet and day-labourer John Clare had expressed a similar linguistic unease, and in his best work had discarded even punctuation, which he called 'that awkward squad of pointings'. It had an extraordinary effect, giving his melancholic descriptions of rural childhood loss a poetic quality, and is one of the secrets of their power and truth. For Catherine, freedom from linguistic analysis helped facilitate an intuitive contact with the creative power in her, of which she was increasingly aware.

Later, after writing the first fifteen or sixteen of her novels in longhand, she developed 'writer's cramp and a frozen shoulder, and thought my writing days were over'. Tom suggested a way out, which would give her further release from the mechanics of writing. 'It was then I resorted to a tape recorder, which I have used ever since.' Catherine cannot recall which was the first novel to be written in this way, only that *Katie Mulholland* (1967) was definitely spoken, not written down. Tom had led her back to the tradition of oral storytelling which Catherine had been part of as a child at number 10, when Rose would tell her stories which led her back nearer to the roots of her culture, back before 1850, stories which Rose herself had heard at her mother's knee. 'I didn't know then what a new world was opening up for me, because while talking my northern characters down I could see them acting . . .' Even today she sits in bed with the characters of her latest novel all around her being themselves in the environment in which she has cast them. When recently I marvelled at the process, she said that it was all very well but a bit difficult when they started to make love to one another.

Writing the short stories about the girl from the North who had no da helped Catherine see that she had been 'over-sorry' for herself, made her realise that the bitterness she felt about her early life had constricted her creativity. Now, with a clearer sense of her own identity, her people had begun to come into clearer focus – 'There was a mass of people crowding my mind that I knew inside out. These were the people I had moved away from, to put it plainly, didn't want any truck with. Yet there they were, dozens of them, hundreds of them, their characteristics shouting at me' – and she began to see her people for what they really were: 'the fact that work was their life's blood; their patience in the face of poverty; their perseverance that gave them the will to hang on'. She acknowledged 'their kindness and open-handedness' as well as 'their narrowness and bigotry . . . And the women. Stoics would be a better name to give to the females of that time, my early time, because for most of them along those river banks it was grind in one way or another from Monday morning till Sunday night.'

From this new, more balanced perspective came fresh insight. She began to see that her people's strength, like hers, was born of suffering, that warmth arose out of the cold hunger of their needs, humour out of the dreariness of their existence, that love blossomed from their seedbed of pain, that a deep-down sensitivity was a facet of their vulnerability to brutal experience and drew them together. A balance of pathos and humour, the antithetical form of her collection of stories, which years later became the Mary Ann series of novels, was intuited out of the same perception of the way the world worked. The first story, 'She Had No Da', won a standing ovation when Catherine read it at the Hastings Writers' Circle. But it was her first novel, *Kate Hannigan*, begun at the end of 1946, which represented the deeper cut.

Kate Hannigan is a triumph of compassion over bitterness on Catherine's road to recovery because Kate Hannigan herself, who is above all a sympathetic character, was inspired by a side of Catherine's mother – a deep-down element which she had first intuited as a little girl of six whirling around a lamppost on a rope in William Black Street, but an element buried ever since under a welter of hate. Catherine may not have forgiven Kate, but she had begun to understand her. *Kate Hannigan* represents Catherine's first literary contact with something fundamental in the make-up of her mother's character, a facet of her spirit which inspired Kate Hannigan and many other of her characters too.

Catherine's female characters 'are strong, they always come through,' but there is much more to them than that. There is a sensuality and womanliness and a generic potential which puts them in charge of her fictional world. Something of this potential has to do with fertility – mammiferous womankind, like Kathie McQueen, with her 'huge breasts', or the buxom Fanny McBride. In *Colour Blind* the young cripple Tony marvels at the 'great cones of flesh hanging out from open blouses as the women sat on their front doorsteps suckling their babies'. In Catherine's fictional world, fruitful, fertile, intuitive women coexist with physically tough, sometimes impotent men whose work is largely uninspirational. The few male artists who do appear are either exploiting dark images of Tyneside for their own gain or drawing on women in some way, usually emotionally. The women, on the other hand, are weavers of the emotional web of life, in touch with its source and not dependent on men in the same way. In the majority of the novels we have a clear sense of men's dependency on women, of the fact that, despite the male, macho myth of the North, the women are in control. Ego is a male problem, a form of hypocrisy which dulls intuition, twists and obscures truth, and is an expression of impotence. Clergyman Donald Rouse's behaviour in *The Garment* is a study in this.

At the root of his wife Grace's emotional problems, which drive her to a nervous breakdown, is Donald's ego. It dominates her life. First, it prevents him admitting to Grace that he is sexually impotent (his name – Rouse – is wonderfully ironic), his weird interpretation of sex carrying bogus religious connotations which keep intercourse at bay. Then it allows him to convince himself that he has achieved acts of union sufficient to explain the appearance of his wife's first two children (by farm worker Andrew MacIntyre, into whose arms Donald's ego has driven her). Finally, on the third occasion that Grace is made pregnant by MacIntyre, when there appears to be no possible excuse for Donald's deceiving himself into believing he is the child's father, Grace revels momentarily in the infusion of honesty and truth into the scene. But even then Donald manages to cast a pall of deceit over their lives, this time from the pulpit. Truth in the novel is confined within the terrors of Grace's breakdown, shut away from the world as she herself is when the asylum gates close upon her.

Catherine has written of the potential in a relationship between a strong woman and a man who is prepared to set himself free of his ego. But she is not a feminist. 'I do not agree with the way the movement tries to denigrate men, to take their manliness away,' she once told me; she likes working with men, though she won't have male bosses. Nor does she glorify women. In *Bill Bailey* (1986) we read that 'men can be vile and cruel but they don't create as much harm as women who are sweet and poisonous', and Bailey's down-to-earth personality and chipper sense of humour overcome cold, ruthless Eva Brown (it takes a careful reading of the novel to connect her name with appropriate Hitleresque images as it is never spelt out in full, both names together, and the surname is only mentioned once). Again, in *A Dinner of Herbs*, Kate Makepeace tells us that all females are bloodthirsty: 'It is as old as the hills . . . where the female of the animals are concerned, they are more fierce than the male. It's the protective instinct in them, I think.'

We see this protective instinct in *The Invisible Cord* (1975). Molly McCabe is a splendidly ebullient character in the mould of Fanny McBride. Her dim son, Georgie, makes seventeen-year-old Annie Cooper pregnant. Their offspring, Terence (known as Rance), kills his own father brutally and becomes involved in pushing drugs. But motherly instinct – the 'invisible cord' which joins Annie to Rance – prevents her from turning him in. Again, in *Fenwick Houses* there is a sense of the aberrant potential of the instinctual, mythic Tyneside mother figure in Phyllis Dowling's suckling of her son, Don, another psychopath, long after he is able to feed himself.

The powerful feminine principle encompassing love and hate, compassion and cruelty, fruitfulness and destruction, on which Catherine draws for women characters as diverse as Fanny McBride, Mary Walton (in *Pure as the Lily*) and Mary's mother, Alice, who, you will recall, brings about the disfigurement of her daughter's lover, the burning alive of her daughter-in-law and the early death through drinking of her son, can be found crystallized in the poet Robert Graves's grammar of poetic myth, *The White Goddess*. His Goddess is the ultimate creative and procreative force, embodying all things and their opposites in the name of truth – kindness and cruelty, beauty and terror, life and death – both sides of Mother Nature, and a rather different concept from the male Christian God, who is all-good and, as a statement of Nature, required the Devil for completeness.

Graves presents the Goddess as the feminine principle which inspires the true Muse poet. As an object of worship, he traces her back to a Sumerian matriarchal civilisation around 8,000 BC, when the idea of a procreative *male* divinity was patently absurd. She occurs in ancient myth under many guises, but her fundamental association is with the goddess Ariadne, the daughter (or younger self) of the ancient Cretan moon goddess, Pasiphae – which brings us back to Kate Fawcett and those strange moments of imaginative release, moon-riding with her daughter along the Slack bank, and the 'primitive weirdness' which Catherine associated with her mother as a child, when suddenly Kate and her friends would dress up in men's clothes and dance crazily through the streets.

Three novels in which Catherine uses the moon as a symbol of imaginative or creative or supernatural power, two of them explicitly connecting it with artistic inspiration, are

The Whip, The Moth and *A Dinner of Herbs*. In *The Whip* Emma Molinero's artistry with whips and knives has its roots in the supernatural. She has a penchant for making night sorties to practise her art, and one night, while throwing her knives against an oak tree in the cold, silver light of a full moon, her special communion with her muse is disturbed by Peggy McFarlane and her illicit lover, a farmer called Hudson. Peggy rises out of the shadows screaming, and it is weird, 'unearthly . . . like someone coming out of the grave'. Peggy describes Emma as a devil with horns and black from head to toe, and claims that her devil's dagger just missed her heart. The scene ends in chaos with the clouds closing over the moon.

Throughout this novel Emma is persecuted, as Catherine was, by the 'something' that set her apart from her playmates and which marks her out as an artist. In her disturbing world of sexual repression and sadistic violence, Emma dictates messages to the subconscious drives of the other characters, arousing envy and resulting in her own exploitation. On the farm she is worked like a horse and her oppressors seem to want to break her spirit as if it were the free spirit of a wild horse, to make her one of them. They try to dominate her, abuse her, even whip her as they would a horse, this creature with a sixth, intuitive sense.

The horse is another symbol of creative inspiration. Hamilton is the name Maisie Carter gives to the horse which appears in her imagination in the novel of the same name, and which later inspires her to write novels. It first appears to Maisie after her mother's violent attack on her, mentioned earlier. It is a black horse with a richly flowing name and a shiny coat like a seal's; it carries a white spot on its nose and has white feet. Catherine had come into contact with horses nearly half a century before the novel was published. Around the time she was taking fencing lessons she had also taken to visiting a stables four or five miles out of Hastings, near Rye. Initially she had run into a bit of trouble with her riding kit. She had answered an advertisement offering for sale a pair of second-hand riding boots. They turned out to be a size too small, but she managed to squeeze her feet into them. When she sent her measurements to a tailor's to make up her riding breeches, they came back many sizes too large. Eventually she sorted it all out and she and her horse came together. She began to enjoy their walks along the cliffs, only one section of the course causing any difficulty. On the way home, horse and rider had to negotiate a gap in a hedge so narrow that Catherine had to take her feet out of the stirrups. Once through the gap, there was a steep descent to the stables, and Catherine would feel the horse tremble in anticipation of the canter home. On one occasion she dared to ride bareback. Horse and rider were as one until Catherine attempted to dismount, threw the wrong leg over the horse's back, over-balanced and fell backwards into a trough of silage.

If you accept that the horse is a symbol of creative potential – which it certainly is for Maisie and elsewhere in literature, myth and psychoanalysis, where it symbolises the 'voice of nature' with which artists, healers and gurus make contact and which rational man has tried to dominate and exploit throughout history – then there are some wonderful allusions to Catherine's struggles to find intuitive contact with her Muse in this story of her relationship with her horse. The horse also brings us back to the moon, because the original horse goddess, Rhiannon, who 'becomes horse' in one of the legendary stories of the *Mabinogion*, and is the forerunner in myth of the Roman horse goddess Epona, is but another 'self' of the inspirational moon goddess.

The Moth (1986) is, to my mind, Catherine's best novel in her later period of writing. Readers, or viewers of its recent television adaptation, will recall that twenty-four-year-old

Robert Bradley, on his first Sunday in the rural hamlet of Lamesley, trespasses on to the Thorman estate near Foreshaw House. It is already dark when he comes upon the estate and sees how wild and run-down it has become. But then a shaft of moonlight catches his eye and lures him in beyond the dilapidated boundary fencing. Once inside, he comes to a lake, and the sublimity of the scene – the still water, the clear night sky and the moon riding high, shining deep into the water – holds him spellbound. He is about to leave when he is suddenly surprised by what looks like a large moth apparently floating towards him through the air from a belt of trees. Mingled with Robert's feeling of wonder is fear, and even as the form is illuminated he remains uncertain whether it is human. Not until the creature comes close does he notice that it is propelled forward by feet and that its supposed wings are the folds of a cape held outwards by human arms.

The hooded figure, a girl, is unutterably impressive. Besides her femininity (dark sweeping eyelashes, oval eyes, pale skin and full but thin-lipped mouth) he senses a strange ethereal quality which defies analysis and possesses him completely. The vision speaks. For a moment he is awed, but she puts him at his ease and he learns that she has a sister called Agnes and that her parents own Foreshaw House. The contrast between Robert's earlier supernatural apprehension and the mundanity of this exchange of information brings to his mind the possibility that the girl (she tells him her name is Millie) is touched in the head. Later we learn that Millie's great-aunt was in and out of asylums. In *The Whip* there is this same connection between artistic inspiration and madness – moon-struck Emma is worried that if she is caught throwing her knives she will be tied up in chains and thrown into the madhouse. And we have already seen how Catherine's breakdown influenced her imaginative perceptions. However, Millie is not mad. She has come out of the little house of her imagination for a while, and because Robert has never found the way into his, it troubles him.

Millie talks to Robert of her love for the moon, and as she does so it disappears from view, leaving only its reflection in the lake, apparently unsourced. She gives the moon mythic status: it has the power of alchemy. He finds what she says strange but at the same time alluringly beautiful. Then she makes physical contact with him: she takes his hand. He finds himself shaking, but she chats to him so normally that he doesn't draw back. She even reassures him that she isn't mad. She is there because the moon is there; when the moon comes out she comes out too. Millie has him in the palm of her hand. It is a masterly performance.

It is Millie, of course, who will draw Robert to his destiny, luring him to work at Foreshaw and inspiring him as he learns to transcend the barriers of the class system of maids and mistresses, manservants and masters, which characterised Edwardian England. Catherine's mainstream themes, explored in the early novels, are all here. But what is new is contained in the dreamlike sequence which introduces Robert to Foreshaw Park and his life's destiny, and is Catherine's recognition, symbolically in the image of the moon, of the power which guides her.

The fourth novel to suggest a supernatural element in what drives Catherine to write, and one which at the same time presents the writer as transformer of the cruel side of her 'goddess inspiration', is *A Dinner of Herbs*, again one of her more recent novels. The title comes from Proverbs xv, 17: 'Better is a dinner of herbs where love is, than a stalled ox and hatred therewith.' *A Dinner of Herbs* is a *tour de force*. In more than 250,000 words, characters and generations come and go, but pace and interest never flag. Throughout, the hatred which clawed Catherine down into the depths of breakdown simmers beneath the surface. It is part of the

The Girl from Leam Lane

landscape of her characters' lives, occasionally erupting in terrible violence. At the centre of the novel is Kate Makepeace, one of a long line of herbalists. Thickset, of medium height, with dark wisps of hair and wrinkled skin, Kate is in her late sixties when the novel opens, but strong of character and wise of mind, a kind of personification of the land in which she dwells – hard, unyielding Northumberland lead-mining country, but 'knowing' of all things which have marked it since creation.

Roddy Greenbank is brought to Kate by his father, Peter, whose wife has died. Kate agrees to keep an eye on him and 'tell him the paths that lead straight in his mind, and where health is to be got from the ground'. Kate becomes a touchstone in the lives of Roddy, his friend Mary Ellen, and a boy called Hal, whose father, Roystan, stands accused of robbery and who is, with Peter, first to suffer at the hands of the Bannamans, for whom hatred will be seen to be an inherited trait.

We first meet Kate as she emerges from the shadows, a witch-like creature, strange, magical. Peter tells us that Kate 'was always a good one with the moon', and he and Roddy watch as the moon comes out from behind the 'black skirts' of the clouds and washes itself in the water. Peter, who once lived and worked here, has watched the moon 'riding alongside us many a night, skipping over the waves'. Later, smelters say that it is as well to keep on the right side of Kate or you'll likely get boils on your neck. Jed Pierce, who chases five-year-old Mary Ellen, develops a huge carbuncle on his backside after a warning from Kate that if he continues to harass her he'll not be able to sit down. 'She had powers . . . it was well to keep in with witches.' This is the classic image of the witch which we all hold in our subconscious and which, in legend, is embodied in Cerridwen, the creature who, according to a recipe contained in the twelfth-century romance *The Vergil of Toledo*, boils up a cauldron of inspiration and knowledge and leaves it to simmer for a year and a day, adding to it magical herbs gathered at the correct planetary hours. She makes a boy – Gwion – stir the brew and one day three drops fly out and land on Gwion's finger. At once he understands the nature and meaning of all things past, present and future. Realising what has happened, the witch Cerridwen pursues Gwion, translating herself from screaming hag first into a greyhound, then an otter, a hawk and finally a black hen.

As *A Dinner of Herbs* gets under way, however, we see fewer intimations of the witch in Kate and the Earth Mother comes to the fore. She becomes all-love, in touch with bountiful, healing Nature, and Mary Ellen, Roddy and Hal all derive their strength from her, its purpose to transform the destructive hatred of the Bannamans. Associations with both sides of Catherine's awesome inspiration, and her resolving role as a writer, are clear.

One special moment with Kate Fawcett, which I have left until now to describe because of its relevance to the character, as well as the source, of Catherine's inspiration, concerns Kate's favourite song, 'Thora'. This song, you will recall, was her 'party piece', enacted at family gatherings at number 10. Aunt Mary and Uncle Alec would be there, 'Mary at her disdainful best'. Also there would be Kate's Aunt Maggie Hindes and her son Jimmy. Catherine would die with shame and disgust as her drunken mother strained to hit the top notes, 'her head well back, that slack lower lip of hers wobbling'.

But one day she and Kate were sitting silently in the kitchen, working on a clippy mat on a weaving frame which stood between them, and in a very soft, quiet voice, the firelight playing on her face, Kate began a rendering of 'Thora' which had an utterly different effect upon her daughter. 'The song, like Kate, was beautiful that day,' and it brought tears to Catherine's eyes. 'I wonder now,' Catherine says, 'whether her "Thora" was speaking out about her kind of pain.' On this occasion Kate was not drunk, nor was she playing to an audience; she was sharing with her daughter a vision of her promised land. The song is worth printing in full in order to appreciate what that meant:

> *I stand in a land of roses,*
> *But I dream of a land of snow,*
> *Where you and I were happy*
> *In years of long ago.*
> *Nightingales in the branches,*
> *Stars in the magic skies,*
> *But I only hear you singing,*
> *I only see your eyes.*
> *I only hear you singing,*
> *I only see your eyes.*
> *Come, come! Come! to me Thora,*
> *Come once again and be*
> *Child of my dreams,*
> *Light of my life,*
> *Angel of love to me—*
>
> *I stand again in the Northland*
> *But in silence and in shame.*
> *Your grave is my only landmark*
> *And men have forgotten my name.*
> *'Tis a tale that is pure and older*
> *Than any the sages tell.*
> *I loved you in life too little,*
> *I love you in death too well.*
> *Speak, speak, speak to me Thora,*
> *Speak from your heaven to me.*

Child of my dreams,
Love of my life,
Hope of my world to be!

'Thora' is one of the songs Catherine sings on the tape which, as I have already mentioned, was issued towards the end of 1996. It is sung from the heart, with power and with an inconsolable longing, as if she would be at one with her mother in her mythic snow-covered land of the North, with its stars and magic skies.

I had read the lyrics before, but I did not know the tune and it was only when Catherine insisted I order a copy of the recording and I heard it sung in that pressing, urgent way of hers that its significance dawned. Immediately I was reminded of a book I had read years before, *Surprised By Joy* by C.S. Lewis. What came to mind was Lewis's description of a particular 'moment of joy' in his childhood. Coincidentally, he, like Catherine, was a fan of Longfellow, and it was while Lewis was idly turning the pages of Longfellow's 'Saga of King Olaf' that he came across his translation of a poem by the nineteenth-century Swedish poet Esaias Tegner, which seemed to the boy to encapsulate the strange spirit of Northernness which the heroic saga was all about.

'Instantly I was uplifted into huge regions of Northern sky,' Lewis wrote. 'I desired with almost sickening intensity something never to be described.' Years later, when he saw one of Arthur Rackham's illustrations in *Siegfried and the Twilight of the Gods*, Lewis recalled 'the stab, the pang' of pleasure-pain that the moment gave him. 'Pure "Northernness" engulfed me,' he wrote, 'a vision of huge, clear spaces hanging above the Atlantic in the endless twilight of Northern summer, remoteness, severity.'

His joy is awe-inspiring, and the poetic image which

inspired his strange pleasure-pain (so similar, I felt, to that implicit in Catherine's rendering of Kate's song, which had cried out her mother's pain and longing) is the very same which all-knowing Gwion gives us of a distant land where countless souls await resurrection in the Fifth Age of the World when Christ will release them. It is an image of the magical, snow-covered grounds of the remote Castle of Arianrhod in the Corona Borealis, a constellation in the northern skies, and the stronghold, no less, of Robert Graves's Moon Goddess of poetic inspiration.

This heroic and yet tragic image of Northernness, yearning for resurrection, seems to encapsulate that element in Northern culture 'that comes from far back and threads the people of this particular area', which Catherine unearths in her novels. She feels it in the voices and emotions of her characters as they speak to her, but it is rooted in Kate, who embodies both the cruel and beautiful aspects of the powerful feminine principle which inspires Catherine's work. It was essential that Catherine was able to come to terms with being part of her mother. She had no need to look for the ground-swell of character in myth and weave it into her novels. Once she had acknowledged her true identity and her creative channels were freed, she had a direct line to it through kinship with Kate, the woman who, as Catherine confirms in the dedication to her first novel, 'found her expression through me'.

A trip Catherine made to the North in 1952 is worth relating because it gave her unexpected contact with this heroic, tragic spirit of a people awaiting transformation. She was visiting her coal-mining cousins in Birtley and had upset them with remarks about the price of coal in the South. Her granda, quick to dismiss anyone else's achievement, had always scorned miners. He 'used to say that all pitmen hewed more coal at the corner end, or at their games of quoits, and pitch and toss, than they ever did down the mine,' and tongue-in-cheek she had taken his part. 'The result of our verbal battle was that they challenged me to go down the mine.' Terrified at the prospect, she was led to the coalface by Cousin Peter, who was a deputy at the Betty pit in Birtley.

In *Maggie Rowan* she gives her experience to Ann Rowan, who is challenged by sister Maggie to go down the pit and face up to her fear for husband David Taggart's safety, and also because Maggie hates her sister, who 'hasn't the guts of a chicken'. Like old John, Maggie thinks of all pitmen with scorn, 'as bigoted, ignorant clods, hewing more coal at the corner ends, in the bars or on the allotments than they did down the pit'. Restless and bitter, plain girl Maggie Rowan is a reject. No one believes that she could have normal desires. She is starved of love. But her unattractiveness clouds the real issue, which has to do with confusion over her identity. She knows she is different, but until she learns that she is not Nellie Rowan's daughter she can't begin to understand why. So she hits back at her people, rejecting their bovine existence, their stupid and coarse boisterousness and humour, while all the time putting her earnings carefully away, waiting for the day she can be shot of the lot of them and get herself a place on Brampton Hill, where the lights shine like stars in the sky. The relevant issue here is not just Maggie's identity but that of the mining community. The pit is the Underworld of myth, 'the darkness and silence of the eternity of the damned'.

Catherine is down there for three hours with the miners, and when she emerges she embraces the daylight and feels ready to pin a medal on every man jack of them. For her, as for Ann, the experience has been nerve-wracking, but it has brought revelation too. Like Maggie, whose experience informs her that 'the pit is like me in some ways, or I'm like it, deep and dark, always clutching at something to lighten the darkness,' Catherine is inspired by her experience to write a novel which apprehends 'the deep, black source from whence all these little contents of lives are drawn'. The phrase is D.H. Lawrence's, but it might as well have been Catherine's.

There are many reasons why the perception of Catherine's work as romance (often by people who have read little or none of it), is ridiculous – for example, the richness of her narrative, the issues involved in it and the characters who drive it. But it is this inspirational contact with the very essence of environment and character which lifts her work out of any category, romance included, and is the fundamental secret of her mass popularity.

The cold violence and cruelty in many of her novels are an essential part of this vision and we should not be surprised or shocked at Catherine's honest but apparently damning claim (which is made in all seriousness) that she is capable of doing absolutely anything that she gives her characters to do. Once, when her mother was staying at The Hurst, she considered having Tom tie her to the bed for fear that she would not be able to restrain herself from walking across the landing in the night and murdering Kate while she slept. Catherine is part of what inspires her, as well as its instrument – a fact which has an unsettling effect even on her husband when she is writing. 'I have to shake my head when I watch her working,' Tom has written, 'the words just come out of her mouth . . . you watch this gift materialise.'

Like the poet John Clare, her inspiration is food and drink to her, but it is not an easy relationship. Clare himself had dreams about his goddess, his 'guardian spirit' as he called her, a 'soul-searching beauty . . . a woman deity [who] gave the sublimist conceptions of beauty to my imagination', identifying her with his lost childhood love, Mary Joyce, his 'simple Enchantress', 'my witching love', 'the Muse of every song I write'. But when his goddess inspiration showed Clare her other side, of cold violence and cruelty, which he describes in his poem, 'The Nightmare' – 'Huge circles lost to eyes, and rotten hulls/Raised with dread groans from the dread "place of skulls" ' – he couldn't assimilate it and began his descent into insanity, never to recover. Catherine made her recovery from a similar descent and the richness of her work is living proof both of that descent and of her return.

It isn't easy being at the beck and call of this inspirational drive, and there have been times when she longed for relief from it. During a particularly desperate period she too had a dream. She had been bleeding badly and had reached rock bottom, and made the decision to give up writing – 'I went to this place,' she told me a decade ago, 'I went to this place and I said to whatever was there that I am tired and that I just want to let go. But as I said it I thought, Why do I ask? Because I knew that I would not get the answer that I want, and this voice said to me, "You are going against your nature. All right, if you give up, you'll give up and you'll go, you'll go very quickly, because it isn't your nature to give up . . ." And this voice went for me, it said, "Tomorrow morning get out of this bed. No matter what you feel like, get out of this bed. Start checking what you have written, get on to that tape."

'And I said, "But I'm too ill to get up."

'And this voice said, "We know how ill you are, but you tell Tom of your decision."

' "But I haven't made a decision," I said.

' "But you have . . ."

'And this went on for an hour.

'The next morning I told Tom exactly what had happened. I told him the exact words because it was still so fresh . . . I could hardly stand on my feet, but I got up and I stayed up for half a day, and when I got back into bed – I always have my tape recorder beside me, but it had been three months since I had finished that part of the story and I had forgotten where I was – and I mumbled into this thing, "Sarah, I'm not sure where I was in this story, but start a new chapter. I know what has to happen. Start a new chapter." And from then it went on . . .'

I once felt bold enough to ask Catherine whether her understanding of the intuitional side of women, as well as her propensity for creating powerful, sensuous female characters, had ever laid her open to lesbian advances. Her reply made me ashamed at my tentativeness. She is so open and honest that no courage is required to ask her anything.

'I have had more trouble with women than with men,' she replied, 'and goodness knows I've had enough trouble with them.' She told me of a secretary long ago, and of the French lodger at The Hurst who had a 'pash' on her and who, after the incident of Kate's mousetrap pie, invited Catherine to France, all expenses paid. I believe it was the only time that Catherine ever set foot abroad, and she couldn't get home quickly enough. Then there were her matrons at the laundry. 'Women seemed to cling to me.' All her matrons had a habit of doing this – she thinks they wanted to mother her, wanted simultaneously to maintain their authority over Catherine and draw on her, rather like some mothers draw on their sons.

It seems they didn't know Catherine very well. Perhaps they sensed that she is a source-figure, a kind of well into which they presumed they could drop their metaphorical bucket. And they were right. She is an inspirational, even spiritual, source, of which love is an integral part, and on which people have drawn since the day she was born. But she is also fiercely independent, and they would be wrong to presume their right to draw on her at will. Indeed, if they did so presume, they might discover things about themselves they would rather not learn.

Life for Catherine is a complex business, and sex is but one way in which the power which interlaces all things may be used – one which transforms little. She is blessed with talents, but has had to fight to release them in herself. Some have derived relief from Catherine's works, but this wasn't what drove her to write; it was relief given almost in spite of herself, for she couldn't but write – it passed as it were through the hem of a garment she never asked or even always wanted to wear. 'When I was returning from France, I was so thankful to be going home that I lay back in the carriage and closed my eyes. Suddenly I felt a hand on my knee. I thought, Oh no!' She had just escaped the unwanted attentions of her French lady and now she was on her way home, sitting in the railway carriage, minding her own business, and there was a hand on her knee. Catherine opened her eyes to see a woman, a stranger, leaning towards her. The woman said, 'You know, you could be a healer.' That was all Catherine needed. She stood up, grabbed her bag and travelled the whole way home standing in the corridor of the train.

Catherine told me about this incident after I had put it to her that her skill as a storyteller was in resolving the fractured lives of her characters. She then told me that on a handful of occasions she had proven that strange woman right, 'but I was afraid of it'. There were instances at home with Tom. He had had a pain in his hand. 'He couldn't play the piano, he had tried all kinds of things, but nothing worked.' She had taken Tom's hand into hers and then placed her other hand upon it. Her fingers had moved over it, not consciously in any particular way. She had done it because she remembered that years before her cat had been in pain and she had done something similar, and the animal had seemed to recover. She had drawn no conclusions whatever from this, but, when all else failed, had slipped into doing the same with Tom without thinking, and it had worked. She found,

223

too, that she had the ability to put Tom to sleep for hours when he was suffering a migraine. Then one night, when she and Tom were living near Hexham, Catherine's solicitor and his wife had a breakdown in their car. The wife was brought to their house in a terrible state, while the solicitor waited by the road for the AA to arrive. Somehow Catherine got the woman under control and, using the same technique she had used on Tom, put her to sleep on the sofa. Hours later, when the solicitor returned, he couldn't wake his wife up. No one could. For some time all attempts failed. Catherine decided never to try such a thing again.

CHAPTER NINE

⚭⚭⚭

Resolution

The period between Catherine's return to The Hurst in 1945, following her discharge after six weeks from St Mary's psychiatric hospital in Burghill, and the end of 1946, when she embarked upon *Kate Hannigan*, was of inestimable importance. In this period she performed the painful psychological surgery which enabled her to go to work on the environment in which her characters subsist and act out their dramas.

However, although it would be a neat conclusion to say that writing *Kate Hannigan* quelled her mental anguish, it did not. Catherine became herself when writing. But not until the early 1960s, after her first twelve novels had been published and the first two films of her work had been released, did she begin to feel more than intermittent relief mentally outside the safe house in which she worked. Nevertheless, what it took to clear the way for *Kate Hannigan* – which amounted to a complete return to self, a dependence on nothing and no one other than herself, and the spiritual/inspirational release which attended this – was the first step along the path to that recovery.

More important to her recovery initially were a series of broadcasts which she gave on BBC Radio's *Woman's Hour*, the first two of which took place before publication of *Kate Hannigan*. Off her own bat she contacted the programme and suggested a first broadcast about learning to draw. This went out in 1949, the same year that Macdonald accepted her manuscript, and it was so successful that it was followed by three others, in 1950, 1951 and 1952, a series of programmes during which she 'came out' about her breakdown and was astonished at the audience feedback she received.

The placing of *Kate Hannigan* with Macdonald, her first publisher, was a speedy and straightforward affair and was occasioned indirectly by her attendance at a lecture at the local library, a talk on how to write a novel. The speaker was Charles Christmas Bush, a successful thriller writer of the time who wrote under the pseudonyms of Major Christopher Bush and Michael Home. The talk was very disappointing. All that Catherine can remember about it is his theme that anyone capable of drawing up a laundry list is capable of writing a novel. The poor man couldn't have known that he had touched on such a raw nerve. Catherine had been drawing up laundry lists for the past decade and a half, yet the writing of her first novel had taken the nightmare of mental breakdown to perform.

She let him have it. There in front of his whole audience, she gave it to Major Christopher Bush on the nose. He must have wondered what had hit him. He had probably thought he was in for a nice cosy evening, no sweat, no bother. He'd earn his fee, serve the good ladies of Hastings the encouragement they craved and depart. But to give Bush his due, later that same evening he would see the error of his ways and play a crucial role in Catherine's rise.

After her outburst she beat a hasty retreat down the stairs and through the door out into the cold, rainy, windswept night. Once outside, she felt so bad about what she had said that she returned to the upper room to apologise. Bush not only accepted her apology, he admitted that the laundry-list theme was an easy solution he had used for years on such occasions, and gave her his assurance that he would not be using it again. Catherine then told him about the three chapters of *Kate Hannigan* she had written, and he suggested that she send them to his agents, Christy & Moore. This Catherine did the very next day. John Smith, a new boy at the agency, read them and wrote to Catherine that she should send him the rest of the novel when it was finished. It was enough to have Catherine devote every single minute of her waking days to the task, which took her a full year to complete.

When John Smith received the manuscript he sent it to Murray Thompson at Macdonald, who, as I have said, read only the first chapter and told his secretary to return it to the agents because he felt it was too strong for any genre he published. His secretary looked at the top page and was caught immediately by the power of Catherine's writing, took it home that night and sat up reading it, unable to put it down until the very last page. The following morning she suggested to her boss that he had made a mistake in rejecting it, and in due course Catherine heard from her agent that *Kate Hannigan* had been accepted for publication. It was a moment of supreme triumph, dampened only by Macdonald's offer, a royalty advance of one hundred pounds of which ten pounds would be retained by Christy & Moore and ten pounds was earmarked for Catherine's typist. Catherine would discover that her agents would also charge her for the postage on submissions sent on her behalf to publishers abroad. In the end her net advance was close to seventy pounds. The book has been in print ever since and has earned Catherine vast royalties, but at the time it did little to supplement the couple's income, which was around forty pounds a month, Tom's salary as a grammar school master. That, however, was hardly the point. She had won through; she had found her *métier*.

In *Hamilton*, we get a marvellous picture of the fledgling author Maisie Carter's relationship with her publishers. Like *Kate Hannigan*, Maisie's first novel is richly autobiographical. Unlike Catherine, however, Maisie falls in love with her first editor, Nardy, whom she eventually marries in *Goodbye Hamilton*. Catherine's relationship with her long-term editor, John Foster White, was indeed close, but only professionally so. To everyone who has been instrumental in her career she is intensely and appreciatively loyal, and in John's case she showed her appreciation by dedicating her award-winning novel *The Round Tower* to him and ensuring that he remained editorially involved until his death in 1997.

What is true to life in *Hamilton* is the excitement of Maisie's first trip to London to meet her publishers – and we also get a taste of the family atmosphere in which Catherine has always enjoyed, and insisted upon enjoying, having her books published, even when publishing them became a business equal in size to a light engineering company and now, when her work earns more thousands of pounds per hour for her publishers than any other single author's. Called to London to meet Murray Thompson, Catherine arrived as excited as Maisie Carter, but on the wrong day: there had been a mix-up of dates by Catherine's agents. She lunched instead with Thompson's secretary, who had been responsible for the book being taken on, and while she enjoyed a pleasant lunch with this woman it had been a great disappointment not to be fêted by her publisher. Today, if she would have lunch with her publisher, I have no doubt that he would be there even if she turned up a week early, and that is not only because she is so important to them from a business point of view – though it is that too and as a businesswoman herself Catherine can appreciate that – but because she has defined the character of her relationship with her publishers, who are in a marketing sense fathers to her fiction.

She has had three main hardcover publishers in Britain: Macdonald from 1950 to 1973, Heinemann from 1973 to 1986, and since then Bantam, who, through their associated imprint, Corgi, have been her main UK paperback publishers since 1957. She has had only two agents. Since Anthony Sheil Associates (now Sheil Land) took over her books from Christy & Moore, Anthony Sheil has personally looked after her literary affairs throughout the world.

Rooney, the story of the Tyneside dustman, was the first novel on which any mass-market paperback publisher dared to risk money. They had all passed up the opportunity of publishing *Kate Hannigan*, *The Fifteen Streets*, *Colour Blind*, *Maggie Rowan*, *A Grand Man* and *The Lord and Mary Ann*, and having been in the paperback business myself, I can say with some certainty that it was no coincidence that paperback rights in *Rooney* were taken up by Corgi in the year (1956) that film rights in the novel were sold to J. Arthur Rank, a film being the best showcase you can have for paperback publication.

The point about the commercial success of Catherine's novels is that it occurred without any great effort on the part of her publishers. From the start it was a pact between a writer and her readers, who eventually persuaded the publishing business to take her seriously. There is nothing particularly unusual in this. It is one of the ironies of the business that vast sums of money are thrown with razzmatazz into publishing 'discoveries' when greater profit may be had from quieter beginnings. I remember Catherine smiling wryly when her publishers paid a huge advance in the eighties for a first author, more even than they were paying her for a new book. Today the situation is as Catherine likes it to be. Anthony Sheil ensures that she is properly valued by her publishers and Catherine ensures that that value is not measured only in money. Catherine's work is her life, they are inseparable, and she would not work with anyone for whom that was not also true.

Early on, her books were consistently sold (by means of cover presentation and other marketing techniques) to the soft market for them, the series romance market, even though Thompson of Macdonald, whose stock-in-trade was category romance, saw immediately that *Kate Hannigan* had flown that pigeon-hole. It was why he hadn't wanted it. Catherine claims that she wasn't called a romantic writer until the hugely successful television adaptation of her *Mallen* trilogy in 1979, and it certainly didn't help her in that sense. But the rot had set in before then.

Recently June Wyndham Davies, vice-chairman of the Romantic Novelists' Association, said that 'Romanticism used to mean something else. It was the opposite of Classicism. But now it is associated with Mills & Boon, Barbara Cartland, and things that are pink and fluffy.' Members of the Association, who include Joanna Trollope and Elizabeth Buchan, might agree. The fact remains that no one who has read both Barbara Cartland and Catherine Cookson could conceivably fail to make a distinction. Links to traditional Romance (as distinct from category romance with a small 'r' – the Mills & Boon genre) include a love interest often connected to a central quest, the juxtaposition of pathos and humour, and catharsis. Her heroines' quests or struggles are Catherine's own – attempts to resolve trauma and realise some element of truth in their lives, which is the substance of her narrative resolutions. Their quests are spurred by loss, disinheritance (sometimes genetic, if their parentage is thrown into question), the hypocrisies of others or their own inability to come to terms with themselves and take responsibility for their own lives (the existential element). Certainly the novels present a reality in which there is hope, but there are no fairytale endings. We are left with the notion that fulfilment lies in the process of resolution, which knows no end. Life goes on.

She begins with character, seeded in the environment which moulded her own character, ensuring a range and depth which lift them out of the simple, plastic, romantic genre: 'I take two, four or six characters and place them in a certain environment, and it is the environment that affects their characters. That started, I then find my end. I always think of the end of the story [the resolution] before I begin it. I compare this to going into a station and asking for a single ticket and I'm asked, "Where to?" And if I didn't know, then why was I asking for a ticket? So what I do next is to go to the pictures. By this I mean I conjure up every scene and every character in it as if I was looking at a film and I act these characters. This is mostly done when I am sleepless. It might take me up to two o'clock in the morning. And Tom will say, "You're not still at it. For goodness' sake, get yourself to sleep, woman!" Do you know, really, I think I am a frustrated actress. Because I act every part. I do every bit of the dialogue and then the following morning I wake up and wonder why I am tired, forgetting that I have lived a number of other people's lives in the night. But I start now and whatever I have thought of last night, I put it down on to tape. It might not be exactly in the same words that I used in the night because my mind at night delivers brilliant answers to questions, but,' she laughs, 'they are very mundane in the morning when I attempt to put them down.'

The close affinity of character and environment is never more clear than in her historical novels, where her characters are of the period, at one with it, not plucked from today and stuck against a historical backdrop. Theatre and painting are involved. Her ability to enact her dramas and literally to see them 'as if I was looking at a film' ensures realism, but she is also the painter whose little brushstrokes here and there build up these pictures like oils on a canvas.

The confusion of Catherine with category romance writers like Barbara Cartland (who is, incidentally, happy to accept her place in the publishing scheme – 'All I can say is that I am still selling well,' she said recently) is partly due to the manner in which they have been published. What people see is the paperback cover on station bookstalls. The move by Bantam away from conventional romantic cover illustrations to the 'big book' look, the more emblematic approach, was designed to rectify that, and has no doubt extended Catherine's market considerably. Her first publishers, faced with the problem of marketing Catherine at a time when romances were bought and sold by the bucketful, and when the market, not the book, was the thing, wouldn't have known otherwise how to sell her. Again, the rapidity with which Catherine produced her novels probably helped to define them in terms of the series romance in the minds of her early paperback publishers (Barbara Cartland, for example, has allegedly written 649 romances in her time). It was quite a tough brief to a marketing man to implement a strategy for *Maggie Rowan* and *A Grand Man*, two such different books, both published in the same year (1954), both written by a relative unknown, without succumbing to the temptation to find some sort of lowest common denominator. No doubt the subsidiary rights manager at Macdonald came to the same conclusion when selling the paperback rights. And so the myth was born. Ultimately it will do her no great harm. It is easy to forget that Dickens' novels appeared first in serial form in a magazine.

It is unthinkable to me now that a writer who has had to delve so deeply and painfully inside herself to create her work should be formularised editorially (as distinct from in marketing terms), and thankfully that didn't happen much.

The Jarrow Slake just yards away from where Catherine had been brought up. Tidal and often a polluted sea of mud, the Slacks, as they were called, became a symbol in Catherine's mind of all the filth and squalor of her early Tyneside environment, images of which crowded her mind in 1944 when the agony of nervous breakdown took hold.

'Ah, Mrs Cookson! The regional writer!' The woman who so described Catherine and challenged her to write about Hastings was to this Sussex seaside town what Fanny McBride was to Tyneside, and might have made a good starting point. But Catherine never was just a regional writer. She discovered that she could only write with strength about the environment of the North which she knew, and only that because of the fears it had bred in her.

Katie Mulholland, Catherine's 'breakthrough novel', had been brewing in her mind but she had been unable to get going with it until Tom suggested it be set against the backdrop of Palmer's shipyard in Jarrow, when all her ideas for it fell into place. In the 1850s Charles Mark Palmer's industrial empire, centred on his shipyard on the Tyne, largely called Jarrow into being. As long as you could see Palmer's cranes there was always the chance of work.

The *John Bowes*, the first profitable iron collier, produced at Palmer's shipyard in 1852, makes an appearance in *Katie Mulholland* and establishes a connection between Tyneside and the Queen Mother, a Bowes-Lyon and one of Catherine's foremost fans.

In 1934 the yard was levelled to the ground. Catherine's novels cover a period from the rise of the mercantile class over the landed gentry in the early nineteenth century (*Katie Mulholland*, *The Glass Virgin*), through the 1930s when financial disaster brought a call for workers' rights (*The Blind Miller*), to recent times (*The Round Tower*) when the social consequences of change, buried deep in the collective psyche, required a psychological adjustment to transform.

The picture shows the fragility of the coal mines, the 'lilliputian halls of hell' in the North-Eastern coalfield, which provided vital energy for the industrialisation and urbanisation of Western Europe. When, in 1952, Catherine was challenged by her cousin to go to the coalface down the Betty pit at Birtley, she emerged from the experience nerve-racked and inspired: *Maggie Rowan* appeared two years later.

In 1976, forty-six years after she left Tyneside, Catherine returned. 'The greatest excitement that I had in coming back was crossing on the ferry from South Shields to North Shields . . .'

Catherine standing on the New Buildings site of number 10 William Black Street after the bulldozers had done away with it, confusion written on her face, perhaps a little helplessness too. 'Everything that I have written since seems to have been bred in that kitchen,' she once told me.

Here, in their home at Langley, up in the hills on the edge of a lake, seven miles from Hexham and in the midst of the most lovely Northumbrian countryside, Catherine and Tom found, from 1981, the privacy to live and work which had been denied them. The great sadness was that ten years later Catherine's illness would force them back into the city to be closer to the hospital.

Catherine at the height of her powers celebrates the crossing of one of many million-copy watersheds with her husband Tom and her UK paperback publishers since 1957, Corgi Books.

The Tyne from Hexham. 'Up here I know that I am in my country. This is my kind of country, not soft like the downs but rugged hills broken up into soft parts, an expanse of sheer mystery.'

Catherine receiving the honorary degree of MA given by the University of
Newcastle.

As the adult comes into the child's time more and more there is recognition and revelation that what we once were and what we have become are mere earthly functions of eternity, which is now.

The only time Catherine came near to being exploited in this way was when her advisers recommended a deal offered by *Woman's Realm* to write romantic serials for them: 'They wanted romances, but with the strength of my writing and my name (because even in those early days I was, fortunately, selling well). I would write short stories for them, I said, but not under the name of Catherine Cookson.' And so Catherine Marchant was born. The first three of her six novels written under the Marchant pseudonym – *Heritage Folly* (1962), *The Fen Tiger* (1963) and *House of Men* (1964) – were published at this time.

There was probably greater editorial input – in terms of what she should write, or at least in what could be published of what she had written – in those early years. The sequel to *Kate Hannigan* was laid aside, as indeed was *Bonny Dawn*, a novel published in 1996, but written in the late 1950s. *Bonny Dawn* was one of a number of manuscripts consigned to Catherine's attic after Macdonald had dismissed it in favour of the kind of thumping great read which was capturing the American market at that time. As a result, we can look forward to a mixed programme of old and new novels well into the third millennium. And I do mean 'look forward', because *Annie Hannigan* – her second novel to be written, is to be published – probably under the title *Kate's Daughter* – at some time early in the next millennium not simply because anything with Catherine's name on it will sell, but because it was rejected in the first instance for the wrong reason, namely that there was too much of Catherine in it and not enough of what publishers were selling by other authors by the bucket full.

Katie Mulholland, which came out in 1967, the twenty-third novel to be published under her own name, is considered to be her breakthrough novel because it was the first to capture the American market – and was to some extent tailored to that end by her publishers. It is a huge, thematically panoramic novel, and was adapted editorially to the American market only in the sense that her publishers insisted she cut it by a third, a request which makes the mind boggle as to its original length.

'Everyone connected with me at this end saw the possibilities of getting into the American paperback world. And so I set about the cutting, which was much more difficult than writing the story in the first place. But it opened up a new era to me: I was, so some people said, discovered.' No doubt her publishers patted one another on the back, but the real secret of *Katie Mulholland*'s success is the same one that will ensure the availability, long into the future, of *Kate Hannigan*, *The Fifteen Streets*, *The Menagerie*, *Fanny McBride* and *The Blind Miller*, all published earlier than *Katie Mulholland* but with a wholly different marketing strategy.

Katie Mulholland coalesced in Catherine's mind one day in Loreto after she and Tom had been out in the garden and come back in to the kitchen to get warm. Tom put the kettle on and they were both standing in front of the Aga waiting for it to boil when Catherine said, 'I've got this big story in my mind but I still don't know where to place it for the best.' Tom lifted the kettle off the hot plate and said, 'You're always talking about Palmer's shipyard in Jarrow. Why don't you just bring the story to the last century and set it there?' That was all it took. Suggestions had been made that she should set it in Roman times, but Palmer's was the lifeblood of Jarrow, the fount. It took Catherine back to her source environment, directly into the main imaginative artery from which all her best works flow.

Her connection with the creative source which gives Catherine no release from writing, even in her ninety-first year, led her, when she first discovered its amazing power, to go with a friend to what was known as The House of Healing in Hastings. In a seance a medium told her that there was an old man standing beside her who was saying that she should return to her own way of working, be true to her instincts. It quite took Catherine by surprise, because at the time she was tussling with Tom over what constituted 'correct English'. The medium also cured a pain under her eye, and it was as a result of these impressive feats that she made contact – by letter – with the faith healer Harry Edwards and happened to share with him the news, which Catherine received from Aunt Mary in 1953, that Kate had been taken ill, indeed had been give only a few months to live by her doctor. Tom had told Catherine that she would never forgive herself if she didn't get Kate back down to Hastings, but when the decision was made the problem arose as to how to get her down, for they had no car. Harry Edwards told Catherine not to worry, it would all be taken care of, and 'what followed', she recalls, 'was on oiled wheels.'

Kate had been living in Brinkburn Street in South Shields, one of the streets to which Catherine had gone as a child to an outdoor beer shop with the Grey Hen. When first she had arrived there, in 1937, Kate had found it difficult to find work, her age and figure, bloated by drink, counting against her, though she was still capable of a ten-hour working day. Eventually she had been taken on by a doctor called Carstairs, who, with his wife, remained Kate's friend and employer right up to her final illness.

By 1953 she was bedridden, puffed up with dropsy; her liver was almost eaten away and she had a bad heart. But 'with the help of ambulances and a night sleeper I brought her back to The Hurst.' It was an extraordinary journey. When they arrived at Newcastle station, a posse of porters jumped to it and winched Kate's great body on to the train, using a luggage lift. At King's Cross an ambulance appeared and raced her across London to Charing Cross station, where the paramedics used more traditional means to get her on to a train to Hastings. Another ambulance made the last leg of the journey, to The Hurst.

'Oh lass, I'm back home,' Kate cried when they laid her on her bed. Catherine's own doctor confirmed that she had only a very short time to live – but Catherine kept her alive for three years. 'Those years were the happiest of her life. But I had to become her gaoler, never left her. I allowed her a bottle of beer a day and now and again, unknown to Tom, I would slip her a miniature whiskey. Knowing what I'd gone through, Tom hated even the thought of whiskey.' Four days before she died she said to Catherine, 'I've been a wicked woman to you, lass.'

'Pity made me contradict her.' Catherine told her mother that the only one she had hurt in her life had been herself. On 23 September 1956 Kate Fawcett died, peacefully.

Two years earlier Tom, Catherine and Kate had left The Hurst, 'which had eaten up my energy and every penny poor Tom and I were earning,' and moved to Loreto, a house on a private road only a few minutes' walk away. 'There were about another four big houses and a bungalow on the road. One of the big houses had been owned by a millionaire. He had three daughters. The family broke up because there was a question of religion . . . the daughters turned Catholic. One became Mother Superior of a convent at St Leonard's. The other built a house for herself quite next to the one she had left. The third one, whom I called "my Miss Harrison", not to be outdone, built her house some distance away down the road and called it Loreto.

'It was beautifully built. She had had the bricks hand made and the pointing was an art in itself. She had something wrong with her skin and as I understand had to wear a mask of white ointment on her face. She was looked after by a nurse (frequent nurses, because they didn't stay), a cook, a maid and a gardener. Finally there was this one nurse who was middle-aged, and the dear lady was also attended by a very acute insurance agent who must have told the nurse that if she meant to stay she should make the old girl see that her future was secure. The outcome was that Miss Harrison left her the house and all the furniture, which I understand held a lot of antiques.

'But I don't think the nurse was there more than a year and a half . . . Anyway, the house went up for auction, but it wasn't sold. Then one day, when I was being driven about by a house agent in search of a new house, I saw a For Sale board outside. There we were, driving along this private road, and I pointed out this sales placard outside the house with its long winding drive. "Oh," he said, "don't go in for that place, it's always up for sale," and he wouldn't stop and show it to me. He had another in mind. But something attracted me to the place and when later I got rid of him I waited for Tom to come home from school and said, "I want to show you something . . ." We walked the ten minutes or so from The Hurst in Hoads Wood Road and as we made our way down the drive to this house, we knew immediately that we wanted it.

'The agent for the house told me its history. It had been built in 1938 and this was 1954.' He also told Catherine that the nurse had turned down a number of people who had made offers on the property; she wasn't just determined to get what she was convinced the house was worth, she wanted it to go to 'the right people,' she said.

By arrangement with this agent, Tom and Catherine were shown around the house by the nurse, and Catherine saw its potential immediately. She loved the wrought-iron framed windows and could see that while some people might be put off by the darkness inside, that could easily be remedied.

'The house seemed dark because everything in it was brown. All the lovely woodwork had been painted brown. But we knew we wanted it straight away. I knew immediately what I would do with it.' As they neared the end of their guided tour, the nurse led them towards two rooms marked 'Private': one was her bedroom and the other turned out to be a sitting room. Recalling what the agent had said about this woman turning prospective buyers down, Catherine immediately went into action. 'I said, "Oh no. No thank you. We can see what the house is like without intruding." That must have got her. Anyway, we made an offer and she got on the phone to the agent.' There was some to-ing and fro-ing about the size of their offer. As far as Catherine could tell from one side of the conversation, the nurse seemed to have taken to them, but the agent didn't advise her to accept their offer at that time.

'As we were about to go a man came in – we had seen him stop his car, a big limousine. Apparently he went round the house and decided he might take it. The nurse was wavering, I understand, when all of a sudden the hall light went out and she asked him would he put a fresh bulb in for her. He was standing on a ladder when the phone rang and it was the agent who at that moment told her that she should let us have the house, as we were the only really earnest ones willing to pay anything near what she wanted. And she said, "All right," and looked up at the man putting the light bulb in and said, "I'm sorry, I've just sold the house." What did he do? He must have been a pig of a fella. He had been about to put the light in, but he didn't do it. He came down and thrust it at her and walked out!

'Anyway, after a lot of legal business we moved our last pieces of furniture into it on Guy Fawkes' night. It was pouring from the heavens. There was no central heating here either, only an electric fire nailed to the wall which the nurse later took down and sold us, together with the mirrors on the back of the bathroom washbasins. She was a very mean woman. Anyway, in the kitchen was an Aga, our first Aga, and that was wonderful, as was the first knock which came to the door.' It was the doctor with the hamper, whose coming I have already described.

'But why, we asked ourselves many times after, had Miss Harrison, this woman with so much money, taken only a half acre of ground on which she built her lovely house, when all around, except for the bungalow that was on one side of us, was thick with woodland that she could have bought for next to nothing? During the years that followed we took three pieces of the woodland. They had been used as a dump during the war, and besides old beds, gas ovens and rubbish of every other description, there was a number of old trees entangled with honeysuckle, some of the branches nine or ten inches across, so strong and entwined that Tom could swing on them from one tree to another. He loved climbing.

'It took a number of years for us to buy those three pieces of land and twenty-two years to make that garden. The labour that we put into it was indescribable. How we did it I don't know: Tom would not have any assistance. I was his labourer in everything he did. This, to me, is Tom's main failing. He will not have help of any kind. He thinks he can do everything himself, and this is part of him right up to this very moment.

'I always regret one mistake I made at Loreto. There was no garage. We couldn't afford a car. All I wanted to buy was nice furniture, and although I was writing I wasn't earning as now. On a piece of land between us and the bungalow was a huge garage that would have held about four or five cars. In it was a sailing boat (the owner of the bungalow was a sailing man). It was now up for sale at £200 (remember, this was 1954). I was for buying it (I always would take a chance), but Tom was against it because it would mean another two hundred pounds on the house payments. He was always terrified about getting into debt. I never was and I never went into debt . . . Fourteen or fifteen years later, we bought that piece of land from the new owner of the bungalow and he charged us eight thousand pounds for it. All that still rankles in my businesslike mind.'

By the time they left Loreto in 1976 Catherine had published forty-one novels, her autobiography, *Our Kate* (1969), and five novels as Catherine Marchant – and she had written many more. It was an extraordinarily productive period, which brought increasing rewards, but it changed nothing in the way she managed their lives. 'We never had separate accounts. We used to divide the money into three parts: a third would go into the bank, a third would pay for new furniture, antique furniture if possible . . .' Always there remained this care about money, born of her past. 'Since the days I put my pennies into the lavatory as a child I was a saver, a planner. I could make a sixpence go as far as a shilling.' The significance of that lavatory in the backyard at number 10, Annie Hannigan's 'little square house', Catherine's bank, her sanctuary where no one could get at her, the room in her mind in which, when she was at her lowest ebb in 1946, she felt safe to write, was such that as she began to gain popularity through her work it even influenced her dreams. When the money started to flow in, incredibly she started having dreams about lavatories. The size of her royalty cheques was presaged in the number of lavatories which appeared – 'and their *condition*'! Perhaps a psychologist would say that these dreams were connected with the success which she could now claim in having cleansed herself of her fears through her novels. For her recovery coincided with this period.

As she had been at The Hurst, Catherine was tirelessly

involved in making the new house the way she wanted it. But this time it was far more rewarding. Everything came together here. In time, they even built a swimming pool. It was begun as a remedy after Catherine had damaged her back and spent three months lying in bed, but later swimming became a great source of pleasure and relaxation when the work was done.

'Looking back at the work that I did in the house . . . Tom was away at school from half past eight in the morning not only till half past four but usually eight o'clock because there were so many meetings, Scouts, parents' associations, sixth-form meetings, there was everything. I remember when his mother and father were paying their first visit, she said in amazement, "Are all your weeks like this?" I said, "Yes." She said, "I would never put up with it. You are never done from morning till night." No, I was never done from morning till night, and on looking back I am amazed how in those twenty-two years I got through the work of looking after that house, clearing it, cooking and doing the washing by hand – we had no electric appliances, no washing machine, dryer, we didn't even have a fridge until about five years before we left there, about the time we also had a beautiful indoor pool made. It was after we had paid the £8,000 for the adjoining land, but, as I said, I was a saver and a planner . . .'

At Loreto, too, Tom first had occasion to understand something of the supernatural world which Catherine encountered in the little room of her imagination. The incident occurred on Christmas Eve 1954, not long after they arrived, and it shook Tom's belief that science and mathematics could explain all. He and Catherine were busily papering a bedroom ceiling. Startled by a strange noise emanating from outside the room, Catherine dropped what she was holding and wrapped Tom in an envelope of wallpaper and glue.

Venturing on to the landing, she saw their bull terrier, Bill, transfixed by something at the bottom of the stairs, the short hairs of his coat bristling with fear. She looked down the stairs but could see nothing. She then tried to coax the dog down with her, but he wouldn't budge. Then, without any prompting by her or Tom, who had by this time joined her, Bill made his own way, warily, step by step, to the bottom of the stairs, where he stood stock still, his head cocked as if someone was standing by him. Whatever was there absorbed Bill completely. Then, unaccountably, because Bill only ever sat when a hand was placed on his rear end, he first sat, then lay supine on the carpet, still looking up at whatever it was that no one could see.

A week or so later, exhausted by the decorating, Catherine was sitting downstairs alone. Resting her back against the chair, her mind in repose, she felt something, a kind of presence which she was convinced was Miss Harrison, the old lady who had built the house and died earlier that year. The following day, as she and Tom listened to the church bells ringing in the New Year, she felt it again, but this time with contentment. Whatever it was – this spirit presence – was departing through the open front door.

CHAPTER TEN

Return to the North

'I confess I never wanted to come back. It was Tom who said to me when I was seventy and we were still working like people in their fifties or even forties, "I think you should go back to the North and die among your ain folk." I know now, and he knew it then, he was using me as an excuse to get away. He was tired of Hastings, which was changing vastly, especially the school that he had once loved.'

Tom had retired from his job at the grammar school seven years earlier. He was suffering increasingly from migraines, which Catherine puts down to the 'strain, because he is a perfectionist. He took so many boys on of an evening to push them through this, that or the other.' There was, of course, no longer any financial need for Tom to work, and in any case he was near retirement age. Also, he could now help Catherine with her post-bag, which was rising to some 3,000 letters a year, and do some of the things he really wanted to do, like working on Loreto, where he turned the garden into something of real beauty.

When I asked Catherine why she had returned to Tyneside, I expected her to tell me that she had at last come to terms with her early childhood and wanted to get back to her roots. But she didn't feel that. The truth is that 'once back, I was homesick, not for Hastings or the south of England but for Loreto, that lovely house and garden . . .' But the truth is, too, that in all the years she was away, and up to the day I write, her early environment never left her, however hard she had tried to rub it out. And she will admit that it is 'strange that from the wider world into which I escaped I have to return, like the eel to the Sargasso Sea, to die where I began . . .'.

This is a theme which she has explored in greater depth in her fiction. In *The Tide of Life*, published seven years before she left Hastings, and in the poem which gave the novel its title, she likens existence to the time it takes for a tide to flow and ebb over the seashore. At the centre of her narrative is a valuable timepiece, a fob watch, to which the fortunes and destiny of her heroine, Emily Kennedy, seem to be tied. Illness and death pervade the novel, and questions are raised about life's futility. But the form of the narrative, which begins and ends in the same location (Pilot Place in South Shields) and, as ever, concerns the resolution of strife, suggests an alternative perception of time to that implicit in the watch symbol of finite time. Finally, what she gives us is not a sense of time as a linear progression from birth to death and then nothing, but of man as his own prisoner and gaoler, of the purpose of life as release from his self-sewn straitjacket, of time as a circular motion, of eternity as *now*.

A similar theme is the subject of a novel she will have been writing around the time that she returned to the North. *The Man Who Cried* (which has to be one of her best titles) was published in 1979. At the start, Abel Mason, a working man, is in his thirties and married to a nasty piece of work called Lena. They are both from the North, but are living just outside Hastings. Their son, Dick, suffers from deafness as a result of frequent slappings by his mother. The situation, which Lena has effectively created, has driven Abel into the arms of Alice Lovina, the wife of a seaman. Lena has discovered the affair and written an anonymous letter to

Alice's husband, who brutally murders Alice. After her funeral, which is where the novel begins, Abel packs a rucksack and takes to the road with Dick, heading north.

Their journey, largely on foot, a gruelling odyssey via Essex, Cambridge, Leeds and Northumberland (close to Hexham), and then back to fictional Fellburn (near Gateshead on the Tyne), occupies the whole of Part I of the novel and contains some extraordinary incidents, including set-tos with a nymphomaniac called Daphne and a religious maniac called Matilda, both brilliant examples of the author's skill in handling plot. When they come upon the 'apparition' of Matilda, Catherine excels. She is indeed a character from another world, her oddness so threatening that we, like Abel, cannot help but spring back as Matilda puts out her fingers and touches his arm.

In Fellburn, Hilda and Peter Maxwell, who run a car and bicycle repair business, install Abel and Dick in an outhouse and offer Abel work on the cars. Abel gives them the impression that he is a widower, and when Peter dies, Hilda persuades him to marry her, an arrangement complicated by her sister Florrie, with whom Abel has an affair and who becomes pregnant.

Abel and Dick's tramp north has a strictly linear feel to it, but Abel's relationships with Hilda and Florrie, and Dick's response to what is going on, in particular his fear of a bigamy charge against his father, which brings Dick to the point of breakdown, mass into a series of busy emotional circles, which it is the author's intention to resolve.

The hero's name, the same as that of the second son of Adam and Eve, and indeed the whole epic feel of Abel's trip north, suggest that this purpose will be achieved with significance beyond the lives of Catherine's fictional characters. The author's own personal odyssey, which led her to Hastings and then, forty-six years later, back to her roots in the North, where I believe Tom did feel Catherine would find fulfilment, parallels the cyclical pattern of Abel's life on an emotional level as well as geographically. That mass of busy emotional circles reminds us of the years 1940 to 1946 in Catherine's life when she, like Dick, arrived at the point of breakdown and through a great effort of will disentangled herself from them. Abel's release, like Catherine's, is like the bursting of a great dam, the flood of his emotions ducted through his streaming eyes, and it brings, if not fulfilment, at least hope.

Catherine has written elsewhere (in an essay called 'Time and the Child') of her perception of life as a circle, the child coming to meet the adult and merging with him before 'the race is run'. As the adult comes 'into the child's time more and more', there is mutual recognition and the revelation that what we once were and what we have become are mere earthly functions of eternity, which has been with us all the time, indeed *is* all time. It is now.

True to the author's vision, various aspects of Abel's past reappear as active ingredients in the present. Among them is Lena, whose arrival does lead to Abel's imprisonment for bigamy. Then, with Florrie dying from injuries sustained in an air raid, Hilda takes Abel's baby in. At the end we are left with Abel and Hilda, their arms around one another, and with Abel's tears . . .

At this stage that is all. For Abel's race is not nearly run, and there is no ultimate resolution in sight. But in his tears lies hope, as his son, Dick, tells us. In shedding his tears this physically strong, stoical northerner, 'who had done nothing with his life except impinge it on four women', shows himself capable not only of release but of transforming his agony into Hilda's joy. His tears wash the scales from his eyes and he recognises a power within him to transform. A more complete parallel with his creator would be hard to find.

Looking back, more than twenty years after returning to

the North, Catherine notes an ironic twist to Tom's suggestion that she come back to die among her own folk. For her return, she considers, has greatly enhanced her life. Three years before making the journey Catherine met a man, a doctor, 'who deserves the greatest honour that could be bestowed on any man. I am sure that if there is a God he is "sitting on the right-hand side of him" . . . No doctor can come up to him, and I met him much too late in life. He was Dr Gabb of St Leonard's.

'I had the breakdown in 1945 and from the time I returned home to Hastings everything I had, from ingrowing toenails to psoriasis of the scalp was, so I was told, a result of nerves, and then after forty-three years of the forty-six I lived there, in desperation I changed over to this certain Dr Gabb in St Leonards. But I knew this man for only five weeks.'

Catherine first met him when he was visiting someone else who was ill at Loreto. While he was there Catherine had a bleeding. By this time she would bleed not only from the nose but from the tongue, and she told Dr Gabb that she had been bleeding since she was eighteen. 'He couldn't believe that nothing had been done for me. So, within a week, he had made arrangements for me to see this specialist in Wimpole Street by the name of Mr Ranger, who looked at my scarred nostrils and the telangiectasis covering most of my tongue. He said nothing could be done for my nose except a skin transplant and this would be touch and go, ninety-nine out of a hundred didn't take. Within another week I was in the hospital and Mr Ranger took three and half inches of skin from my hip and inserted it into the nostril, at the same time cutting a big wedge out of my tongue –

' "Eeh, my, what if I'm never able to talk again!"

' "You will talk, Mrs Cookson," Mr Ranger assured me, "Don't worry!"

'The touch and go happened that it went. The skin grafting

took. It was rather a painful fortnight, but I was back home, and this dear, dear, dear Dr Gabb came to see me. He was delighted that it had been done. He also came to say goodbye. He was going to London to have an operation, he said. This was the fifth week of our acquaintance. He had heard about Tom's migraine and he had already sent to America because he had heard of some kind of treatment for migraine, and he would let me know from London. We said goodbye. I can see him holding my hand warmly. When at the end of the week I heard he was dead I just could not believe it. I could not believe that for the last five weeks he knew he was dying of cancer, that he knew he had one more operation to go through and that he would probably die. Yet he did all that for me and even from his bed in the last week he wrote to Tom and sent him the particulars for his migraine he had received from America. Just think, in those five weeks that he knew me, he knew his time was short and yet when he saw this woman bleeding profusely he was astonished that nothing had been done for me . . . There is a doctor, and nobody in his profession will ever come up to him.'

Catherine still bleeds from the nostril above where the skin graft was made, but rarely from where it used to occur. The more critical development since Dr Gabb's passing is that she now also bleeds internally. Moreover, a year or so after she returned to the North she suffered a series of heart problems, and in 1990 suffered two heart attacks. But she believes that had she remained in the South, where no doctor other than Dr Gabb ever did anything for her ill-health, she would now be dead. She told me earlier this year, 'From coming back to the North I know that I am only alive today because of the attention that has been paid to my blood disease. Today I have six doctors who see to different parts of me . . . finally to be kept alive by blood transfusions every three weeks. And at every turn I have endeavoured to make research possible so that some day this awful, devastating, if rare, condition will be alleviated.'

A year before arriving in the North, Tom and Catherine purchased a property at number 39 Eslington Terrace in Newcastle. They bought it ostensibly for somewhere to stay when Catherine was researching her books, and it was initially to this house that they went to live in 1976 after they had sold Loreto.

Three years earlier Catherine had been granted The Freedom of the Borough of South Shields, which was a good welcome home. It was the first of a number of tributes, from both inside and outside the area, including an Hon. MA from Newcastle University and a D.Litt. from Sunderland University, which thrilled her particularly, and then of course the OBE in 1985 and the DBE eight years later.

'We landed in Newcastle and we lived in this very nice house for about a year, but it had no garden, and so when we heard of this house on the outskirts of Corbridge [Northumberland] we went after it.' One important plus point of Town Barns, as the house was called, was that it had a beautiful swimming pool, something which Catherine sorely missed since leaving Loreto. But it was here that for the first time in her life Catherine would discover the downside of being famous.

The man who sold the house to them had built another house in what should have been its large garden, leaving a relatively small garden plot for each building – 'Ours had the least and it ran down the side of the house. But next to it was a great, long, dirty field which belonged to a farmer, who kept a sick cow in there. The only thing that grew in there was thistles, and part of the field was terribly steep. We bought this from the farmer, who said it was building land and of course charged us accordingly. I think in those days we paid about twenty-seven or twenty-eight thousand for it.

'Then Tom could see it filled, because his heart was in gardens, and, well, he engaged a designer, whose men came in and Tom told him what he wanted done. He himself helped and soon there was a wonderful surrounding of trees, and one of those steep banks was covered with hundreds of beautiful crocuses. It was a wonderful sight in the spring, for he had planted thousands of daffodils around the roots of trees forming an avenue right across this field. But it didn't please all the townsfolk. Some said, "Why stick daffodils all over the place and azaleas and rhododendrons?" etc., etc. Anyway, by the time we finished, with the land, the trees, and paid the designer, it cost a straight £50,000.'

When four and a half years later Catherine and Tom left the house, in order to recoup the investment they agreed to sell the entire property to a builder, who intended to build three houses in among the gardens. The land was only worth that amount if it was built upon and the properties sold. The builder couldn't afford both to build the properties and to pay what they wanted for the land, so they came to an arrangement whereby Catherine and Tom would receive the money for the land once the houses were built and sold. Unfortunately, 'by the time that happened he had gone bankrupt and I'm still waiting for the £50,000. Anyway, that's by the way.'

The real story about their short stay at Town Barns is the reason why they left it. 'Well, I hadn't been in Corbridge more than six months or so (which I spent mostly in bed because the cold weather did nothing for me and I ended up with very bad bronchitis) when a lady from the town came to tell me that people really weren't very pleased with me living here because I didn't show myself in the town. Why didn't I?

'That was the beginning, and yet not really the beginning,

for when we first took the land we had an anonymous letter telling us that members of the community weren't pleased that we had dug up an ancient patch of ground that went back to the building of the moat around the "town". Then I had a filthy telephone call, one of these mad sex men, and this upset me very much. There was also a pub on the opposite side of the road, a very old pub, where the visitors to the town used to go, and of course they were told about this Catherine Cookson and so I had people at the door at all hours wanting autographs.

'The climax came when one day Tom yelled up from the hall, "What are you doing?"

'I said, "I'm getting dressed."

' "Get away from the window," he said.

'Well, there was a high wall that divided our land from a path to the river and there, going along the wall, was a man with a cine camera. Believe me, I couldn't believe I was all that famous.

'Then Tom was stopped in the street one day by a beaming lady who told him gleefully that she had me on the rota of the sightseeing bus in Durham. Twice before this we'd had a busload of people unload at the gate, and as I said, it wasn't a very big garden and it wasn't a very big yard leading to the garage, so they were almost on top of us. This lack of privacy did not endear Corbridge to us . . .

'After four and a half years we found a bungalow in Langley by the side of a lake – originally dammed to supply water to the one-time smelting works there. Today, it is probably one of the most beautiful areas in Northumberland.' It is indeed an exquisite location and the place where I first met Catherine and Tom. I was amazed to hear her refer to it as a bungalow, until she explained that it had been yet another of their major building projects, possibly the biggest of all: 'Attached to it was a two-hundred-year-old cottage. We gutted the old cottage, and made it into a nice apartment. We built upwards on top of the flat roof and made a forty-foot study, and we turned an awful, dirty swimming pool, which was attached to the conservatory, into a fifty-foot drawing room, and above that made a forty-foot bedroom en suite which was really a beautiful piece. Tom took over the garden, as always, and I the house, and there we were, and our privacy was respected, no one troubled us . . . and we would have been there yet but I was bleeding more and more.'

This was the great sadness of Bristol Lodge, for it was an incredible house, beautifully furnished and designed. I had had no idea that they had done it all themselves. But of course by this time they were well practised. The Hurst had been their apprenticeship, done on a shoestring, the hundred-pound cheques in those early days papering over the cracks of a building that needed a complete overhaul. They had loved that house and had given it their all. At Loreto, where at last their life had come together, they had been able to give the house what they had longed to give to The Hurst but had been unable to afford, a beautiful garden, with many rhododendrons and azaleas. On all their houses they lavished the love, care and inspiration of parents for their children, and with the benefit of all the lessons they had learnt since giving life to The Hurst, Bristol Lodge rewarded them most generously during the decade between 1981 and 1991.

The day I arrived, Tom met me at the front door and showed me up to the study, where Catherine was standing in the middle of the room. At the time I had read *Our Kate* and a handful of the early novels – *Kate Hannigan*, *The Fifteen Streets*, *Maggie Rowan* – and I was in the middle of *Katie Mulholland*. I had spoken with Catherine on the phone and we had corresponded, but I carried with me only a sense of her early life, of the girl from Leam Lane, and among all the interior splendour of Bristol Lodge it was this phrase that occurred to me as Catherine came towards me with her hand outstretched. Indeed, she hadn't changed. I said something about the beauty of the house, but as we sat down to talk she straightaway steered me back to the kitchen in number 10. 'Why I am sitting here today talking to you is thanks to our kitchen there,' she said. 'There have been other things bred in me and they are the niceties, but the rawness of life came from that kitchen. That's why I am able to write about the rawness of life, though there was in me, inherent, this other side, something that led me to a place like this, to a room like downstairs [she was referring to the magnificent drawing room]. And this other side of me sort of levelled off the raw experiences of when I was young. If I had just kept that side I don't know what would have happened, I may not have been a writer. It was the other side that pushed me out of that environment, that said that this is no place for you; get out of it. And yet it's always the early environment that sticks with you until you're a very old woman. But there it was, that is the hub, the kitchen . . . You see, I believe everybody is a result of their environment and no matter what was in me, what was passed on to me, it was the environment that set me on and made me what I am today. Without that kitchen you wouldn't be sitting there and I wouldn't be talking to you.'

Much later, when she told me that the big houses in her novels were all products of her imagination, and I suggested that she must have had some real-life reference points for them, Catherine referred me back to the time when she was five and she would turn her face to the wall and imagine for herself a better life, big houses, servants, horses . . . She had had no reference points then and the houses in her fiction are a representation of, 'a part of my "picture on the wall" . . . So perhaps I owe my descriptions of big country houses to the gentleman in me, "the other half", which knew just what was needed.'

The problem with Bristol Lodge was that it was thirty miles from Newcastle, where Catherine's nose specialist, Mr Hugo Marshall, lives. 'It meant that I had longer distances to travel when I bled. It was nothing for Tom to have to drive me to his private house four times a week when I'd be bleeding like a pig. Then, two years before we left Langley and Bristol Lodge, I had long spells in bed.

'As I have said before, you never get rid of a breakdown. Well, come this day [in 1989], I was in a very, very low state. The bleedings had been bad, I had flu, and cystitis had affected my kidneys. I was taken into hospital for a time and there it was found that I was also bleeding from the stomach. Topping all this, I had what is now called ME. This could affect me, really paralyse me, for an hour or two, when I would be unable to speak or move. I realised this state was ripe for a return of the breakdown and it came . . . the aggression . . . I couldn't walk down to the bathroom. I had to be practically lifted from the bed to the commode. And I knew now that my mind was in such a state that I couldn't fight it with my slogan "I can and I will". I would have to have help. I could not confide this to Tom. He was worried enough. But I knew that I must go away and have mental treatment. I knew this would distress him above measure, because when I went into hospital he always came with me. He would take a room so that he could be near me all the time. But on this sad day my mind became clear in a way, and I planned what I would do. On the morrow, which was the day my doctor visited me and we chatted for an hour or two (we had become friends), I would tell him to make arrangements to have a treatment. I was no longer able to right all these ills, both mental and physical.

'It was as I lay there, thinking this, that a voice from

somewhere said, "Get up." I took no notice. A still small voice that speaks to me very loudly at times. Still it went on, until I cried at it, "I can't get up, you know I can hardly stand." I have written about this in *Plainer Still*, but I think it is worth telling again. The voice now said, "Put your feet out of bed." I took no notice. Again it came, "Put your feet out of bed. Sit up on the edge." Slowly I obeyed. But when the following order came – "Go into the sitting room and look at the television," I cried out at it, "Stop this! Stop this! I could never walk to the sitting room. I'm ill!"

' "Go to the sitting room and look at the television."

'I found myself staggering down a long room. When Tom opened the door, in amazement he cried, "What on earth are you doing?" And I said to him, "Take me into the sitting room to the television." Blindly he obeyed me.

'*The Railway Children* was on. I didn't mind them, but I rarely looked at television. It disturbs me. What followed next I don't remember. I only know that Tom knelt by my side, gripping my hand, and I sat dumb, really dumb, not uttering one word, not even when he said, "I'll go and make a cup of coffee, eh?"

'I was left alone and there came on to the screen the Sunday evening religious programme. It was showing the inside of Buckfast Abbey. There were the great pillars the monks had built years ago. Tom and I had visited the Abbey . . . The camera now was moving slowly down the aisle towards the stained-glass window, which got bigger and bigger until the whole picture filled the screen with the face of Christ. It wasn't a nice face, because you can't make a nice face out of stained glass. But there it was, staring at me. What I did next I have no explanation for because, remember, I had thrown off the Catholic Church and all its man-made dogmas and doctrines. I had no belief whatever in God. Faith was the last thing I thought of. Then what prompted me to thrust out my hand until it covered his face and I cried aloud two words, "Help me"?

Now there's no way that I or anyone else can describe what happened because it was so swift, swifter than a flash of lightning . . . There's no way to describe it, but I only know that in that unknown instant of time I was filled with a peace that only St Paul's words can bring down to earth – "the peace that passeth all understanding". I was enveloped in it. It filled every pore in my body. In all my life I had never experienced anything like it, nor even hoped to. I turned my head and saw Tom standing at the drawing room door; his face was alight and what he said astounded me even more. "Oh," he cried, "I felt it!"

'Then Tom came up to me and held me. I said to him, "I believe in him, not in the doctrines or the religious jargon, but I believe in the man Jesus." Tom held me close. My face was wet. So was his. I sat on in a state of wonder. There was not a fear left in me. There was not a worry left in me. There was a calmness in me that it is impossible to describe, a wonderful, wonderful peace. I had been born out of trouble. The only solace that had been given to me was the love of Tom and his help. No one else's. And now he was sharing my peace. That it was to be tested within a matter of hours I wasn't aware. I only knew that if I could live in this state for the rest of my life, all that I had gone through had been well compensated.

'It was four o'clock in the morning when I started to bleed – what I call one of my stinkers. You could hold a full pack of tissues to my nose and within minutes they would be sodden. Such was the case. Tom went through his usual routine. I would have to be got into Newcastle and to my consultant's. He rang, then dashed round seeing to the security, seeing to the dog, my beloved friend, dressing me in what I call my bloody coat because it had been sodden so much with blood over the years, wrapping around my shoulders and head a big woollen shawl. Then he went out to get the car. He got as far as the door and came back saying, "I can't see a finger before me, fog, it's as thick as ice."

'I said, "It'll be all right."

'He said, "Can't you understand, the fog, I can't see anything."

'Again I said, "It'll be all right." I wasn't worried in the least. Nothing could worry or touch me any more.

'When Tom saw that I might bleed to death he groped his way to the garage and got the car out. I have described the journey in other places. It usually took a full three-quarters of an hour from our house to the specialist's home, that is, in the night when there is very little traffic. But this journey, what with the fog, the ice and the hold-up at the entrance to Newcastle, took us nearly three hours, by which time my specialist was at work in the hospital.

'I was still calm, still at peace, but he couldn't stop the bleeding. He had to plug it temporarily before I was taken to the theatre. When I have a cauterisation or a plugging I can't have any anaesthetic, so I have to put up with it and very often it is sheer hell. This time wasn't any different, but what did it matter?'

Telling me this, Catherine was at pains to make me understand not only her exquisite feeling of peace, but precisely where this extraordinary experience had finally led her: 'I do not believe in the tenets of the Catholic Church or any other sect or religion. You understand me? I believe in him, the man, the thinker, the healer, the man who recognised the great spirit that was in him, and used it, used it to the extent of dying for his principles. He needn't have died on the cross, because he knew what that meant – the death penalty, crucifixion – and there were rows of victims hanging from trees along the road. He knew what he was doing, he was carrying out what he believed in. And so he will help me from now on. But he only. No false gods.

'I look upon him as a man born of a woman under the same circumstances as I was born, and he was a man who knew at the beginning he possessed a spiritual urge, and he used it. He was a healer, there have been many since. He was a deep thinker and knew humanity in and out, and he talked to the ignorant so that they could understand: he made his truth into stories, what are called parables. Above all, he was a magnetic character. He drew people to him. He drew the twelve followers to him. There have been many such since. There have been men in history for whom a friend or a person would die, give their last breath, follow them to the ends of the earth. Some people are born with this magnetism. And above all this man was a rebel. And as such he died for his own opinions. That is what I admire about him. And in my childhood every Good Friday, about three o'clock, I used to cry about him. Well, whatever he had is in more or less degrees in all of us. It is a spirit, and if I believe in nothing else I believe in that, or it, or whatever you would like to call it – this power that can sometimes create what you can term a miracle.

'I did not return home from hospital until two days later. I was still in the after-effect state, but I felt I must tell someone, and who but my dear friend, Father Tom Power. I have a number of friends who are priests. One is dear Father Tom of Haydon Bridge. Poor Tom, he did his best to get me back [to Catholicism], until I had to emphasise that he was flogging a dead horse. Twice he has written to the Pope about me, and the Pope has signed plaques, one for my eightieth birthday and one for my ninetieth. Dear soul, he had tried for years to win me back to the Catholic faith until he realised that, as I said, he was flogging a dead horse. But he maintained that I was more with God and more religious than anyone he knew.

'Well, I told Father Tom. Was he ecstatic? He said he knew that God would work his way in the end. But it was from this time that the peace faded, and you can say that I returned to ordinary humanity, but with a difference. I have with me now the knowledge of a spirit, a great spirit belonging to perhaps the greatest man who ever lived. This great healer, this man who understood human nature so well, and, so that his wisdom would reach the minds of the fearful and the ignorant, he turned it into parables.'

The ferrying of Catherine from Bristol Lodge to Newcastle and back again became such a frequent occurrence that it was clear something had to be done. 'It couldn't go on. My specialist advised that I must get into the city or somewhere near him and the hospital. It was either I die there [in Langley] or get attention to my bleeding. So in we came. Five and a half years ago, my specialist's wife, Ann, found us a lovely little house, so secluded in the centre of the city that no one would believe that it wasn't in the depths of the country. It broke my heart to have to assent to a sale. Most of the beautiful things I had collected since 1930 had to go. But as Tom said, they would be of little use to us if I was dead.

'I wouldn't buy this house till I'd seen it, so one day they carted me here from the hospital, and the poor woman who lived there couldn't believe it when three times I asked for a bowl and vomited blood. I tried not to spoil her carpets, but she had been a midwife and she understood.

'As soon as I walked in I saw it was open plan and knew what I wanted done. Inside there were, altogether, only eight rooms and I realised I would only be able to get one-third of my furniture, the good pieces, in. The kitchen had to be gutted, and there was no en-suite bedroom. There was, however, a garage big enough for four cars.'

Catherine drew up a plan and acted swiftly. 'Eighteen Geordies worked for a fortnight, close on three weeks – "Wor Kate" is what they called me – and I had the garage cut into two and one part turned into a utility room. Outside, where they kept the dustbins and the oil tank and coal-houses, I had another room built on . . . So now here we are in this transformed, beautiful little house.

'Since we arrived here [in 1991] I have been out of the house on only three occasions, special events, other than to go to the hospital; and in the past three years not at all. I have only been out in the garden twice this year – and then had to be carried out. But my corner, where the bedroom is, is really beautiful and likely I shall have to pass the rest of my days here.'

During these, the years of her great success, Catherine has donated a vast proportion of her earnings – millions – to educational and medical establishments, as well as to all kinds of people she would encourage. She retains a healthy indifference towards money for its own sake – 'I don't think about figures' – and money has not changed her one iota. Tom and she look forward to their weekends, free of business when they can be alone, as once they always were. And despite her failing eyesight her work continues, propped up in her bed in White Lodge in the heart of the city, with her faithful Grundig Stenorette by her side.

Of late, owing to her illness, this Grundig has been our main means of communication. Nothing, it seems, will keep her down. When her spirit is low, her WP as she calls it – her will power – comes into play. Indeed, as I have said, she has just completed her latest novel, *The Silent Lady*, and she continued to record tape after tape for me during the final writing of this book.

Often she would make these tapes early in the morning,

her most creative time, with the result that each tape delivers not only answers to my questions, but a symphony of feelings which range over the near century of her life. The final tape was long in the making. Catherine had been very ill, she hadn't even the strength to pick up the microphone. Yet when it came through, that resolving note of humour which rings out and triumphs over suffering in so many of her best works, can be heard right through to the end: 'It has been some days since I have talked to you . . .

'It is six o'clock in the morning. I have been awake for the past two hours, as usual thinking back, and I ask, Piers, why are some people born to fight? It's been a tough life. But the last stage has been more than trying. In 1977 and 1978 my timekeeper played up five times and the only way I won, my heart specialist said, was because I was a cantankerous old woman. I admitted to the cantankerous, oh yes! – but not to the old. Anyway, it's at it again, not only threatening to go on strike, but it's got its associates in all my other depart-ments to back it up, and they will unless I raise their wages by giving them two pints of blood every two or three weeks. And so I am faced with an ultimatum. But I've still got one ace up my sleeve, and that's my WP, so we'll only have to wait and see who wins . . .

'Well, there goes the buzzer, and this is the end of these reels of rigmarole, and I doubt that you'll get a lot out of them. But nevertheless I hope you'll learn more about this old girl.'

Epilogue

Dame Catherine passed away peacefully at her home in Jesmond, Newcastle, on Thursday 11 June 1998, eight months after publication of her biography and just nine days before her ninety-second birthday. Tom was with her, holding her hand. Always Tom was there when Catherine needed him; his devotion was absolute.

Immediately the news broke, the media circus began and Ann Marshall, her closest aide, was swamped with condolences and, of course, birthday cards from those who hadn't heard. It was a testing time. Tributes were legion. She had been an inspiration to many – actors, writers, friends and readers. Unfortunately, journalists rushing into print after deadline-beating interviews can be prone to paraphrasing, which is disappointing to a biographer whose subject, in pursuit of accuracy, had made herself so generously open to scrutiny.

Catherine was always a stickler for accuracy. I remember an error cropping up in the first book we did together in the 1980s. Both she and I had missed it in the proofs, but when it appeared in the finished book her searing response took more than ninety minutes to deliver on the telephone. In *The Girl From Leam Lane* she had been so frank that on sending her the manuscript I was worried less about mistakes than that she would want to back track or tone down some parts of it. But she didn't. 'I think it is splendid,' she wrote to me in March 1997, 'and Tom cannot speak too highly of it,' adding a trifle more darkly, 'He has made remarks here and there. There are one or two points I may want to discuss with you later.' Preparing my defence like a guilty schoolboy about to be brought up before the Head, I anticipated that these 'points' might have to do with my cutting a sliver more deeply under the skin than she had expected, as when marking her out as capable of all that even her cruellest characters do. I was wrong. She had particularly enjoyed the analysis of herself in terms of her principal fictional characters: 'Your transposing of my character into the characters in the book is simply amazing,' she wrote, and went on to satisfy both her own dignity and every biographer's desire to reveal more than is proferred by his subject by concluding: 'You know too much about me, Sir!'

Now she was gone and there would be no more banter over the phone, which she loved so well. Had it been possible, I know what would have been on the agenda. Before her death she had been given the last rites, even though only two years previously she had told her dear friend Father Tom Power that he 'was flogging a dead horse' trying to save her soul. Her life-long battle with the Roman Catholic Church had been about its dogma which she felt concealed rather than revealed the naked truth. I believe that this arch-storyteller, understanding the manner in which her own stories dispensed truths about the human condition – we spoke about this a lot – found a way to accept the Christian story as a vehicle, its purpose to awaken a response in our subconscious to the truths that inspired it. From this position, intellectually, it is but a short passage to accepting her anointing as the symbolic affirmation of these truths, the challenge of which she had long met. Given the ferocity of her own struggle to arrest truth it would be a harsh judge who saw her acceptance of the last rites as an example of the hypocrisies she had spent a lifetime rejecting.

Between Catherine's death and her funeral on the following Tuesday (16 June), Hugo Marshall, her consultant surgeon for the past twenty-five years, took Tom for a haircut. (Apparently the gardener usually cut his hair – I can just imagine Catherine insisting on it: he keeps the grass well enough, why shouldn't he cut Tom's hair?) It was the first time for many a year that Tom had left the house, other than to go to hospital, and the trip, which also included choosing and ordering flowers, was a poignant reminder of how isolated from the world both he and Catherine had become. When Tom came to pay he discovered that he had no money. Neither he nor Catherine carried any; they had no need to, they never went out. Money simply didn't figure in their lives, except as a happy opportunity to encourage others.

The funeral itself was deliberately low key and private. A close friend told me that in the period leading up to it Tom had not seemed unwell. Afterwards, he sat in Catherine's chair and welcomed a small circle of friends. Eventually, of course, he was left alone, though a nurse was in the house overnight. It was the first time for many decades that Catherine and Tom had been apart, even for a short while.

On more than one occasion Catherine had said to me that she hoped he would go first because she knew that when one of them died, the other would follow and she wanted to spare Tom those few, painful, intervening days. I took this as a statement of their devotion to one another rather than as a prediction. When Tom did in fact die just seventeen days after Catherine, I had occasion (yet again) to marvel at her perceptiveness. Tom had been quoted as saying, 'Life without Kitty would be no life at all,' which was why one journalist asked me if it had been suicide. The facts are that Tom had been admitted to hospital for a check-up on Tuesday 23 June and died peacefully of heart failure the following Sunday.

So it was just three weeks after Catherine's funeral I found myself at Tom's funeral. It proved to be an enlightening experience. Tom had always refused to discuss his life before he met Catherine, beyond the fact that he was the son of a parish verger in Essex and had attended grammar school and Oxford University. Talking to one of his sisters after the service I learned that he had not replied to her letters for the past twenty-seven years. As we were speaking, a nurse who had attended Tom introduced herself. Tom's sister was amazed to discover that this nurse knew all about her. Whatever reasons there may have been for Tom's silence through nearly three decades, he had not forgotten his family. Why then had he never replied to his sister's letters?

Catherine and Tom's was an all-consuming relationship. They had friends and numerous acquaintances, they had publishers, agents and doctors by the score, but since their first meeting in 1936 until the end of it all there was only really the two of them against the world – only 'thee and me', which was how Catherine described it in a poem read at Tom's funeral. So what was it that bound them together to the exclusion of all others?

Frantic sleuth work by close friend Alex Morris and Canon Frank Dexter faced with the difficult task of delivering Tom's funeral address with precious little to go on, revealed some interesting facts hitherto unrecorded. I hadn't been aware that Tom's father had died early and that his mother had married again, this time to a plumber's mate. Tom had adored his step-father and learned from him practical skills put to good use when he and Catherine were tackling The Hurst, the cavernous, run-down house in Hastings. More significantly, Canon Dexter resolved a quandary of mine that Tom seemed perfectly unaffected by his Oxford University education. Characteristically, Oxbridge graduates tend to evince a confident or superior air, which was notably absent in Tom. Now, for the first time, Tom's college was revealed as St Catherine's (where else?). This confused me because I knew that St Catz was founded in the 1960s, long after Tom graduated. On speaking to the college authorities I discovered that in Tom's day it was a non-collegiate society, which offered an opportunity to win an Oxford degree to underprivileged students without the means to pay college fees. As a society it had no buildings of its own and none of the trade-mark Oxbridge college traditions. He gained a first in Mods and two years later, in 1935, graduated with a good second-class honours degree in mathematics. Tom, like Catherine, had come from a poor background. When they met, the following year, he was a man who had overleaped enormous social barriers but without any of the pretensions which Catherine believed were required in her planned rise, and which so primed her for breakdown. I had never before considered the impact of this successful but classless young man on Catherine who was so riddled with affectation. A decade after meeting Tom, the pseudo-lady was cast aside and, as I have described, she became free to be herself and write about her people. It seems likely that Tom was her educator in more than syntax, therefore, and that this encouraged a dependency. At his funeral I was moved by fresh evidence of Tom's ability to get through to people as an educator. When Catherine died he received letters of condolence addressed to 'Dear Cookie' from pupils he had taught nearly half a century earlier.

The polaric difference between Catherine and Tom was in their personalities. On introduction to Tom one met Catherine's projection of him – a shy, studious, gentle man – which indeed he was. Because he was physically also a small man and she was forceful and extrovert, some have concluded that in Tom, Catherine found someone to bend to her extraordinary will. Undeniably, hers was a powerful personality, indeed ruthless if need be. As I have written, 'the cold violence and cruelty in many of her novels is an essential part of her vision and we should not be surprised or shocked at her honest but apparently damning claim (made in all seriousness) that she is capable of doing absolutely anything that she gives her characters to do'. This includes, you will recall, such as Alice Walton's disfigurement of her daughter's lover and the burning alive of her daughter-in-law as well as much worse in many other of her novels. Catherine, who came within a whisker of murdering her own mother, was, on her own admission therefore, quite capable of taking the role of all-devouring spider to Tom's fly. But that is not in fact how it was. Without Tom, she may never have found herself or emerged from breakdown, and it is worth remembering that she didn't write anything worth reading until she had faced 'the Kate in her'.

Working with Catherine I had a glimpse into how mesmerisingly inspirational, how compelling and demanding she was. Her relationship with Tom may have deprived him of a 'normal' life, but on the plus side, life with Catherine was more electric than he ever imagined it could be. The point is that Tom revered (as strongly as Catherine did) the nature of what inspired her to create characters as diverse as Fanny McBride, Mary Walton, Mary Ann Shaughnessy, Anna Brigmore, Kate Makepeace, Alice Walton. He was always the champion of the projects I undertook with her because he understood that I was as fascinated as he about the nature of her inspiration.

'Do you know, really I am a frustrated actress,' she once said. Then, eighteen months before she died, when she was completing her final novel and I asked whether the actress in her was still working, she replied rather irritably, 'I *am* the part'. Her kind of acting was of the Method school. She *was* her characters, the warm, humorous Fanny McBride, the spiritually true Mary Walton, the cheeky innocent Mary Ann Shaughnessy, the sensual, highly self-disciplined Anna Brigmore, the strange, wise, bewitched Kate Makepeace, the ruthless Alice Walton. With Tom's help, Catherine brought all of these alive from within her. No wonder she said he met her 'searches'.

Inevitably, after Tom's death, journalists seized on a quote from a friend that he had died of a broken heart, but it is too slick. As with her best novels, any attempt to construct a romance out of Tom and Catherine's relationship will fail. After sixty years together they could not live without one another, but the nature of the binding was deeper than romance. Catherine wrote best from the heart, from within herself, from her own being, a being that was enormously loving and generous, but not romantic. As she admitted, she was the instrument, sometimes an unwilling one, of what inspired her to write. In that sense, she and Tom (who rescued and sustained her) both took the role of fly.

When she was gone there was a moment or two when Tom nearly returned to himself. There were attempts to integrate him into the world – one of which, to my certain knowledge (an invitation by Alex Morris to visit his home) was met with almost boyish enthusiasm. But it was not to happen. The call from Catherine remained the stronger.

Books by Catherine Cookson

1950	Kate Hannigan	1965	Matty Doolin
1951	The Fifteen Streets	1966	The Unbaited Trap
1953	Colour Blind	1967	Katie Mulholland
1954	Maggie Rowan	1967	Mary Ann and Bill
1954	A Grand Man	1968	The Round Tower
1956	The Lord and Mary Ann	1968	Joe and the Gladiator
		1969	Our Kate
1957	Rooney	1969	The Nice Bloke
1958	The Menagerie	1970	The Glass Virgin
1958	The Devil and Mary Ann	1970	The Invitation
		1970	The Nipper
1959	Slinky Jane	1971	The Dwelling Place
1959	Fanny McBride	1971	Feathers in the Fire
1960	Fenwick Houses	1972	Pure as the Lily
1961	Love and Mary Ann	1972	Blue Baccy
1962	The Garment	1973	The Mallen Streak
1962	Life and Mary Ann	1974	The Mallen Girl
1963	The Blind Miller	1974	The Mallen Litter
1964	Hannah Massey	1974	Our John Willie
1964	Marriage and Mary Ann	1975	The Invisible Cord
		1975	The Gambling Man
1965	The Long Corridor	1976	The Tide of Life
1965	Mary Ann's Angels	1976	Mrs Flannagan's

Trumpet
1977 The Girl
1977 Go Tell It To Mrs Golightly
1978 The Cinder Path
1979 The Man Who Cried
1980 Tilly Trotter
1980 Lanky Jones
1981 Tilly Trotter Wed
1982 Tilly Trotter Widowed
1983 The Whip
1983 Hamilton
1984 The Black Velvet Gown
1984 Goodbye Hamilton
1985 A Dinner of Herbs
1985 Harold
1986 The Moth
1986 Catherine Cookson Country (memoirs)
1986 Bill Bailey
1987 The Parson's Daughter
1987 Bill Bailey's Lot
1988 The Cultured Handmaiden
1988 Bill Bailey's Daughter
1988 Let Me Make Myself Plain
1989 The Harrogate Secret
1989 The Black Candle

1990 The Wingless Bird
1990 The Gillyvors
1991 My Beloved Son
1991 The Rag Nymph
1992 The House of Women
1992 The Maltese Angel
1993 The Year of the Virgins
1993 The Golden Straw
1994 The Tinker's Girl
1994 Justice is a Woman
1995 A Ruthless Need
1995 The Obsession
1995 Plainer Still (Anthology)
1996 The Branded Man
1996 The Bonny Dawn
1996 The Upstart
1997 The Bondage of Love
1997 The Desert Crop
1997 The Lady on My Left
1998 The Solace of Sin
1998 Riley

As Catherine Marchant
1962 Heritage of Folly
1963 Fen Tiger
1964 House of Men
1975 Martha Mary Crawford
1976 The Slow Awakening
1977 The Iron Façade

INDEX

Index